Bad Girls & wicked women

Bad Girls

& wicked women

JAN STRADLING

THE MOST POWERFUL, SHOCKING AMAZING,
THRILLING & DANGEROUS WOMEN OF ALL TIME

PIER 9

4

Contents

Introduction

In telling the stories of the 'bad girls' of history, an interpretive approach is usually required. Most of the women included in this book lived in times and cultures so vastly different to ours that they cannot be judged by today's standards and expectations. Some committed terrible crimes for which there is little apparent excuse, but others were victims of circumstance who dared to be different.

In some cases it is extraordinary that their stories were recorded at all, living as they did in days when women and what they did were seldom seen as holding historical significance. If their exploits did make it to paper, their stories were penned by male historians whose biased attitude toward powerful and independent women usually ensured that they were portrayed as evil harlots, the facts distorted to fit the preconceptions of the time. In past centuries women had little choice as to how they were perceived, almost inevitably falling into the categories of daughter, mother and/or wife, or whore. Royal or commoner, it made no difference. The women who attempted to deviate from these positions and take their place alongside men were harshly judged, depicted as unfeminine, manipulative, self-serving and generally wicked.

The women in this book were often extraordinary individuals who in a multitude of ways broke with tradition and challenged their male counterparts. Identifying their motivation brings us a step closer to understanding why they did what they did. To ignore or shatter sexual conventions, the desire to escape poverty, to achieve position and power, to take on the harsh responsibilities which often accompany leadership, to take revenge, or acute mental disturbance seem to be the key factors.

History has portrayed many high-profile women as evil temptresses with insatiable sexual appetites. Going by the accounts we receive from historians, the Roman Empress Messalina considered it no mean feat to bed twenty-six men in one night for a wager. Catherine the Great of Russia was an enlightened politician but it is alleged that her sexual appetite was voracious. Then, of course, there's the Queen of the Nile,

The feisty and intelligent Catherine the Great of Russia plotted with her lover and their followers to overthrow her imbecilic husband, Peter III, so she could seize the throne for herself.

Cleopatra, one of the ultimate temptresses of all time. Cleopatra was seen as having almost hypnotic powers, capable of reducing men to mere putty in her hands. But was she really such an evil seductress? By the end of her life she had only taken two long-term lovers—albeit two of the most powerful men in the world, Julius Caesar and Mark Antony. It seems, in fact, that she was startlingly intelligent and selective in her choices.

None of these women was judged more harshly for her sexual activity than femme fatale Mata Hari, who attempted to make a living in war-torn Europe when all hopes of a glittering acting career had faded. Known to have slept with officers from both sides of the conflict in World War I, she was accused of being a double agent, hated and despised by the Germans, French and English alike. But the question lingers: was she really a double agent, or just a convenient scapegoat for the Allied forces then taking a beating from Germany? In the end it is debatable whether she was on trial for spying or simply because of her promiscuity.

Perhaps some of the women in this book did make the most of the perks that went with the job, in the same way that today power and sex often go hand in hand. But for others sex was the means to a livelihood, something they could fall back on when times were hard and they were unable to support themselves any other way due to lack of education and the absence of other forms of employment. Abject poverty drove many women to attempt to escape their bleak existence by clawing their way to comfort and into a position of power. However, with power often comes corruption. Once some of our bad girls experienced the privileges that went with position, they became determined to hang on at any cost.

The Dragon Empress maintained her control over China for fifty years. Having been ignored by her own family and done her time as an Imperial concubine, when she became mother to the heir and later regent, she fought hard to retain her status. She was liable to execute anyone who challenged her and, like all dynastic Chinese rulers, had a plethora of servile court eunuchs who would willingly administer poison or throw offenders into deep wells. The Philippines' Imelda Marcos eventually succumbed to decadence and greed; having ogled Malacanang Palace as a child from an impoverished family running barefoot through the streets of Manila, as an adult she hated anything which reminded her of that poverty. She surrounded herself with luxury—unfortunately all financed by the national purse at a time when the average Filipino lived on two dollars a day. Australia's Tilly Devine began working the streets of London at the age of sixteen. Sick of being the one doing the hard graft, when she spotted an opportunity to exploit others she took it. Swathed in furs, dripping garish jewellery, she set up brothels throughout Sydney and made huge money through real estate. But she had an even darker side. As she became further submerged in the Sydney underworld, she took gang warfare to an

THESE WOMEN used whatever skills they had to focus on their individual goals. Their lust for power sometimes resulted in intrigue, murder, and a burning desire to be number one in a dog-eat-dog world.

unprecedented level through a personal feud with a woman she believed was trying to usurp her. Chicago May was another opportunist, although her fame was a great deal greater than her crimes might warrant.

Then there are women such as Georgia Tann, whose crimes are still affecting her victims. Starting off concerned with the plight of orphans, she single-handedly introduced adoption to America. But the wealth and power accompanying her activities became so addictive that she ended up 'stealing' five thousand babies and running an extremely lucrative black market adoption agency. In the South China seas, Shi Xianggu, selected from a group of prostitutes on one of Guangdong's floating brothels, negotiated her way to leadership of the largest pirate fleet of all time. Having terrorised the seas with a flotilla of 1800 ships and eighty thousand men, she set herself up for life financially before negotiating an amnesty and pardons for all involved. What a politician she would have made!

Many of the past's great women leaders held loftier ideals in leading their subjects and fighting for a cause. Queen Boudica embarked on a bloody crusade against the Romans, rallying the tribes of Britain and eventually responsible for at least eighty thousand deaths. Seen as a champion of freedom, she's one of the few women in this book that history treats quite kindly, yet recent evidence points to appallingly indiscriminate acts of revenge. England's Tudor monarch, 'Bloody Mary', massacred many Protestants and failed to understand why her people wouldn't come to her Catholic heel. Having received neither compassion nor understanding from the time she was very young, she was bereft of both qualities.

Madame Mao was allowed to marry Chairman Mao on the strict condition that she would stay out of politics for thirty years. When the muzzle was removed her thirst for power escalated, resulting in the implementation of the Cultural Revolution, a movement that condoned senseless killings and the tearing apart of Chinese culture and tradition.

Revenge was a strong motivation amongst women who felt they had been badly done by. Palestinian terrorist Leila Khaled grew up in a refugee camp in Lebanon, surrounded by thousands of families like her own who had been thrown out of Palestine by the Israelis. Filled with hatred, she was so politically passionate that she became the first female terrorist, even undergoing plastic surgery in order to retain her anonymity on later missions for the PFLP. India's 'Bandit Queen', Phoolan Devi, embarked on a personal vendetta which resulted in many men being subjected to torture and, most often, death. Phoolan Devi had been married off at the age of eleven and raped and tortured throughout her life. We can't vindicate what she did, but we can at least begin to understand why.

Then there were the women who felt on the outside and who exhibited non-conformist behaviour. Never truly fitting in, New Zealand conwoman Amy Bock's most notorious con was to pose as a man and marry an unsuspecting bride. It is probable that she was a lesbian at a time when lesbians were considered 'inverts'. Another outsider, the Aztec woman known as Malinali, was sold by her family as a slave—no longer feeling any allegiance to her people, she assisted the Spanish in their conquest of Mexico. In late nineteenth-century New York, Typhoid Mary was exiled for being a 'healthy' carrier of typhoid. Forced to live in isolation for an interminable length of time and shunned by society, she had little to lose when she finally rebelled by sneaking back to work in New York's kitchens.

But there were also the bad girls whose stories read like Gothic horror tales. These women also had clear motivations but their actions may well have been largely affected by mental disturbance. When the unfortunate combination of power and madness came together, tragedy ensued. Queen Ranavalona of Madagascar committed a holocaust which wiped out at least one-third of her own people who were bent on embracing Christianity. Elizabeth Bathory of Hungary, known as the 'Blood Countess', believed that the blood of youthful virgins was the elixir that would bring her everlasting youth. It is thought that she tortured and murdered more than six hundred young women before her ghastly crimes were discovered. Serial murderer Mary Ann Cotton saw her many children, and her husbands, as mere commodities to be cashed in on her way to a comfortable lifestyle. These are some of the women for whom time and place have no bearing on their terrible acts.

Belle Starr alone fits none of these categories. Originally led astray by poor choices in husband material, she ended up with a reputation for wickedness that far outstripped the reality—an early case of the press gone into overdrive.

These women's stories spring to the page from all corners of the globe. Despite their differences, one thing draws them together and connects them through the centuries—an irrepressible spirit. Most of them refused to be seen as victims. No matter how they've been depicted or how they were treated at the time, they took matters into their own hands. Some suffered untimely deaths, but in pushing the conventional boundaries they made defiant choices and accepted the consequences. As a group, all these women leave the reader with a sense of wilfulness. One can imagine the moment as Amy Bock marches cheekily up the aisle with another woman, as Mata Hari blows a final kiss to her executioners, as Queen Boudica sips from a poisoned chalice, choosing death over captivity, moments that capture an air of defiance which still resonates.

Known as the 'Bandit Queen', Phoolan Devi joined a terrorist gang while still a teenager in order to fight the caste war, as well as to wreak revenge on the men who had abused her as a child.

Cleopatra VII

Serpent of the Nile, last of the Pharoahs

69/70–30 BC

Drunk with destruction,
dazed with dark delights,
She dreamt herself a
deity at Rome.
– Horace (Roman poet)

Cleopatra VII Thea
Philopator (meaning,
'Cleopatra the Father-Loving
Goddess') ruled Egypt from
51 BC until her death
in 30 BC.

Under cover of darkness, Cleopatra's boat slid into the river bank near the palace where Julius Caesar had taken up residence. Silently, she stepped ashore and with the help of her loyal servant, Apollodoros, rolled herself securely in a Persian rug. She was carried past the guards and into the palace over Apollodoros's sturdy shoulders. As they moved through the corridors, Cleopatra heard the muffled challenges that Apollodoros successfully shrugged off, claiming the carpet was a gift for their glorious leader.

At last they arrived at Caesar's quarters. Bowing low at Caesar's feet, Apollodorus gently unrolled the rug. Out stepped the twenty-one-year-old Egyptian Queen, flushed no doubt at the success of her plan, and immediately turning on the full force of her not inconsiderable charm. The fifty-year-old Caesar was delighted with this unexpected and highly exotic gift, and rapidly succumbed to the charm offensive. That night, it is alleged, they became lovers. Cleopatra had found herself the most powerful ally in the world.

At the age of seventeen, Cleopatra had become joint ruler of Egypt with her twelve-year-old brother and husband, Ptolemy. By the time of her death at the age of thirty-nine, she had shown herself more than a match for her power-hungry family and their hangers-on in the corrupt Ptolemaic court, had murdered all her siblings, and secured Egypt's position as the largest and most important client-kingdom under Rome's domination. She was much admired, being able to speak eight languages and the first of the Ptolemaic pharaohs, rulers of Greek descent, able to communicate with her people in Egyptian. She was also a scholar, a philosopher and a great alchemist, writing several books upon the subject. She took as lovers two of the most powerful men in the world, Julius Caesar and Mark Antony. She was regarded by the Roman people as the 'serpent of the Nile', a sorceress who possessed hypnotic powers which she used to snare their greatest leaders and manipulate them to her advantage. To this very day her name conjures up an image of bewitching, sphinx-like beauty, and throughout history she has been thought of as both witch and whore. But her true power lay in her intelligence and charisma, and her flair for the intricate game of politics, which she played with consummate skill and grace until the bitter end.

Sibling Rivalry

Born in 69 or 70 BC, the second daughter of Ptolemy XII and his sister–wife Cleopatra V, Cleopatra spent her early years trying to survive in the whirling currents of intrigue, back-stabbing and sibling rivalry of the Ptolemaic court in Alexandria. The Ptolemaic pharaohs were the successors of Ptolemy, one of Alexander the Great's generals, who had seized control of Egypt after Alexander's death. Because combined male and female rule was believed to be blessed by the Egyptian gods, the Ptolemies followed the Egyptian practice of 'keeping it all in the family', in which siblings, sometimes even parents and children, married, sometimes with a huge disparity in ages, to consolidate power. Cleopatra spent her early years with her head in as many books as possible, acquiring the knowledge and the skills that would serve her well in later life.

In 51 BC, around the age of eighteen, following dynastic tradition Cleopatra married her much younger brother Ptolemy XIII and as Cleopatra VII became joint ruler with him of Egypt. But dynastic tradition clearly did not carry much weight with the ambitious young queen. As co-regent, she proved herself resourceful and wise beyond her years, succeeding in guiding her country through a disastrous drought and instigating much-needed economic reform, and as Egypt's fortunes improved she mounted a campaign to become sole ruler. Cleopatra knew Rome would be casting interested and no doubt greedy glances in her country's direction and that to maintain her position she would need to massage the egos of her Roman masters. But the threat was not merely from Rome. Within her own court, Cleopatra was surrounded by conflicting factions, all vying for power. They were incensed at her autocratic ways and intent on putting a younger, more naive, and more easily manipulated ruler in her place.

Matters came to a head in 48 BC when the supporters of Cleopatra's husband and their sister Arsinoe staged a coup. Her life in grave danger, Cleopatra was forced to flee from Alexandria. But it was not in her nature to give up easily—and when word reached her that the Roman consul Julius Caesar was on his way to settle the dispute, she returned to the outskirts of the city to await his arrival. She was confident of her powers of persuasion and sure that if she could only win an audience with Caesar, she could turn the situation to her favour. But entering Alexandria would mean certain death at the hands of her brother's murderous supporters. Deciding that the prize was worth the risk, Cleopatra devised a plan.

The Queen staged one of the most famous entrances in history, described in loving detail by Plutarch in his *Lives*. With the help of a servant, she wrapped herself in a Persian rug and gained entrance to the palace where Caesar was staying. When the rug was unrolled and the nubile young Queen lay at the feet of the startled consul, Cleopatra must

Queen Cleopatra with her handmaidens on the terraces of the Temple of Philae.

have known she had staged the perfect coup. The middle-aged Caesar, who had always placed huge value on honour and the respect of his peers, was immediately enchanted. Cleopatra sprang up, seeming in that moment to transform herself from slave, making her obeisance at her master's feet, to mistress.

When Ptolemy and his retinue arrived next morning, he found that his sister–wife had outmaneuvred him on every front and was enjoying the Roman leader's undivided attention. Furious, Ptolemy indulged in what must have looked like a childish rage, hurling his crown across the room. Caesar now took matters into his own hands, reinstating Cleopatra on the throne and quickly disposing of the opposition. Ptolemy was killed in battle and Arsinoe taken prisoner. Cleopatra married her even younger brother, Ptolemy XIV, to consolidate her position, but it was Caesar who was the recipient of her favours. At any point he could have made Egypt a Roman province run by a Roman Governor, but Cleopatra's seductive charms and ingenuity continued to hold him in thrall.

Having regained her throne, Cleopatra set about using her partnership with Caesar to provide her with the political leverage she needed to expand her lands. To celebrate the victory against Ptolemy, Caesar spent the winter with the Queen, indulging himself in a lifestyle that contrasted starkly with his rather austere habits in Rome. Cleopatra used her powers of persuasion to her country's full advantage and procured gifts of vast territories from her lover—her liaison was protecting Egypt and allowing it to grow as a wealthy autonomous state. She further cemented the connection when, in 47 BC, she gave birth to their son, Caesarion ('Little Caesar'). Cleopatra had dreams that one day Caesarion would rule both Rome and Egypt, making her, in effect, the mistress of the world.

Caesar, politically astute, knew Rome would never accept a foreign Queen—or Caesarion. A Roman citizen could not legally marry a citizen of another country, and Caesarion would always be illegitimate in Roman eyes. Reluctantly Caesar returned to Rome, and Cleopatra was dismayed when he chose to recognise his adopted son and great-nephew, Octavian, as his official heir. But Cleopatra was not to be so easily cast off, and a year later visited Rome with Caesarion. In their honour, Caesar paraded his prisoners through the streets in triumph, with Cleopatra's sister, Arsinoe, among them. The Roman people became increasingly resentful of the presence of the Egyptian seducer, a woman whose subjects worshipped reptiles and whose extravagance represented everything they most abhorred. The mood got even uglier when Caesar, in a moment of uncharacteristic rashness, had a statue of gold made in her honour. His enemies seized on his weakness and on the Ides of March, 44 BC, he was assassinated on the steps of the Senate. In his will, there was no mention of Cleopatra or their son.

Cleopatra fled to Egypt with Caesarion, her grief mingled with keen disappointment that her dreams of empire seemed to have died on the Senate steps with Caesar. She now focused her considerable energy on the future of the Ptolemaic dynasty. Having already had Arsinoe executed, her young brother–husband seemed just one more irritating obstacle in the way of the succession. No doubt feeling that fratricide could be justified if it meant Caesarion's future was ensured, she had Ptolemy XIV poisoned. She then appointed her son joint ruler but did not make a husband of him. Cleopatra was keen to consolidate her power as quickly as possible for, without her powerful protector, Rome might try to remove her from the throne and capitalise on the wealth and strategic position of Egypt for mounting military campaigns in the East. The idea that she might find a replacement for Caesar also began to preoccupy the Queen.

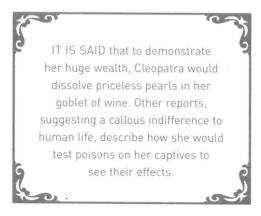

IT IS SAID that to demonstrate her huge wealth, Cleopatra would dissolve priceless pearls in her goblet of wine. Other reports, suggesting a callous indifference to human life, describe how she would test poisons on her captives to see their effects.

By 33 BC, the contest in the Roman world was between Caesar's designated heir, Octavian, and the powerful military leader Mark Antony, who had spoken so movingly in the wake of Caesar's death. Cleopatra knew of Antony's reputation, and when a military campaign brought him to nearby Tarsus (in modern Turkey) and he requested a meeting, she was determined not to waste the opportunity.

Temptress of the Nile

With her usual sense of drama, Cleopatra staged another of her famous entrances. Plutarch describes the scene that was to enchant Mark Antony:

> *She came sailing up the river Cydnus in a barge with gilded stern and outspread sails of purple, while oars of silver beat time to the music of flutes and fifes and harps. She herself lay all alone, under a canopy of cloth of gold, dressed as Venus in a picture, and beautiful young boys, like painted Cupids, stood on each side to fan her. Her maids were dressed like Sea Nymphs and Graces, some steering at the rudder, some working at the ropes.*

That night, she invited him to dine with her, having prepared yet another theatrical setting.

When Mark Antony arrived, he was dazzled by the display of royal opulence. Lights hung from every tree, wine was drunk from golden goblets, and a sumptuous banquet was served from dishes decorated with precious stones. The sophistication and extravagance which seemed to characterise the Egyptian Queen must have served to highlight the differences between the two. Antony was a rough and ready soldier while Cleopatra revelled in extravagant display and in the stage-managed glamour of the scene.

At the end of the evening, she presented him with the glittering goblets and plates that had been used to serve the banquet. Even in his bedazzled state, Antony must have recognised that the Queen was displaying such choice treasures to impress on him how rich she was—and how useful she might be to Rome, whose coffers were so often drained by its imperial ambitions. The next evening, Antony attempted to return Cleopatra's hospitality, but quickly realised he could not compete. Shortly afterward he went with her to Alexandria, where the Egyptian Queen deftly organised the entertainment. Every evening a banquet was held, each accompanied by an ever more breathtaking show of opulence. And when Antony arrived at the final feast, he found the floor knee-deep in rose petals. Like Caesar before him, he had fallen hopelessly in love, and soon his fabled sense of duty was entirely forgotten. Together they set up the 'Society of Inimitable Livers', dedicated to debauchery, and despite their very obvious differences became inseparable. Days were spent in hedonistic pursuits and nights in languorous voyages down the Nile, enthusiastic feasting and passionate love-making. Often they would take to the streets of Alexandria, masquerading as a servant girl and slave. Although Cleopatra may have begun the liaison with an eye to its political benefits, it seems that the 'temptress of the Nile' was herself ensnared.

But once again, Rome exerted its irresistible pull. A reluctant Mark Antony returned home to his commitments—and a prearranged marriage (his fourth) to Octavian's sister, Octavia, the most virtuous of Roman women. Shortly after he left, Cleopatra gave birth to twins, Alexander Helios and Cleopatra Selen, and was in agony at what she saw as his desertion. Antony was haunted by those months in Alexandria—four years later he returned and, to the fury of Rome, rekindled the affair. This resulted in Cleopatra bearing him another son, Ptolemy Philadelphus. By his actions, Antony had publicly spurned the virtuous Octavia, and Rome took her humiliation to heart—as did her furious brother, who had brokered the marriage in the first place.

Octavian now began a propaganda war against Cleopatra, depicting her as manipulative, ambitious, and an ever-present danger to Rome. Hadn't she already seduced the great Julius Caesar? Wasn't she turning yet another pillar of Roman society into a love-sated slave?

In 34 BC Antony, apparently oblivious to the coming storm and infected by Cleopatra's love of opulence, made a fatal mistake. Plutarch vividly describes the scene:

Although Cleopatra has the reputation of being one of history's great temptresses, contemporary portraits on coins and reliefs tend to reveal her as striking rather than beautiful, with a strong chin, broad forehead and prominent nose.

He [Mark Antony] had two thrones of gold, one for himself and one for Cleopatra, placed on a silver dais, with smaller thrones for his children. First he proclaimed Cleopatra Queen of Egypt, Cyprus, Libya and Syria and named Caesarion as her consort … Next he proclaimed his own sons by Cleopatra to be Kings of Kings.

He made matters even worse by handing out to his sons kingdoms that still belonged to Rome. Cleopatra, dressed in sacred robes, was hailed as the new Isis, the goddess of Magic and the Giver of Life. Octavian reported these actions to the Senate and declared war. Antony was seen as an emasculated puppet and an enemy of Rome.

A fierce sea battle began in September of 31 BC off the coast of the Roman colony of Actium in Greece. The two sides were evenly matched in terms of force, but Antony was less experienced as a naval commander and distracted from the beginning by the presence of Cleopatra. As was the custom of the time, she had brought with her the family treasure and was waiting impatiently at anchor for Antony to win the day. We are told by the Roman historian Cassius Dio that on seeing Octavian's ships making headway and Antony's men beginning to desert him, Cleopatra fled the scene for Alexandria. Instead of staying to face Octavian, Antony followed her, confirming to the Romans and to his own forces that he was in her power. On reaching Alexandria, he heard that his forces had surrendered and many of his allies had joined Octavian. Time was running out for the lovers.

The Club of Those Who Die Together

Determined, it seems, to enjoy life to the end, Cleopatra encouraged Mark Antony out of the depression into which he sank as he recognised the enormity of what he had done. With misplaced bravado they revived the Society of Inimitable Livers, changing its name to the 'Club of Those Who Die Together'. Hoping to secure the Egyptian throne for her descendants, Cleopatra held an elaborate coming-of-age ceremony for Caesarion and Antony's eldest son by his former wife Fulvia. This was her last political act and possibly her most misguided one, for once the boys were recognised as men and claimants to the throne, Octavian could never allow them to live. Hearing that Octavian was now marching toward Alexandria, Cleopatra, the orchestrator of so many dramatic entrances, began to set up her final exit.

The Queen began building a mausoleum, into which she moved all her treasured belongings. Hoping to trick Octavian, she told her servants to spread the word that she was dead. But the false news reached Mark Antony—with catastrophic results. Devastated, he begged his servant Eros to kill him, and when Eros refused he fell upon his sword. Too late he learned that Cleopatra was still alive, and was carried to her mausoleum, where he died in her arms. Cleopatra, knowing she had lost both the throne of her beloved Egypt and the man who was her soulmate, was inconsolable. Octavian, wanting to emerge as a benevolent victor, allowed her to take charge of her lover's burial, determined that she should stay alive at least until they returned to Rome. But Cleopatra was several moves ahead of him.

Assisted by two maids, she dressed herself in regal attire and ordered a feast to be prepared. When a poor peasant arrived at the mausoleum carrying a basket of fresh figs, the Roman guards saw no reason to suspect him. But concealed within the basket lay a number of asps, the small deadly snakes which Cleopatra had decided should help her execute her plan. Meanwhile, a letter was delivered to Octavian from Cleopatra, containing a desperate plea that she be buried beside Mark Antony. Alarmed that she was going to forestall his plans, Octavian sent his guards to the mausoleum. But they were too late. Cleopatra was already dead, reclining regally on her golden couch with one of her two maidservants dying at her feet. The other maidservant was faithfully adjusting her Queen's crown for the last time as the guards rushed in. It was no coincidence that Cleopatra chose the snake as her agent of death. A symbol of the Royal House of Egypt, the snake was also the symbol of rebirth and regeneration. Even in her death, it seemed, Cleopatra sent a signal of hope to her people.

The death of Cleopatra meant the Ptolemaic dynasty came to an abrupt end, for Caesarion was murdered shortly afterward, along with Fulvia's son. Oddly, Cleopatra and Mark Antony's three children were taken to Rome and raised by Octavia. While Cleopatra was represented by Octavian propagandists as indolent, self-indulgent and cruel, in Egypt she was admired and respected. She had tried to solve the country's economic problems, encourage the arts and a new building program, and stamp out the corruption that had been endemic in the Ptolemaic court.

The Meeting of Anthony and Cleopatra, 41 BC, by Lawrence Alma-Tadema

In many senses, she was a captive queen in a captive country who succeeded in restoring Egypt to its former glory and resisting Roman oppression for almost her entire reign.

Cleopatra presented a dangerous challenge to the Roman ideal of virtuous womanhood, and to achieve her aims she enlisted the help of two of the most powerful men in the world. Her love affairs with Julius Caesar and Mark Antony have been the subject of countless plays and films. Shakespeare's description of her in Antony and Cleopatra still holds true: 'Age shall not wither her, nor custom stale her infinite variety'. By painting her in the darkest of colours to serve his political ends, Octavian, her sworn enemy, succeeded in immortalising the very person he despised, and ensured that the last of the Pharaohs would be forever remembered as one of the most complex, enigmatic and sexually powerful women in history.

Messalina

Roman empress who took self-indulgence to the limits

c. AD 22–48

Let her live and be happy with her lovers, three hundred of whom she holds in her embraces, loving none truly but again and again rupturing the loins of them all; and let her not count on my love, as in the past, for through her fault it has fallen like a flower at the meadow's edge, after being lopped by the passing plough.
– Catullus

Messalina was delighted to hear that her husband, the Emperor Claudius, was leaving Rome for a lengthy military campaign in Britain. In his absence there would be no need for her trysts to be clandestine. Deciding that the situation called for a celebration, the Empress summoned her lover, the actor Mnester, to help her plan it. As they joked that the Empress was truly the mistress of depravity, Messalina thought to herself, why not prove it? She would issue a challenge to Rome's most famous prostitute, Scylla, to see who could bed the most men in one night. Mnester immediately made off for the brothels to ensure Scylla's participation. Hardly in a position to refuse the Empress, Scylla accepted the unusual challenge.

The following evening, an unruly crowd gathered to witness, and perhaps take part in, the much talked-about event. Arriving at the palace to the sound of jeers and wolf whistles, Scylla insisted that she be paid for her night's work—it might be sport for the Empress, but for Scylla this was a job. Far from refusing her, Messalina liked the idea, announcing that she too would be paid for every man she slept with.

The contest continued throughout the night. At daybreak Mnester announced that the two women had bedded an equal number of men—twenty-five. Scylla had had enough; she took her payment and staggered away. Messalina declared that she had not yet tired, and carried on for several hours.

The lascivious, scheming Messalina was the Roman Emperor Claudius's third wife.

Unlike the idealised Roman woman, who seldom had an identity other than that of loyal wife, obedient daughter or devoted mother, Messalina practised none of the virtues that this patriarchal society demanded. Instead, she exploited the power of her position to acquire lovers and stock her personal coffers, to benefit her allies and eliminate her enemies. For seven years her political game-playing, brazen debauchery and strong streak of manipulative cruelty took a stranglehold on the citizens of Rome, severely damaging the reputation of her husband, the Emperor Claudius, in the process.

Caligula's Practical Joke

Messalina Valeria was the only daughter of Domita Lepida and the consul Marcus Valerius Messalla Barbatus. Her grandmothers had been at once half-sisters and nieces of Rome's first emperor, Augustus, and thus Messalina was a member of the nobility. Although she was a regular visitor at the palace during the reign of Emperor Claudius's predecessor, Caligula, it was rare for Messalina to be summoned into Caligula's presence. Consequently, when she was told that the Emperor wanted to see her, she approached the audience chamber somewhat fearfully.

It was common knowledge that Emperor Caligula had declined into madness. He suffered from unpredictable, often violent mood swings, he was a sadist, a sexual deviant and severely delusional, considering himself one of the gods. Messalina had no idea what lay in store for her—but it seemed that Caligula had called her into his presence for a purpose other than debauchery or death. Giggling insanely, he announced that the young and beautiful Messalina would be the perfect match for his uncle Claudius. At fifty years of age, with an uncontrollable laugh, a slobbering mouth, a running nose, a stammer, a persistent tic of the head and a stumbling walk, Claudius would have seemed far from 'perfect' to Messalina. But there was no refusing Caligula.

The grandson of Mark Antony, the unfortunate Claudius was despised by his family, and even his own mother referred to him as a 'monster of a man'. How then was Messalina expected to feel anything for him? Reports regarding Messalina's age at the time vary wildly; some say she was fifteen, others that she was thirty. Whatever the case, Claudius was much taken with his proposed bride; it was apparently love at first sight on his part.

Messalina quickly realised that she could turn the situation to her advantage. Well used to the ways of Rome, she had long craved the power that came with position. By marrying Claudius her ties to the imperial family would be strengthened, so she chose to hide her feelings of repulsion. They were married in AD 38, and Messalina soon bore

Claudius a son, Britannicus, and a daughter. But destiny was about to deal a surprise hand to Messalina, one beyond her wildest dreams of ambition.

On 24 January AD 41, Caligula was stabbed to death in the narrow corridors of the palace. There had already been several assassination attempts on the unbalanced Emperor, but the fatal hit was carried out by his own bodyguards, the Praetorian Guard, in a conspiracy involving palace officials and members of the senate. His wife and child were then sought out and murdered. Terrified, being also a member of the imperial family, Claudius ran for cover. He hid behind a curtain, where the Praetorian Guard found him, shaking and stammering. But to his astonishment, Claudius was proclaimed Emperor the very same day. Believing him to be incompetent, the conspirators had made the assumption that Claudius would be a puppet emperor and give them no trouble. To some extent they were right, for his reign might have been free of controversy were it not for the woman he had married. On 25 January AD 41, Claudius became Emperor Claudius Caesar Augustus Germanicus, and Messalina became Empress. As the Emperor's wife, and mother to the heir apparent, Messalina had suddenly become the most powerful woman in Rome.

A Reign of Tyranny

Messalina soon became aware that her position was somewhat insecure. Because of his age, it was extremely likely that Claudius would die before his son could acquire political power. Other potential successors, with a stronger connection to the bloodline of Caesar Augustus, might well step forward and lay claim to the imperial title. Messalina's chances of survival in such circumstances would be slim; as the mother of Britannicus, she would doubtless be assassinated along with her son in any coup. Messalina decided that she must take pre-emptive action, and herself annihilate anyone who could threaten her son's succession and hence her own survival. And she was prepared to use any measure available.

It was quite common for women of the Roman nobility to use sex for political advantage, and Messalina rapidly came to understand the power she possessed. But none was as proficient at sexual intrigue, or seemed to revel in it quite as much, as Messalina. She formed liaisons with a host of men, at times just to gratify her natural appetites, at others to protect her position. Often she managed to elicit sensitive information from her lovers. If they were rich, she would later have them executed for treason, confiscating their property to add to her already overflowing personal treasury.

Constantly on the lookout for new conquests, Messalina's roving eye alighted upon Mnester, a handsome actor. At first Mnester was happy to comply with her sexual demands, but as time passed she required his presence more and more, eventually insisting that he give up acting and be at her beck and call, day and night. When Mnester turned down her proposition the Empress was furious, and told Claudius that a lowly actor had refused to carry out her orders. Oblivious to what these 'orders' were, Claudius decreed that Mnester must do whatever she demanded. So it was that Mnester was forced to give up acting and submit himself to the Empress's carnal desires whenever and wherever. This success reinforced Messalina's notion that her activities were justified.

Despite his physical failings (possibly caused by a form of cerebral palsy), Claudius was definitely not a stupid man, but rather one of great intellect. When it came to women, however, particularly his beloved wife, he was a fool. Messalina's influence over him was so strong—compounded with Claudius's own suspicions, fears, and distrust of other people—that she managed to secure death sentences for great numbers of her enemies. It is known that thirty-five senators and more than three hundred other people were executed during Claudius's reign, many at Messalina's instigation.

Shortly after being declared Emperor, Claudius recalled from exile his nieces, Caligula's sisters Agrippina and Julia Livilla. Messalina was furious when Julia refused to accord her the respect she believed she deserved.

MESSALINA IS SAID to have had one man killed simply because she wanted his gardens. Consul Valerius Asiaticus owned the Gardens of Lucullus, one of the Empress's favourite places. The much admired and experienced consul was charged with failing to maintain discipline within his regiment, and with homosexual acts. Condemned to death and allowed to choose his own demise, he opted for suicide. The gardens were later passed on to the Empress. Ironically, it was here that Messalina would later meet her own death.

She was also jealous of Julia's beauty and of Claudius's obvious affection for her. On a trumped-up charge of adultery, she managed to have Julia banished once more. In fact, by accusing Julia of having an affair with Seneca, one of Rome's most accomplished authors and philosophers—a man who incidentally was strongly opposed to Messalina's immoral way of life—she managed to rid herself of two enemies at once. Under Messalina's orders, Julia was starved to death in exile. The Empress then arranged the poisoning of Julia's husband, since not only did he suspect her role in his wife's death, he'd also had the audacity to refuse her amorous advances. She was becoming a monster drunk with her own importance.

The people who might have stepped in to oppose her were simply too afraid. Even a number of Claudius's advisers had recognised Messalina's power and offered her their allegiance, including Narcissus, one of the Emperor's most trusted confidants. Though devoted to Claudius, Narcissus was an astute man who valued his own skin. Messalina was aware of his influence over her husband, and decided to involve Narcissus in her next devious scheme.

Suggesting that the military commander Appius Silanus would be a great match for her widowed mother, Lepida, Messalina encouraged Claudius to summon him back to Rome. Soon afterward, the real reason behind the marriage became apparent when Messalina tried to coax Silanus into her own bed. Infuriated when he turned her down, Messalina was also alarmed, for Silanus's loyalty to the Emperor was such that she feared he might report her behaviour, and now she involved Narcissus. Messalina and Narcissus spoke with Claudius independently,

THEN LOOK AT THOSE who rival the Gods, and hear what Claudius endured. As soon as his wife perceived that her husband was asleep, this august harlot was shameless enough to prefer a common mat to the imperial couch. Assuming night-cowl, and attended by a single maid, she issued forth; then, having concealed her raven locks under a light-coloured perruque, she took her place in a brothel reeking with long-used coverlets. Entering an empty cell reserved for herself, she there took her stand, under the feigned name of Lycisca, her nipples bare and gilded, and exposed to view the womb that bore thee, O nobly-born Britannicus! Here she graciously received all comers, asking from each his fee; and when at length the keeper dismissed his girls, she remained to the very last before closing her cell, and with passion still raging hot within her went sorrowfully away. Then exhausted by men but unsatisfied, with soiled cheeks, and begrimed with the smoke of lamps, she took back to the imperial pillow all the odours of the stews.

– Juvenal, *Satire VI*

both telling him of supposed dreams in which Silanus intended to assassinate him. Claudius firmly believed in the prophetic power of dreams, and Messalina and Narcissus were two of his most trustworthy and beloved sources, so he saw no reason to doubt them. When Silanus made a sudden entrance into Claudius's chamber one morning, for what he'd been told was a scheduled meeting, the Emperor took fright, certain that he was about to be killed. He shouted for his guards, and Appius Silanus was dragged away and executed.

Messalina cuckolded her husband continually. It seems unbelievable that she could behave in such a manner without his being aware of it, but because of the clever allegiances she had formed with many of Claudius's close advisers, talk of her infamies never reached the Emperor's ears. Even had he known, it is unlikely that he would have stood up to her outrageous antics, since he was often seen to behave more like a servant to his wife than her Emperor.

Twenty-five Men in One Night

In AD 43 Claudius led the Roman legions into Britain, and Rome was basically left to the whims of his wife. In his absence she conspired to turn the city into one huge brothel, forcing many women to prostitute themselves with other men in front of their husbands. The men who were prepared to see their wives degraded received honours and offices, and those who refused were offered the grim alternative of death.

It was at this time that Messalina is thought to have issued the challenge to Scylla. The general populace assumed that Claudius knew of his wife's excesses, and his support began to wane as a result, but it seems that he remained unaware of the true state of affairs, for in AD 44 he returned from Britain still holding nothing but adoration for his young wife. As proof of his love, Claudius obtained permission from the Senate for her to ride in the ceremonial chariot, an honour previously forbidden to women.

From AD 41 to 48, Messalina was the Achilles heel in the otherwise respected reign of her husband. Claudius had no reason to distrust his wife since her power was totally dependent on his position. But when she set eyes upon an alternative husband and emperor, her downfall was set in train.

A Hurricane from Ostia

Not long after the Emperor's return from Britain, word reached Messalina that a young consul-designate named Caius Silius was the most handsome man in Rome. As soon as she saw him, Messalina was besotted. She tried every trick in the book to woo him away from his wife and finally succeeding in seducing him. She then embarked on an outrageous plan to marry him. The historian Tacitus is quoted as saying, 'She craved the name of wife because it was outrageous and thus the greatest satisfaction to a sensation-seeker'.

Although the idea may seem preposterous, it is possible that there was method in this madness. The fact that many of the people who owed allegiance to Messalina appeared to support the marriage points to a political motivation. Caius Silius was from a well-respected family, he had the support of the Praetorian Guard, and was popular with the people. If he could marry Messalina and take the throne, she and her children would be safe from the machinations of other claimants. It is possible that the lovers planned on installing the youthful Britannicus as Emperor and ruling together as regents. Regardless, it would appear that the assassination of Claudius was now a possibility—ironically, partly due to the machinations of his wife—and that Messalina, although not the main instigator, was certainly party to the murder plot.

While Claudius was again away from Rome, on a visit to the port of Ostia, Messalina moved into action. She 'married' Silius in a huge public wedding, which was followed by a great feast. According to Tacitus, wine was flowing freely as Messalina led the guests in a wild dance. At her side was Silius, crowned with an ivy wreath. In the midst of the proceedings, one of Messalina's former lovers climbed up a tree. The guests asked playfully what he could see. His answer shocked them all: 'A hurricane from Ostia'—a cloud of dust in the distance announcing the return of Claudius and his retinue to Rome. The wedding guests were terrified, and fled the festivities.

Once Messalina's accomplice, Narcissus had become anxious that the Empress was about to seize power with Silius, and had travelled to Ostia to warn Claudius of the events unfolding. As the entourage approached, Messalina set out on foot in an attempt to intercept her husband. The people of Rome, used to seeing the Empress fly past in her royal chariot, looked on in amazement as she stood in the road. As his chariot hurtled toward her, Claudius was sorely tempted to stop, but Narcissus reminded him of her treachery and to Messalina's dismay he raced on by.

Aware that Claudius could change his mind at any moment, Narcissus showed the Emperor the imperial treasures that Messalina had appropriated and given to Silius. With this proof of his wife's attachment, Claudius could no longer ignore the situation. Death warrants were immediately signed for Silius, Mnester, and all of Messalina's accomplices. In a last attempt to avoid execution, Mnester is said to have showed Claudius his back, ravaged by Messalina's fingernails, claiming that she had forced him to sleep with her. But not even the impassioned words of an actor in the performance of his life could change his fate.

Even at this point Messalina's mood was still one of hope, combined with rage. Her mother knew that all was lost, however, and pleaded with her daughter to do the honorable thing and take her own life. Messalina refused, certain that an audience with Claudius would persuade him to forgive her. In fact, his resolve was weakening and Narcissus, seeing this, took it upon himself to give the order for Messalina's execution.

The soldiers found Messalina in the Gardens of Lucullus, lying hysterical on the ground. They insulted her, addressing her as if she was a mere slave. Messalina understood then that the end had come and that it might indeed be better to die with dignity. Pathetically scraping at her throat with her dagger, she found she did not have the courage to kill herself, and the guards unceremoniously beheaded her on the spot. When the news of her death reached Claudius, as it soon did, he did not ask how she had died, but simply demanded another cup of wine.

Whether Messalina was an astute player in court politics, a quasi-psychopath, or merely a misguided woman who fell victim to her own weaknesses and excesses, is subject to debate. Whatever her motives, in an era where lust, incest, murder, debauchery, madness and corruption were seemingly commonplace, Messalina has been reported as one of the worst. Her notoriety remains legendary, and her name has entered our vocabulary as a synonym for the ultimate immoral temptress.

Following the death of her husband, King Prasutagus, in AD 60, Queen Boudica became ruler of the Celtic Iceni tribe in East Anglia, Britain.

Boudica

The Celtic warrior queen who took no prisoners

AD 30–62

It is not as a woman descended from noble ancestry but as one of the people that I am avenging lost freedom ... This is a woman's resolve. As for the men, they may live and be slaves!

– Boudica

Stepping from her chariot, Queen Boudica reached into the folds of her tunic and pulled out a wild hare. She held the animal up for all to see, then lowered it gently to the ground, her 200 000 warriors looking on expectantly. The hare froze for a second, as if turned to stone by the intensity of that collective gaze, before exploding into life and racing up the hill toward the enemy. Surely this was the signal that the gods were on the side of the Britons and wished them to vanquish the Romans. Boudica led the charge into battle.

In AD 60–61 Boudica, Queen of the Iceni, outraged at the brutal treatment of her people at the hands of the Romans, performed what, at the time, must have seemed like a miracle. Through the sheer force of her personality and her courage, she united a number of warring Celtic tribes and led a fierce revolt that almost defeated the well-oiled fighting machine that was the Roman army, and came close to destroying its power base in Britain. Three major cities were destroyed and an estimated eighty thousand citizens and 'collaborators'—as Boudica regarded them—were massacred. The Roman historian Tacitus describes her merciless onslaught: 'It was not on making prisoners or selling them or any of the barter of war that the enemy was bent but on slaughter, on the gibbet, the fire and the cross'. The Roman Governor of Britain, Gaius Suetonius Paulinus, was busy quelling rebels in Wales when Boudica cut a swathe through southeast Britain. What humiliated the Romans about this revolt was that the rebel hordes of wild Celts were led not just by a Roman subject, if only a Briton—but by a woman.

A Troubled Legacy

Boudica (also Boudicca, Boadicea) was born into a high-ranking family in the Trinobante tribe in AD 30. Her rank meant that from an early age she would have been trained to ride a horse and later to drive the heavy two-wheeled chariot that tested the skill of even the strongest man. At that time, Britain was made up of countless warring tribes, forever discovering new reasons to attack each other. The neighbouring Iceni in East Anglia, among the largest of the tribes, were led by the much-loved King Prasutagus, who had found a way of successfully operating under an oppressive Roman rule while ensuring that the dignity of his people was respected. The striking, flame-haired Boudica, tall and distinctly Amazonian in appearance, caught his attention and they were married in AD 48. The Iceni enjoyed a relatively trouble-free period under the guidance of this King and Queen, and celebrated the birth of their two daughters—whom the Celtic people regarded as being as worthy as any male heir to carry on the royal line.

This peaceful period came to a sudden end when Prasutagus fell gravely ill. In an attempt to take care of his Queen and to ensure his daughters were given a proper dowry, the King made a will in which he left his land and most of his money and possessions to the Emperor and bequeathed his remaining fortune to his wife. To the Iceni this seemed a fair distribution of his worldly goods but it was to prove a fatal mistake. Like all the leaders of the Celtic tribes following the Roman invasion under Claudius, Prasutagus was a client ruler and there was a strict code to be observed. It was against Roman law to leave any part of a personal fortune to anyone other than the Emperor. Prasutagus passed away peacefully—but almost before the last funeral rites had been observed, the wrath of Rome under Nero, the new Emperor, was unleashed.

Roman administrators in Britain took furious issue with the will of the dead Iceni King and sent troops to make an example of the troublesome tribe and their Queen. It was decreed that all the Iceni chiefs have their hereditary titles taken from them and that all the relatives of Prasutagus be forced into slavery. Boudica watched in horror as the Roman soldiers ransacked her palace, taking with them everything they could carry. Adding terrible insult to injury, they dragged the struggling Queen to the market place, stripped her, and flogged her with rods in front of a horrified crowd. As she screamed in rage and agony, the soldiers turned on her daughters, the teenage princesses, and subjected them to ritual rape. The message from Rome was loud and clear: the Britons were Rome's subordinates and in future they must adhere to the rules laid down by their captors or suffer the awful consequences.

Comforting her distraught daughters, Boudica watched the soldiers rampaging through the town, lashing her people, young and old, driving them helter-skelter through the streets as if herding cattle. This moment was a turning point for the Iceni Queen. Consumed by fury, she swore to bring the Roman invaders to their knees. The largest indigenous tribe in

Britain, the Iceni had always had a reputation for being relatively peaceful —but now it was to be all-out war.

Blood in the Water

Boudica forged an alliance with the Trinobante, themselves a large tribe, and turned to the scattered smaller tribes in the region who were habitually at war with each other, realising that if she could get them to work together they had the potential to become a serious united force. Secretly she travelled between the tribes, displaying the wounds she had received at the hands of the Romans and telling of the atrocities they had committed. She was a persuasive and inspirational speaker, able to pass on her vision of the tribes acting as one, capable of overthrowing the occupiers, seizing back power. From contemporary descriptions she must have made an impressive figure as she harangued various groups. Roman historian Cassius Dio wrote: 'In stature she was very tall, in appearance most terrifying, in the glance of an eye most fierce, and her voice was harsh; a great mass of the tawniest hair fell to her hips; around her neck was a large golden necklace; and she wore a tunic of diverse colours over which a thick mantle was fastened with a brooch'. The warring tribes began to share the vision Boudica offered, of a Britain free from Rome's tyrannical yoke. Putting aside years of bitter disputes and rivalry, they pledged their allegiance to the Iceni Queen.

Boudica had undergone a metamorphosis since the death of her peace-loving husband, discovering the passion and the skills she needed to transform herself into a tribal leader and orator. She succeeded in amassing a huge army, with the whole of East Anglia taking up arms. While to the Romans the thought of a woman leading an army, or even fighting alongside men, was laughable, the Britons held no such prejudices. In Celtic culture, goddesses were revered and women were seen as equal to men. Of a battle in 102 BC between the Romans and the Celts, Plutarch had remarked: 'The fight had been no less fierce with

Boudica fires up her 200 000-strong army of Celtic warriors, both men and women, with a stirring speech before leading the charge into battle against the Romans.

the women than with the men themselves … the women charged with swords and axes and fell upon their opponents uttering a hideous outcry'. Boudica's Celtic sisters threw themselves into the fray with enthusiasm. To the Romans, used to prim matrons who took care of the children and the household gods, waiting patiently for their husbands to come home from war, these women were the stuff of nightmare.

Boudica was not only to prove herself a great warrior but was about to show she was an accomplished military strategist as well. Leading an army of more than 100 000 warriors, the Queen set her sights on Camulodunum (modern-day Colchester), the new administrative capital of the imperial province. Camulodunum, in effect a colony of retired Roman soldiers, was the center of Roman religion and authority in Britain. The tribes around the city had been cruelly mistreated by the veterans; many of their people had been banished from their homes and forced into slavery. They hated their Roman masters but had never had the numbers to mount an attack. When the red-haired Boudica called them to arms, they rose as one, convinced that this was the moment they had been waiting for.

As Boudica was marching on Camulodunum, Suetonius was cornering rebels on the island of Mona (modern-day Anglesey), unaware that his rule was about to face its most serious challenge. As the Queen drew nearer the city, it seemed that the gods themselves were on her side. The Roman historian Tacitus tells how the statue of Victory, erected by the Emperor Claudius as a symbol of Rome's domination, suddenly fell, landing with its back facing the direction from which Boudica was approaching. The citizens of Camulodunum were horrified, interpreting this to mean that they were destined to flee from the oncoming enemy. More foreboding omens followed, seeming to warn that death was imminent. As the Warrior Queen came closer, strange moans were heard in the Senate House and there were rumours of screams echoing across the stage. Some frightened witnesses said they had seen the river change to the colour of blood. Even the sceptics among them were silenced by reports that when the tide ebbed, it left behind the likeness of human forms and the ruins of a ghostly city.

On being told of the rebellion, a badly rattled Suetonius immediately sent part of his forces to march on the beleaguered city. But he was too late, and the prophecy that the river would change to the colour of blood was to be horribly fulfilled. Despite all the omens, the veterans and their families were not prepared for the savagery of the British attack. Boudica razed Camulodunum to the ground and every man, woman and child,

Romans and collaborators alike, was put to the sword. She was utterly merciless, determined to take no prisoners, preferring instead to sacrifice them to the Celtic gods of war. It is estimated that some seventy thousand people were massacred, in what today might have been described as 'ethnic cleansing'.

Suetonius had sent a legion of five thousand troops, thinking that this would be enough to quell the rebellion, but Boudica was ready for them. Experts at ambush, the rebel forces attacked the Romans outside Camulodunum. News of the rebel success spread through the country and the smaller tribes, who had wavered at first in their resolve to take on the Romans, now joined the Warrior Queen on her mission to drive the invaders from their land.

Unmoved by Tears and Prayers

Boudica now led her triumphant forces toward Londinium (modern-day London), the largest city in the British Isles and a thriving centre of commerce. Unlike Camulodunum, Londinium had no official Roman settlement but was full of those who had prospered under Rome's rule, mainly peaceful traders, merchants and moneylenders. To Boudica, they were nothing more than collaborators and therefore must suffer the consequences of their betrayal. Learning of the Queen's approach, the terrified merchants sent pleas for help to Suetonius. Londinium had no fortifying walls to hide behind, and its people were more used to handling money than wielding swords. Suetonius reached Londinium before Boudica, but on making a swift assessment of the city's strategic weaknesses realised he had no chance against the Warrior Queen. 'Unmoved by tears and prayers,' reports Tacitus, 'Suetonius gave the signal for departure.'

Unopposed, Boudica and her army rampaged through the city, massacring between thirty and forty thousand people. According to Cassius Dio:

Those who were taken captive by the Britons were subjected to every known outrage. The worst, most bestial atrocity committed by their captors was the following: first, they hung up naked the noblest and most distinguished women and then cut off their breasts and sewed them to their mouths, in order to make the victims appear to be eating them. Afterward they impaled the women on sharp skewers run lengthwise through their entire body.

The attacking tribes were living up to their barbaric reputation, appearing to be driven by a bloodlust that nothing could sate. Whatever righteousness was on Boudica's side at the outset of her mission must surely have been stripped away in the pitiless massacre of the innocents that followed.

Word of the rebels' success was spreading to tribes throughout the country and their numbers were increasing daily. Leaving Londinium in flames, Boudica turned her army toward Verulamium (modern-day St. Albans), which was made up entirely of Roman sympathisers. She was bent on total destruction. As she was by now leading a massive force of up to 200 000 warriors, it must have been difficult to imagine how anything could stand in her way. But Suetonius was waiting. Recognising that Boudica posed an increasingly serious threat to the Roman presence in Briton, he had chosen to sacrifice Londinium, anticipating her move on Verulamium. Ready to fall on his sword if he failed this time, he marched to confront the Warrior Queen and her hordes.

In the face of Boudica's approach, the people of Verulamium fled. Anyone who remained was killed and the city was totally destroyed. But here it seems that Boudica may have allowed her frenzy for revenge to override her undoubted skills as a strategist. Had she paused on her headlong rush to Verulamium, she might have intercepted Suetonius at a point along the way where his soldiers were exposed and unable to resist the advantage of the numbers she possessed. So why did she fail to confront her adversary? It is possible that as her army grew in size the Warrior Queen was beginning to lose control, or that communicating a change of plan was impractical. In any event, this missed opportunity was to have fatal consequences.

Conquer or Die with Glory!

Suetonius chose a battleground outside the city of Verulamium, positioning his troops in an open space at the top of a slight incline, a forest shielding him on one side. This gave him a clear advantage, since Boudica could attack from only one direction—the bottom of the hill. But looking down toward a ground darkening with the gathering army of Celts, Suetonius's ten thousand soldiers might have been forgiven if their nerve had failed. The war cries floating up to them seemed more like the cries of wild animals. Many of the 'barbarians' were naked, their skin painted blue. Suetonius tried to rally his men for what lay ahead, ridiculing the rebel force, stressing that the Celts were nothing more than a bunch of 'runaways' and that many of them would be fighting with their bare hands. But his soldiers' eyes could not help but fix on the figure that rode into the clearing, gripping a spear in one hand and the reins of her chariot with the other—the flame-haired Amazon whipping her forces to even greater fury.

Boudica drove among the ranks of her army, now 200 000 strong, watching while families gathered on the plain at the rear. Grandparents, wives and children took their places in wagons to witness the glory and reclaim the freedom that had been so cruelly seized from them. On that fateful morning in AD 62, there can be little doubt that by now Boudica was battle-scarred and weary, and that the effort to hold herself erect as she gripped the reins of her plunging horses was immense. Nevertheless, she delivered a rousing speech to her warriors, telling them that heaven was on their side, assuring them that the Romans waiting above them thought only of flight and would not sustain even 'the din and shout of so many thousands, much less our charge and blows'. With the hare released, the signs augured well—the gods were on their side. Her battle cry rang out above their heads: 'Conquer, or die with glory!'

Suetonius waited until the last moment. When he gave the order, javelins flew through the air in a disciplined wave, decimating the front line of the advancing rebels. The Romans moved in from all sides, pinning Boudica's forces back against their horrified families, the circle of wagons preventing them from taking flight. Crushed together, the

A bronze sculpture of Boudica stands outside the Houses of Parliament in Westminster, London.

rebels were unable to use their long swords and the scene descended into carnage as the Britons were brought down by Roman swords. It was Suetonius's turn to be ruthless, ordering his soldiers to slaughter the families trapped in the wagons as well, determined that such an uprising would never happen again.

THERE ARE MANY CLAIMS as to where Boudica's body lies. Some believe it is buried deep under the earth below Platform 10 at King's Cross Station in London.

With defeat staring her in face, Boudica slipped from the battlefield, her dream of liberation from Roman rule in tatters. She knew a crowing Nero would parade her through the streets of Rome and her daughters would be raped and tortured. The Warrior Queen chose death over captivity. Boudica filled a chalice with poison, passing it first to her daughters before raising it to her own lips.

History has been determined to find in Boudica a worthy British heroine—one who almost triumphed against the might of Rome. The life-size bronze statue of Boudica standing tall in her chariot, her daughters at her side, occupies pride of place opposite the Houses of Parliament in London, reminding passers-by of her heroic stand. But it cannot be denied that although she had enormous courage, and for a brief period succeeded in welding warring factions into one cohesive force, Boudica was also, in the tradition of her people, the most savage and ruthless of leaders. Merciless in battle, it was on her orders that thousands of innocent civilians, including women and children, were tortured and slain. Despite this, her fight for freedom has continued to resonate. Some of the worst atrocities of those battles have been edited out of the collective memory by those who see in the Warrior Queen a proud feminist icon and fierce champion of the oppressed.

The seated Spanish conquistador Cortés, with his interpreter Malinali at his side, negotiates with the Aztec emissaries.

Malinali

The Mexican slave who consorted with Cortés

c. 1500–1527

Doña Marina, although a native woman, possessed such manly valor that though she heard every day that the Indians were going to kill us and eat our flesh with chillis ... she betrayed no weakness but showed a courage greater than that of a woman.

– Bernal Dìaz del Castillo (Spanish historian)

Malinali listened as the Aztec emissaries tried to make themselves understood by the Spanish conquistadores. They spoke a dialect that the Spanish interpreter could not understand, and without his help there would be no negotiation, only violence. Malinali could understand what the Aztecs were saying, and she also spoke the dialect that Jéronimo de Aguilar had mastered. She was the link they needed, but it was difficult for her to speak up since she was a mere slave, who had been presented to the invaders as a prize in an effort to persuade them to move on. Malinali had been betrayed into slavery when she was a little girl, and sold on at least twice. Why should she help a people who treated her with such contempt?

But the desire to break this impasse was stronger even than her resentment. Perhaps she understood that her unusual language skills would give her a power she had never enjoyed before. Taking a deep breath, she began to speak. Cortés looked across at the native girl whom he had already decided would be the property of one of his most trusted generals. As he listened to her now, he began to change his mind.

Malinali Tenepal, christened Marina by the Spaniards and called La Malinche (the 'Captain's Woman') by the Aztecs, is reviled by many Mexicans, who see her as acting as Cortés's accomplice, helping him to destroy the great Aztec empire and engaging with him in a bloodthirsty quest for power and gold. The term *malinchista* came to be synonymous with one who loved foreigners and betrayed their own country for profit or because of a feeling of inferiority. But the demonising of Malinali and the portrayal of her as traitor, temptress and whore began only in 1821, some three centuries after her death, when Mexican nationalists became determined to give their newly independent country a proud new identity and wipe out any trace of the Spanish and those who had defected to their side. The fact that Malinali bore Cortés a child reinforced their picture of her as a 'Mexican Eve', sexually consorting with the enemy and leading her own people to destruction. There is a belief still prevalent that the reason women are often mistreated in Mexican society can be traced back to Malinali. But while to the nationalists she was the ultimate betrayer, to others she was a strong woman, fighting for her independence at a time when women were often treated as slaves and had no voice in affairs. Malinali's voice was to change the history of her people for ever.

Sold into Slavery

A certain mystery surrounds Malinali's early life, the exact date and place of her birth being unknown, perhaps adding another layer to the legend for subsequent eager historians to weave their own stories around. It is known, however, that she was born between 1502 and 1505 on the day called Malinal, that she was brought up in the Veracruz region of southern Mexico, and was the daughter of a *cacique*, meaning she belonged to a noble Aztec family. There is no doubt too that she received an education and showed an early aptitude for language skills. This relatively privileged life came to an abrupt end when her father died and her mother took a new husband. Malinali was the natural heir to her father's estate, but when her mother gave birth to a son, her stepfather decided she should be hastily removed. According to Bernal Dìaz del Castillo, an historian who had been a soldier during the Spanish conquest and who knew Malinali, her parents sold her as a slave to some passing traders—'Indians from Xicalanco'—and then pretended she had died in the night. The callousness of her mother's behaviour must have left an enduring mark on the young child. It was the ultimate betrayal and the beginning of years of servitude and abuse.

The Mayan traders who had bought Malinali soon sold her on to some Tabascas and so, treated like a commodity rather than a human being, she found herself finally in the city of Potonchán, where a wealthy lord bought her services. Hour after tedious hour, she was forced to weave textiles and listen to the chatter of the local women, who were undoubtedly a notch above her in the pecking order. With her natural ear for languages, Malinali found herself drinking in the sounds and soon picked up the local Mayan language. Unwittingly she had acquired the key that would eventually release her from slavery, but for the moment she knew with a grim certainty that her destiny was mapped out for her—as soon as she reached adolescence, she would become a concubine. Before long, however, she was to find herself being offered once again as a prize for a very different master—and at last the opportunity arose to take charge of her fate.

Conquistadores

In 1519, as Malinali spun and wove and listened to the rise and fall of the voices around her, Hernán Cortés, the leader of six hundred Spanish conquistadores, attacked the city of Potonchán, determined to execute the orders of his royal master and bring these troublesome Indians under the yoke of Spain. The Catholic religion was of course part of that package, and the search for the fabled wealth of the Atzecs acted as a keen

The nineteen-year-old slave girl Malinali is presented to Cortés by the Mayans as a peace offering.

spur to their endeavours. The Mayan warriors, inadequately equipped to deal with the more sophisticated Spanish weaponry, quickly sought other measures to appease their foes. To Malinali's dismay, she and nineteen other young women were presented to the Spanish as a peace offering.

The Spanish informed the women that to equip them for their new role as concubines, they must first be baptised into the Catholic religion. For Malinali this was not the ordeal it might have been, since her own gods had always seemed resolutely oblivious to her plight. Her defiant air combined with her striking beauty caught the attention of Cortés, and after her baptism he 'gave' her to his close friend, Alonso Hernández Puertocarrero. Once again she must have felt a fierce frustration at her helplessness, but at least she had moved one step closer to the source of power.

It appears that Malinali quickly took to the rituals of her new faith and enjoyed the sense of being born again as she received her baptismal name of Marina. At least human sacrifice was not on the menu of this god, who seemed content with bread and wine. Others may have looked askance at how readily Malinali, now Marina, turned her back upon the sacred rites of her people. Perhaps there were whisperings. Trained to be submissive, to cook and spin, to always obey, the treatment she received at the hands of these bearded foreigners armed with their crucifixes and swords probably seemed no worse than anything she had endured before. When Cortés travelled to the Aztec capital of Tenochtitlán, now the site of Mexico City, Marina, as the mistress of Puertocarrero, went with them.

The Emperor Montezuma, all-powerful leader of the Aztecs, sent emissaries to intercept the advancing Spanish army and discover their intentions. Cortés was anxious to negotiate but at the first meeting interpreter Jéronimo de Aguilar struggled to understand them, for while he spoke Mayan, he was not acquainted with Náhuatl, the Aztec language. Watching Cortés's frustration grow, Marina stepped forward and managed an apparently effortless translation. That a mere woman had such sophisticated language skills came as a shock to the powerful men who had been moving closer to a violent resolution while they fumbled to understand each other. Marina spoke both Mayan and Náhuatl, Aguilar spoke Mayan and Spanish, so a complicated chain of translation began with Marina acting as the conduit for negotiation.

Cortés was captivated, knowing he had found the tool he needed, and he adopted Marina as his interpreter and secretary. She had made herself irreplaceable, but it was from this point that her actions were later to be traduced by the nineteenth century Mexican nationalists, who gave her the reputation of turncoat and betrayer of her nation. (In fact, Mexico wasn't a nation at that time but a region of warring kingdoms, many of which, like the Cholotecas, the Campeolans and the Tlaxcalans, hated the Aztecs and the tributes they exacted.)

Before long, Marina had added fluent Spanish to her repertoire and was able to dispense with Aguilar's help, standing beside Cortés at his meetings with the local people, confidently negotiating and laying out his political agenda—perhaps even adding a few flourishes of her own. It must have been clear to the conquistadores that this slight native girl possessed impressive leadership skills herself. But in the eyes of the Indians she was guilty of a dangerous deviation from the norm, for women of that time, in their cultures, were allowed no voice at formal occasions.

By now, Cortés had taken back the 'gift' he had given to Puertocarrero and taken Marina to his bed—a fact made much of by subsequent historians intent on deriding her as the Mexican Eve, ready to sell herself to the devil himself. But did she have any choice in the matter? In any event, it is certain that Cortés became increasingly dependent on her loyal assistance as she helped him navigate his way through unfamiliar territory, negotiating with the Indians as they went. His troops were dangerously thin on the ground and Cortés hoped to persuade the tribes in the vicinity to join him, always using Marina (now respectfully addressed as Doña Marina) as his 'voice'.

The Cholula Massacre

Cortés soon worked out a way of conquering those Indians who failed to come to heel. First his soldiers would go in hard on the attack, wielding their weapons with consummate skill and ensuring that the damage they inflicted was enough to demonstrate their strength. Then, when the chastened Indians were retreating in disarray, Marina would approach the negotiating table and offer them the option of joining the conquistadores. In this way Cortés managed to conscript large numbers of Tlaxcala warriors, who agreed to assist in the conquest of their old enemies, the Aztecs. No doubt, Cortés was able to exploit the fact that the Tlaxcalas were angry that it was from their numbers the Aztecs often chose the victims to be sacrificed to their gods. Marina had advanced to a position of main player and in later centuries was regarded as the root cause of the bloody events that followed.

On their way to Tenochtitlán, the capital of the Aztec kingdom, Cortés and his growing army marched towards Cholula, 'one of the most beautiful cities imaginable', and also the wealthiest trading centre in the region. The Cholulas seem to have decided not to put up a fight and welcomed the conquistadores into their city, while stipulating that their old enemies, the Tlaxcalas, should camp outside the walls. For the first few days the Spaniards were treated as honoured guests, housed within a palace and provided with lavish feasts. Marina seems to have baffled the Cholulas. After all she was an Aztec like them, and surely was being held against her will. A Cholulan noblewoman warned Marina that she should escape immediately because there was a plot to massacre the entire Spanish army. But Marina, by now his faithful companion and servant, warned Cortés of the danger, beginning the chain of events that was to have fatal consequences for the Cholulas.

Fired up by the warning, a furious Cortés gathered his men around him, swearing that this time there would be no damage limitation when they attacked. While the Cholulan warriors waited unarmed in an enclosure near the pyramid temple of Quetzalcóatl, the Spanish army descended upon them to slaughter without mercy. It was to be the bloodiest of massacres, a tragedy in which a triumphant Cortés estimated that three thousand Cholulas were killed. Mexico's nationalistic historians believed it was at least twice that number.

News of the massacre travelled quickly to Tenochtitlán where, as Bernal Dìaz said, 'If we had a reputation for valour before, from now on they took us for sorcerers'. The Aztecs were terrified of the Spanish, and Cortés marched on toward the Valley of Mexico and the home of Emperor Montezuma II, meeting no resistance. Many Aztecs knew of the Aztec woman who travelled with the Spanish; for some, Marina symbolised the hope that perhaps the conquistadores came in peace. For others, her role in the slaughter by the temple of Quetzalcóatl meant that she was evil personified. On 8 November 1519, as Cortés marched into the lake-island city of Tenochtitlán with six thousand Indians in his ranks, it seemed he had achieved a bloodless coup. Riding beside him into the Aztec capital, knowing she was assisting in the destruction of her people's heritage, Marina must have questioned her role. Perhaps she hoped that she could encourage them to embrace the Catholic faith and that she could use her talents of diplomacy to find a peaceful resolution. Or did that moment feel like sweet revenge for the abuse she had suffered at the hands of her family and her tribe?

La Noche Triste

Marina was present at every meeting between Cortés and Montezuma. At first the Aztec leader lavished gifts on his Spanish guest and made promises that seemed to imply that he would eventually offer him the city. (It is sometimes suggested that Montezuma and many others at first thought the white-skinned Spaniards were gods, as foretold in an ancient myth.) Marina watched as the days passed and the two men circled each other like wary lions, each trying to assess the strength of the other. She was privy to things no Aztec woman had ever experienced, accompanying Cortés and Montezuma to the temple of the city's supreme deity, Huitzilopochtli, the god of war and the sun. The stench of human sacrifice hung in the air, for the most recent victims were still burning, suspended in the temple braziers. The horrifying nature of the temple was a scene usually witnessed only by priests and victims. Maintaining her composure, Marina informed the Emperor that the human sacrifices and the worship of the Aztec gods—referred to by Cortés as 'devils'—should cease. Montezuma was furious, insulted by such blasphemy, and from that moment all pretence of cordiality vanished.

Montezuma's army was now only held in check by their fear that the Spaniards were foreign gods with supernatural powers, while the Spanish army, in effect made up of disparate Indian tribes, was exhausted and potentially unruly. One tiny spark might result in a terrifying conflagration. Attempting to control the situation, Cortés placed Montezuma under house arrest, but in doing so excited the fury of the population, who gathered on the streets baying for his blood. Cortés implored Montezuma to speak to his people and for a moment the unruly mob stopped to listen. Then a volley of stones thrown by impetuous hands struck the Emperor; seriously wounded, he was carried from the scene.

It was Marina who now seemed to take control. Standing erect before the crowds, she appealed to their leaders and appeared to calm them. But Montezuma died of his wounds shortly afterward. A day later, knowing his forces were outnumbered, Cortés decided to flee. Under cover of night, the Spanish army wrapped the hoofs of their horses in thick cloth and attempted a silent retreat. But to no avail—an old woman raised the alarm. In the chaos that followed, many of the Spanish drowned in the lake, weighed down by their armour; others were captured and triumphantly sacrificed to the gods. Marina and Cortés managed to escape alive, clinging together on the back of his horse and disappearing into the night.

The Spanish called it *la noche triste*—the sorrowful night—but victory for the people of Tenochtitlán was short-lived, for smallpox began to ravage the city. The conquistadores had left the disease behind them like a Trojan horse that would ensure the destruction of Tenochtitlán. Since the Aztecs had no immunity, thousands died. The Spaniards who'd survived the battle took to the hills and worked alongside their Tlaxcalan allies, preparing to lay siege to the city. By 1521, when the attack finally came, the people of Tenochtitlán could put up little resistance, their bodies riddled with disease and putrefying corpses piling up in the streets. But it was the six thousand Indians whom Marina had enlisted who were to prove the deciding factor as they stormed the city for the final time and put it to the torch. In the event, destroying the city of Tenochtitlán may have prevented the deadly disease from ravaging the whole country. In a strange twist of fate, Marina had indirectly been her people's saviour.

After the Conquest

In 1524, Marina set out to accompany Cortés on an exhausting march to Honduras in order to wrest it back from Cristobal de Olid who had claimed it as his own. Yet again her skills as a translator and negotiator were to prove invaluable. But it seems Cortés was preparing himself for his return to Spain. It was on this expedition that he married Marina off to one of his respected officers, Juan Jaramillo, despite the fact that in 1522 she had borne Cortés a son, Martín. (Don Martín de Cortés is on record as the very first Mexican, a mix of Spanish and Indian blood. He was sent to Spain to be educated and in 1548, at the age of twenty-six, was executed for conspiracy.) Marina later had a daughter, Maria, to Jaramillo.

After the conquest of Honduras, Marina asked to be reunited with her mother and her half-brother, whom she had not seen since she had first been sold into slavery. Her terrified family assumed that she was going to have them killed for their betrayal of her, knowing how powerful she had become. But it seems that Marina, still only in her early twenties and now a mother, had seen enough bloodshed to last a lifetime, and she met her family with gifts and forgiveness, practising the doctrine of her new faith.

It seems, also, that Marina's usefulness to Spain had reached its end. Following her marriage to Jaramillo she disappears from the historical record, and it is thought that she may have died a victim of plague at the

NEGATIVE IMAGES OF MALINCHE are to be found in the work of the artist José Clemente Orozo, whose 1926 painting shows her naked, embracing Cortés as she stands upon the piled-up corpses of the massacred natives.

age of twenty-five. Ambiguity and mystery surround her death just as they did much of her life, fuelling the legends and the myths that were to gather around her.

Cortés mentioned Marina very rarely in the letters he wrote to his master, Charles V, perhaps embarrassed that a woman had played such a vital part in his conquest, referring to her rather off-handedly as 'my interpreter, who is an Indian woman'. But the nationalist historians of the nineteenth and twentieth centuries ensured that she had a leading part in terms of her responsibility for the colonisation of Mexico, even claiming that without her the conquest would have failed. She became an empty vessel into which those with their own political agendas and vested interests poured their venom, depicted as a woman who could never get enough of the white man, perhaps even sexually voracious. In recent years, there has been a more sympathetic portrayal of her, and a recognition that without her interpreting skills and ability to make Cortés understand the customs and temperament of her people, there would have been even more bloodshed. That such a small force succeeded in conquering the mighty Aztec empire must have been a bitter pill to swallow for those determined at a later date to glorify the traditions and prowess of the pre-Hispanic Indians. Perhaps it helped to soothe bruised male egos to believe that an evil temptress had been at work.

Mary Tudor was the daughter of King Henry VIII and his first wife, Catherine of Aragon.

Mary I of England

Queen, defender of the faith, and executioner of innocents

1516–1558

Always remain steadfast to the true faith.

–Mary I on her deathbed

Queen Mary stood beside the water at Greenwich Palace, downhearted as her beloved husband Philip approached to take his leave of her. She wondered whether, if she were as beautiful as her half-sister Elizabeth, he might not be leaving. Banishing the traitorous thought, she achieved a warm smile. Apart from Mary's father, who had cruelly let her down, her husband, Prince Philip of Spain, with his delicate features, blue eyes and sensitive nature, was the only man she had ever, and would ever, love. Just when Mary had begun to despair in her quest to find a suitable husband, Philip had been suggested to her—and not only was he suitable, she fell in love with him as well. But now he was going away—and apparently heartbroken by Mary's failure to give him a child.

Philip was not quite as heartbroken as he appeared, however. He was planning to enjoy the amorous attentions of younger, far less neurotic women in Amsterdam while he took care of Spanish business in the Netherlands. With a final solemn bow to his Queen, Philip turned his back on England and stepped lightly aboard his ship. Mary trod briskly up the steps into the palace and paused at a window which overlooked the water, away from the prying eyes of her courtiers. There, as she watched the wind filling the sails of Philip's convoy, Mary gave way to grief. Through her tears she watched the ships sail toward the horizon, taking with them the love of her life and leaving her alone with nothing but her prayers.

Mary is one of the most infamous of British monarchs, earning herself the unenviable title of 'Bloody Mary' for zealously hunting down those who failed to convert to Catholicism during her reign and 'purging' what she saw as their heresy in fire. She was responsible for the execution of at least three hundred people, many of them poverty-stricken peasants whose only sin was to remain loyal to their Protestant faith. Her successor, Elizabeth, learned a lesson from Mary's overzealousness, promising she would never 'make windows in to men's souls', where Mary had battered down the doors and put those who resisted her onto the rack and into the flames. A devout Catholic, Mary ruled for only five years, but in that short time she acquired the reputation which has made her one of the most despised rulers in England's history.

Fall from Grace

It would be difficult to find a child who began life more privileged than Mary Tudor. Born in 1516, the only daughter of the English king, Henry VIII, and his Spanish queen, Catherine of Aragon, Mary was adored by both parents and extravagant gifts were lavished upon her. By the age of nine, she even had her own court at Ludlow Castle, full of little courtiers the same age. Although Henry made it clear he needed a male heir, he was a doting father and would insist that nothing was too good for his little princess. Catherine had suffered many miscarriages and the loss of a baby prince before Mary's birth, and viewed her as a special gift from God. So it was that until the age of fourteen, Mary enjoyed an idyllic childhood, secure in the knowledge that she was one of the most important of all the European princesses, offered several times in marriage in attempts to form alliances.

THE GREATEST PEARL
in the kingdom.
– Henry VIII

How shocking then it must have been when Mary's much-loved and loving father began to direct his attentions elsewhere. What had she done to displease him? And what could she do to regain his affections? Mary chastised herself, trying to work out how she had failed. The answer was simple, of course—she was not a boy.

Increasingly desperate for a son, and convinced that Catherine was now barren, Henry had begun to look elsewhere for the mother of his heir. His gaze fell upon one of Catherine's ladies-in-waiting. Anne Boleyn—young, beautiful, cultured and sexually alluring—made the loyal Catherine seem staid and old by comparison. The lustful Henry was bewitched by the tantalising Anne, but she refused to bestow any sexual favours on him unless she became his wife. Not a man to be thwarted, Henry embarked on an effort to break up his marriage that was to have far-reaching implications for the Church and for England.

Mary watched in growing confusion as her father begged her mother to agree to an annulment of their marriage. Catherine refused, not only because of her religious beliefs, but also keenly aware that if she did, her daughter would be seen as illegitimate and thus forfeit her right to the throne. Increasingly frustrated, Henry came up with what seemed to him a 'cunning plan', arguing that since Catherine had been briefly married to his brother Arthur, his own marriage to her was incestuous and as such, null and void. An educated young woman, well read in Christian theology, Mary bravely joined battle with her father, questioning his attempts to ground his argument in the scriptures of Leviticus and Deuteronomy. She pointed out that this provision had only applied to Jewish marriages, and should not be manipulated to fit Henry's own situation. The father did not take kindly to the daughter's attempts to educate him.

Henry now asked the Pope in Rome to officially annul the marriage. The Pope refused, criticising him for even entertaining such a notion. Furious, Henry took a step that was to forever change the course of English history. In 1533 he outlawed papal power in England, declared himself the Head of the English Church, and secretly married Anne. Furious in his turn, the Pope immediately excommunicated him. Thomas Cranmer, appointed Archbishop of Canterbury by the King, decreed his marriage to Catherine void and his marriage to Anne legal.

Mary watched as her mother's position was usurped by Henry's new wife, and was to feel pushed even further back into the shadows when, in 1534, Anne gave birth to a daughter, Elizabeth. She was not the son Henry wanted, of course, but his new daughter quickly became his new favourite.

With Catherine still steadfastly refusing to agree to divorce, Henry focused his anger on the previously much-loved Mary. He was in for a surprise. These turbulent years had altered her, and she was no longer the sweet, compliant girl and devoted daughter she had once been. Henry stripped Mary of the title of princess; to his fury, she refused to accept the demotion and stood up to him with the same steady resolve as Catherine. Both women were asked to sign a document accepting Henry as the Head of the English Church but, determined not to betray their Catholic faith, neither would acquiesce. Enraged by what he saw as insolence and insubordination, Henry banished Catherine from court and persuaded Parliament to pronounce his firstborn child illegitimate, thus removing her from the line of succession. Mary's fall from favour was swift and absolute.

The once privileged princess now found herself imprisoned for long periods of time with little food and few companions. A psychological game was played in which rumours of her projected painful demise at the orders of Anne Boleyn were purposely fed to the already distraught young woman. To add to the humiliation, when Mary wasn't imprisoned she was forced to take up duty as a humble lady-in-waiting to her half-sister Elizabeth, the little girl who had inherited her father's indomitable personality and resilience—not to mention his flaming red hair. Mary's proud Aragon blood made her feel this insult keenly and she found it hard to entertain sisterly feelings toward her rival. When Henry proclaimed Elizabeth his heir, Mary was devastated. Only her faith helped her survive.

Through this faith, Mary managed by an enormous feat of the imagination to convince herself that her father was merely a puppet in Anne Boleyn's hands. Loyalty, steadfastness and devotion were Mary's great attributes, but they were of little use in a court where everyone seemed to be plotting against each other and jostling for power. The heartbreak of her situation was taking its toll on her, however. Now in her twenties, her health started to fail and she became plagued by nervous anxiety.

In 1536, Catherine died and Mary was left alone to witness her father's increasingly scandalous and unpredictable behaviour. That same year, Henry had Anne Boleyn executed on almost certainly trumped-up charges of treason and incest, and Elizabeth was also declared illegitimate. Henry took a third wife, Jane Seymour, and suddenly Mary's star seemed to be in the ascendant again. Within a fortnight she was miraculously back in favour, having struck up a good relationship with the new Queen.

Seduced perhaps by the renewal of her father's attentions, and without her mother's influence, Mary finally gave in and signed the document that recognised Henry as Head of the Church in England and her parents' marriage as illegitimate. When Jane Seymour gave birth to a son, Henry finally had everything he had wished for. It was of little importance that Jane died from puerperal fever shortly after the birth. With a son safely established as his heir, Henry announced the order of succession as Edward, then Mary, then Elizabeth. Mary took no pleasure in taking precedence over Elizabeth, unable to forgive herself for signing the document in which, in her eyes, she had betrayed both her mother and her faith. Her intense piety would ensure that when she had the opportunity she would later defend her faith to the bitter end. Only thus might she atone for what she saw as a cardinal sin.

The Rightful Queen

Henry died in 1547, and at the tender age of nine Edward VI acceded to the throne as England's first Protestant king. It was a heavy weight to descend upon such childish shoulders. Following Henry's rejection of papal supremacy, Protestantism had become the dominant faith and his Catholic subjects had found themselves at bay and increasingly forced underground. Mary, bolstered by a widespread public belief that she had been mistreated and was the rightful heir, openly practised mass, ignoring her half-brother's protests. Despite her Catholicism, there were growing murmurs that Mary should be queen; consequently when Edward died of tuberculosis in 1553, the public was shocked when, under the terms of his will (although it was constitutionally invalid), Lady Jane Grey, the Duke of Northumberland's daughter-in-law, was declared Queen of England. Never crowned, Jane was no more than a puppet for her father-in-law's ambitions, and her 'reign' lasted only nine days. Mary was taken by surprise when the outrage of the English people was such that Jane was executed, and Northumberland suffered the same fate. The throne was Mary's—her time had come at last.

The bells rang out for Mary's coronation and the streets of London were packed with well-wishers. It seemed that justice had finally been done and Henry's firstborn daughter was now the country's rightful queen—and England's first queen regnant, the first queen to rule in her own right. But what sort of queen would Mary make, following the traumas and upheavals of her upbringing? She had as a child been closeted in the court, witness to the plots and back-stabbings and malicious rumours that dominated life there, and later kept in solitary confinement with nothing but her prayers for company.

The Roman Catholic Queen Mary I earned herself the name 'Bloody Mary' for her massacres of Protestant 'heretics'.

Mary wrongly interpreted the jubilant approval of the crowds as an acceptance of everything she embodied, most importantly her Catholic faith. But if there were two things that incensed the English above all else, they were papal power and Spain. Ten days after her accession, when Mary publicly celebrated her first mass, riots broke out. This only served to make the new Queen even more determined to restore England to Catholicism, to force her subjects back to the one true faith. This was to prove a fatal error of judgment.

When Mary shortly announced she intended to marry, unseen, twenty-six-year-old Prince Philip of Spain, she alienated her subjects even further. While to Mary the marriage meant a chance to provide a Catholic heir for the English throne, Philip's agenda was rather different. He saw an opportunity to gain England as an ally for Spain against the much-hated French. On the surface, Philip appeared to be one of the greatest matches any Queen could hope for. Heir to a powerful empire, he was said to be charming and handsome, although envoys overseas spoke of his cruel, calculating behaviour and his harsh treatment of heretics. Following Mary's announcement, the streets of England ran with blood as Protestants everywhere took up arms against Catholics. Priests were beaten and even Mary narrowly escaped death in an uprising. Elizabeth, now a figurehead for the Protestant revolt, was becoming ever more popular.

Despite the civil unrest, Mary stubbornly went ahead with her plans. Entering into the marriage purely for religious and political purposes, she was completely unprepared for the feelings her new husband was to inspire in her. On 25 July 1554, she married Philip at Winchester Cathedral, and it was said that by the end of the ceremony she was madly in love. After years of solitary devotions and rigid self-discipline, the thirty-seven-year-old Queen became besotted with her much younger bridegroom. However, while she saw a dashing prince, he saw a physically unattractive older woman—who dressed badly and had no eyebrows (a trait apparently shared with Henry and Elizabeth). The marriage was consummated and a month later it seemed that the Queen's dreams of a Catholic heir were to be realised. A joyful Mary announced she was pregnant.

Into the Flames

Mary now turned her attention to dealing with her rebellious Protestant subjects. Driven by the fierce conviction that she was doing God's will, she began to earn the title that was to follow her down through history. 'Bloody Mary' reintroduced the medieval heresy laws, which meant that anyone denouncing the Catholic faith would be burned at the stake. In February 1555, the first 'heretics' were executed, marking the beginning of her reign of terror. Over the next four years, more than three hundred people were put to death, many of them ordinary men and women, farmers, labourers and churchgoers, who over the years had become confused by their rulers' changing religious allegiances. Heretics had certainly been burned during Henry's reign, but always in the past they had been given the opportunity to recant and save themselves from the flames. Mary took this right away—once a person was charged, there was no forgiveness.

Perhaps Mary's years of mistreatment at the hands of her father had chilled and hardened her heart. In those dark days she had clung devoutly to her faith and been traumatised when she was forced by her bullying father to reject papal authority. She was determined to bring England back to the one true Church and in so doing absolve herself of her terrible betrayal of her faith. But her subjects were torn apart while she sought to absolve herself, and her Protestant victims were hailed as martyrs. Instead of re-establishing the religion she loved, Mary was destroying it. Her unborn child was her greatest hope for converting England—a Catholic heir and future king.

The Phantom Pregnancy

By April 1555, the preparations for the royal birth were complete and Mary restlessly paced the halls of the palace, hands clamped to her swollen stomach, awaiting the delivery. Latin and English verses proclaiming the birth had been carved in wood, and the Queen and her servants had stitched a comforter and matching headpiece for the baby's bed. Clothes were laid out and midwives stood ready. The court held its breath. In late April, rumours spread that Mary had given birth to a boy and her Catholic subjects lit bonfires in celebration of the news. But the rumours were ill-founded. Mary continued to pace and the court to hold its breath. May came and went with no royal issue. By August, Mary was forced to face the terrible truth. She was not pregnant. She had experienced a phantom pregnancy, and the longed-for child was no more than a figment of her imagination. Devastated, Mary turned to her husband for comfort and support.

But Philip's patience with his dowdy, clinging wife had long run out, and he announced he must leave on urgent business to the Netherlands. An almost hysterical Mary became even more limpet-like, begging him to stay. To calm her, Philip muttered vague promises that he would return, and left posthaste for Amsterdam. He left behind him an inconsolable woman, counting the beads of her rosary as she feverishly murmured her prayers, and writing letters to him each day.

Philip did return, but it seems his sole aim was to enlist Mary's aid in Spain's war against France. In need of funds, he turned to Mary, confident he could charm her into providing support. Mary was pathetically grateful for these crumbs of affection and, despite the government's fierce opposition, in June 1557 declared war on France. Satisfied, Philip beat a hasty retreat—and England breathed a sigh of relief at his departure. There had been growing concern that Mary was planning a coronation for Philip that would recognise him officially as King of England.

Six months later, Mary again announced that she was pregnant, but again it was only her body playing tricks. With her prayers unanswered, Mary's health deteriorated further and she sank more deeply into melancholy, oblivious to the fact that England was being torn apart by the ongoing efforts to re-establish Catholicism. The nation was plagued with burnings, taxes, hangings, beggars and fines. In addition, the unimaginable had happened—English forces had lost the port of Calais to the French. Calais had been in English hands for over two hundred years and its loss would be remembered as one of the worst failures of Mary's reign.

Gravely ill, Mary retired to her chamber, nominating Elizabeth as her heir and amending her will to state that Philip's involvement in English government should cease on her death. It must have been particularly painful to recognise the Protestant Elizabeth as her heir, an heir, moreover, born of a non-royal mother while she herself came from such a distinguished royal line.

As Mary's depression deepened, she was plunged back into the whisperings and plots of her childhood, and developed a paranoid belief

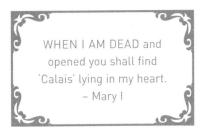

that everyone was conspiring against her. She rarely left her chamber and when she did, she was encased in a suit of armour. Her final hours were spent weeping and wailing, and it was thought that her tears were for the child who remained a phantom of her fevered imagination. They might also have been for the country she had failed so abysmally to serve.

By the end of Mary's reign, with heretics still being consigned to the flames, she was both feared and hated by her subjects. As her health grew worse (it is thought that she was probably suffering from ovarian or uterine cancer), she pleaded for Philip to visit her one last time, but he declined, pleading pressure of official business. With her dying breath, she summoned her ladies-in-waiting and asked them to 'always remain steadfast to the true faith'. On 17 November 1558, aged forty-two, Mary died. For centuries to follow, the date of her death was a cause for national celebrations.

Mary I was a tragic figure, mistreated by all who knew her, and given brutally short shrift in the history books for her cruel treatment of Protestants. But perhaps the first and most cruel betrayal lay with her father, Henry VIII, whose arrogance in seeking a son ultimately proved her undoing. The princess who showed so much promise and the queen whose country felt that she was the rightful ruler was in the end ill equipped to take the throne.

The treatment Mary received at the hands of the people she loved had fostered intolerance and hardened her heart, leading to a reign scarred by violence and persecution. As her world fell apart, she clung ever more devoutly to her faith, never understanding why her people refused to convert. Mary failed at the three things she most wanted to be: a Queen, a wife and a mother; and while the title 'Bloody Mary' may be justly bestowed, she is perhaps most aptly referred to as 'the unhappiest of Queens, and wives, and women'.

Elizabeth Bathory

Real-life female 'Dracula' who loved to bathe in blood

1560–1614

The Lady is so wicked that it is impossible to account for her actions and cruelties.
– Witness Benedict Deseo, court chamberlain to Elizabeth Bathory

It is thought that Elizabeth Bathory may have murdered more than 650 young women.

Countess Elizabeth Bathory checked her reflection in the mirror as the young servant girl brushed the shining, jet black hair on which she prided herself. The tiniest lines were beginning to gather around her eyes and the Countess regarded them with alarm. The servant girl was annoying her too, with her clumsy brush-strokes. Scared that her mistress might fly into one of her legendary rages, the girl nervously pulled the brush too hard through the long hair. The Countess screamed with rage. Turning on the cowering girl, eyes blazing, she lashed out, her long nails gouging a deep scratch in the maidservant's hand. Enough blood was spilt to splash her own hand before she banished the girl from her presence with an angry tirade.

But a few days later, the Countess noticed that this same patch of skin seemed to be looking particularly radiant. She felt a delicious thrill of excitement. It seemed to the enchanted Elizabeth to have 'the translucent glow of a candle illuminated by another one'. She smiled at her mirrored face and that troublesome network of tiny lines. Blood was easy to come by. Could she have discovered the secret of eternal youth?

Elizabeth Bathory is reviled as a sadistic monster and serial killer, her crimes so hideous that even in a period where brutality was the norm and human life held cheaply, she shocked and repelled her contemporaries. During the early part of the sixteenth century, she allegedly murdered more than 650 young women, mostly servant girls, having first subjected them to hideous torture. It is claimed by some that she even bathed in their blood in the hope of holding back the ravages of time. Perhaps it will come as no surprise that, with her insatiable appetite for blood, she lived for many years in a gloomy castle perched upon a rock in the wilds of Transylvania.

Early Signs of Instability

Elizabeth Bathory (Erzsébet Báthory), daughter of Baron George Bathory and Baroness Anna Bathory, was born in 1560 into a powerful Hungarian Protestant family, many of whose members held high office. Elizabeth, surrounded by indulgent sycophants, was brought up to believe in her innate superiority; servants were there only to fulfil her every whim. Her cousin Stephen became Prince of Transylvania in 1571 when she was eleven years old, and was later elected King of Poland; another cousin was appointed Lord Palatine of Hungary.

Perhaps partly because of the family's aristocratic background, there was evidence in the Bathory family of the kind of extreme psychotic behaviour that would attract medical attention today. Intermarriage with relatives, common at the time and known to be favoured by the Bathorys, was seen as a way of maintaining the purity of noble blood, and almost certainly increased the likelihood of any deviant behaviour appearing. One of Elizabeth's aunts was famous for her cruelty; an uncle was a homicidal monster with no grasp on reality. Elizabeth appears to have showed early signs of mental instability, being prone to uncontrollable rages. She also suffered epileptic seizures. A stable childhood might have helped to keep her demons at bay, but she was frequently witness to torture meted out by officials on the family estate, and to public executions. To Elizabeth, servants and peasants were 'lesser people', barely human, and from an early age she showed a callous indifference to their pain.

Elizabeth was extremely well educated for a woman of that era, with a particular aptitude for languages. While many belonging to the upper classes were illiterate, she could read and write Hungarian, Greek and Latin. She was said to be a great beauty with an alabaster complexion and large dark eyes—although it would probably have been foolish to have said otherwise.

Outside her studies, Elizabeth was soon experimenting sexually, bestowing her favours on a peasant boy. In 1574, aged fourteen, she became pregnant and was forced to give her baby daughter away to be fostered by peasant parents. Abandoning her baby to grow up as a peasant may have taken a toll on her fragile mental health. It is possible to speculate too that she felt humiliated at having lost her virginity to someone from a class for which she felt such contempt. In 1575, shortly after she had given birth, she married twenty-five-year-old Count Ferenc Nadasdy, to whom she had been engaged since she was eleven. Nadasdy's family was not quite as prestigious as the Bathory family; it was his mother, Ursula, who had pushed for the engagement. No doubt she imagined she would acquire a biddable new daughter-in-law. It would not be long before she learned of her mistake.

The wedding was a gala occasion with many European dignitaries, including the Holy Roman Emperor Maximilian himself, invited to attend. Elizabeth retained her maiden name, her new husband adding it to his own to increase his prestige. The young bride left her family home to live with Ferenc in Castle Sarvar and become mistress of the remote Nadasdy estate, deep in the mountains of Transylvania (now central Romania). Confined to the gloomy castle with a husband who was respected as an athlete and a warrior, but whose own mother admitted he was 'no scholar', Elizabeth initially found time hanging heavy on her hands.

Sadistic Games

Elizabeth was surprised to discover that she and her illiterate husband had more in common than she had imagined. To her delight, Ferenc introduced her to the grisly methods of torture he had learned to use in warfare. He was often away for long periods, fighting against the Turks, but while he was home it is said that he spent hours devising new ways of causing his enemies to suffer, designing specialist tools capable of inflicting unimaginable levels of pain. Soon he and Elizabeth began to act out sadistic fantasies on their hapless servants, secure in the knowledge that as members of a noble and powerful family they were above the law, that no one would question what they did. Selecting a poor servant girl at random, they are claimed to have smothered her in honey and forced her to lie outside for days as a feast for hungry insects. In his absences the Count left behind an under-occupied wife who paced the shadow-filled corridors, devising yet more sadistic entertainments.

Bored by her husband's lengthy military excursions, and missing her partner in crime, Elizabeth took a number of lovers. On one occasion she even absconded with a young nobleman, but the affair was short-lived—perhaps he discovered that the Countess had tastes he did not share. In any event, she returned to Castle Sarvar and begged her husband for forgiveness. The Count demanded that she fulfil her duty as a wife and provide him with an heir. In 1585, Elizabeth gave birth to their daughter, Anna, and over the next nine years bore two more daughters and a son, Paul. Count Nadasdy's next requirement, that his mother live in the castle to keep an eye on his philandering wife, was not quite so easy to cope with. Countess Ursula Nadasdy duly arrived, and Elizabeth hated her from the first. But although her sadistic activities may

ELIZABETH WAS SAID TO HAVE ordered the construction of a torture device called the Iron Virgin. Carved in the shape of a woman's body, it was dressed in a rich costume, and draped with a long wig. A maidservant would be asked to adjust a jewel, at which point the Iron Virgin would snatch her up and stab her with the spikes attached to its chest until the poor girl bled to death.

have been curtailed by the arrival of her disapproving mother-in-law, they did not stop. The doors of her bedchamber and the dungeons were thick enough to muffle the screams.

An Evil Coven

It was unfortunate that Elizabeth had no role models who might have exerted a calming influence upon her, associating instead with people who merely seemed to make her feel that her deranged behaviour was perfectly normal. Her aunt, who was known to be bisexual and who also claimed to be a witch, seemed to take great delight in her niece's cruel practices. Elizabeth was intrigued by this aunt's sexuality and ready to explore the possibilities on offer. Her immediate circle now consisted of Iloni Joo, her childhood nurse, Dorothea Szentes, known as Dorka, a peasant woman who claimed to be a witch, and the sadistic manservant Johannes Ujvary, known as Ficzko, reported to have been a dwarf. It is unlikely that Elizabeth's sadistic behaviour would have seemed untoward in this unsavoury group and they became her chief confidantes and accomplices.

The entertainments enjoyed by this gruesome coven included beating servants with whips and cudgels until they screamed with pain, and burning them with hot irons should the ironing not be properly attended to. Another torture was to force an unfortunate girl to sit outdoors, naked in the freezing cold of the Transylvanian winter, while buckets of icy water were poured over her from a window above. Most of these girls soon died of hypothermia. The dark passageways and dungeons below Castle Sarvar echoed with the groans and cries of the victims, while in the comfort and luxury of their quarters upstairs Elizabeth's children played and looked forward to the visits of their smiling, indulgent mama. The Countess was reputed to be a devoted mother, but when she shut the door behind her children she turned into the cruel mistress the servants had learned to dread.

Elizabeth began to invent her own tortures, as well as devising satanic spells against people who owed her money. She wrote often to her husband, sharing with him the details of her latest cruel deeds. In one letter she describes with relish how:

Thorko has taught me a lovely new one [spell]. Catch a black hen and beat it to death with a white cane. Keep the blood and smear a little of it on your enemy. If you get no chance to smear it on his body, obtain one of his garments and smear it.

How far the Count encouraged his wife's vile activities will never be known, but he had certainly been her first mentor. When he died of an infected wound in 1604, he was hailed as a national hero, the 'Black Hero of Hungary'. Elizabeth, now one of the richest landowners in the country, revelled in her new power. Her first act was to banish her interfering mother-in-law from the castle; it is thought that Ursula wisely took her grandchildren with her. Elizabeth, now free from all restraints, was able to indulge every whim of the monster that lurked within her.

A Taste for Blood

Elizabeth first took herself to the royal court at Vienna, but was later to spend a good deal of time at what had become her favourite home, the castle of Cachtice, a towering fortress above the River Vah in northwest Hungary. There she found a kindred spirit in a woman called Anna Darvula, whose taste for sadism appears to have equalled her own. The two women became lovers, and Anna may have introduced Elizabeth to satanic rites and diabolism. But the Countess became increasingly obsessed with the fact that despite the power she wielded, she had no control over one thing—for the beauty on which she had prided herself for so long had begun to fade. She spent long hours staring at herself in the mirror, her long, black hair coiled sleekly against her head, her pale complexion glowing in the candlelight, her hands smoothing the silk encasing her voluptuous figure. But when she brought the candles closer, the mirror told her a different tale. At forty-three, it showed the first cracks appearing. If only she might discover the secret of eternal youth.

At what was to be a pivotal moment in her descent into the depths of depravity, Elizabeth lashed out at the maidservant who'd accidentally tugged at her hair as she brushed it. The girl's blood splashed onto the Countess's hand. Days later, she noticed the whiteness and tone of the skin where the blood had spilled was much improved. In her madness, she decided that virgin blood was what she needed to restore her youthful appearance. Assisted by Dorka, she scoured the countryside for unsuspecting girls and offered them positions as servants at the castle. For the impoverished peasants such an offer was an opportunity too good to miss, and few questions were asked as the girls were bundled into the carriages. Elizabeth would take them to a small cottage at the foot of the rock on which the castle stood. From there they were taken through a maze of underground caves to a secret passageway that led straight to the dungeons where the girls would meet their horrific end. Legend has it that the Countess bathed in the blood of the girls she had killed. Whatever the case, there is no doubt that by now she had cast caution to the winds.

> COUNTESS BATHORY IS SAID TO BE the inspiration, along with Vlad Dracula, for Bram Stoker's Gothic tale of Count Dracula, a vampire who inhabited a castle in Transylvania and drank the blood of the terrified maidens he had lured to his lair.

Elizabeth's activities could not have gone unnoticed for long. It is possible that the Lord Palatine of Hungary, Count Thurzo, one of her cousins, knew about them but had turned a blind eye in an effort to protect the Bathory name. But in 1609, after her lover Anna Darvula died, Elizabeth upped her game.

Not long after Anna's death, Elizabeth found an equally enthusiastic accomplice, a woman named Erszi Majorova. Together with the other members of her inner sanctum, she devised a plan to target the daughters of noble families who were in financial difficulties. She had decided that peasant blood was not having the desired effect upon her ageing skin, and was in need of a superior 'claret' to effect the miracle. Elizabeth's noble court at Cachtice was highly organised, and was seen as an ideal place for any young girl who wished to better herself. When the Countess publicly proclaimed that she was starting an academy for young ladies, her aristocratic neighbours were delighted. Proper etiquette was essential if their daughters were to make good marriages. Elizabeth announced there were twenty-five places on offer for the best candidates. Like bringing lambs to the slaughter, the carriages started rolling up to Castle Castiche. Many of these girls were related to the Countess, but this would not save them. Clearly, for Elizabeth, the old saying that blood is thicker than water failed to resonate.

The Castle's Secrets

As the Countess's murder spree spiralled out of control, she seems to have given up any efforts at concealment. In the beginning, when a young woman was killed she was buried on the Cachtice estate by a local pastor. As the numbers of dead rose to extraordinary levels, pastor Janos Ponikenusz began to voice his concerns. He refused to bury any more girls and would eventually testify in court. He must have seen the distinguishing marks and burns they bore. Another pastor once asked the arrogant Countess why there were so many. She replied haughtily, 'Do not ask how they died. Just bury them'.

One tale relates how a love-struck man from Cachtice was so devastated by the loss of his betrothed that he crept into the castle and discovered what was going on. He bravely denounced the Countess to her cousin Thurzo, the Lord Palatine. Everyone knew that peasants had been disappearing, but now that the daughters of the aristocracy were going missing the situation could no longer be ignored. It was Elizabeth's uncle, the King of Poland, who eventually demanded an investigation, and

The fortress-like Castle Cachtice in northwest Hungary, where many of Elizabeth's victims met their fate.

the Lord Palatine chose to lead it personally in an attempt to save the family's reputation. On 30 December 1610, Thurzo led a raid on Castle Cachtice. The Hungarian Parliament was not sitting over Christmas, which meant he was able to act without referring to them. The door to the castle creaked open and its terrible secrets were revealed at last.

What the investigating party were faced with was said to have been too depraved and terrible to put on record. It was claimed that dead and dying girls lay all around, and that others awaiting torture were found in the dungeons. The horrified group managed to release some survivors before going upstairs in search of the Countess. They found a drunken orgy and a torture session in progress. Elizabeth's accomplices, Dorko, Iloni Joo and

Ticzko were arrested and taken away. Elizabeth was held prisoner in her own castle, her fury at being restrained falling on deaf ears. Her gruesome game was finally up.

In the seventeenth century it was extremely unusual for a member of the Hungarian aristocracy to be put on trial, because the aristocracy was generally considered above the law. But on 2 January 1611, before a special tribunal, Judge Theodocius de Szulo began to hear the evidence against Elizabeth Bathory and her accomplices, with twenty-one judges at hand to assist with the mounting evidence. Over the days and weeks that followed, statements were gathered from servants and survivors. Each day up to thirty-five witnesses appeared; they were asked the same eleven questions relating to who, how, what and where the incidents had taken place. Elizabeth's presence was never requested. Her son Paul wrote a letter begging that she be forgiven. His was a lone voice. Her daughters refused to have anything to do with her.

At the end of the trial, Countess Bathory was found guilty on eighty counts of murder. Her diary was presented as evidence, for in it she had recorded the names of more than 650 women. It was thought that investigating officers would have uncovered even more deaths had they travelled to other parts of the country. Although it was impossible to trace all the names, her guilt was evident and she became known as 'Hungary's National Monster'.

Her accomplices were beheaded or burned at the stake for witchcraft and vampirism, but Elizabeth was never formally sentenced. As a member of the nobility, she could not be executed; instead, the Prime Minister decided that sentencing was to be delayed indefinitely, which amounted to solitary confinement for life. She was walled up in a small room in Castle Cachtice, surrounded by her mirrors and treasures. It was bricked up with only a narrow slit in the door for food and above it, a tiny window. No one knows if enough light stole into the room to allow her to watch in the mirror as her beauty faded. No one came near her, apart from the jailer who brought her food. The only sounds she heard would have been those of the castle's scurrying rats. She died four years later at the age of fifty-four, having shown not one sign of remorse.

Quite apart from the evidence of her sickening depravity, other factors may have been involved in the Countess's downfall. Elizabeth Bathory voiced opposition to the ruling Hapsburgs and had openly declared her vision of a more autonomous Transylvania; her cousin George, on the other hand, was a staunch supporter of the Hapsburgs. The King owed her money, which she was demanding that he pay. Perhaps it was in the family's interests to have the Countess out of the way, but the stories and witness accounts of the murders are too many to think that they might have been fabricated.

Some historians have suggested a difficult menopause as a reason for her behaviour, but it is more likely that Elizabeth Bathory was insane from an early age and that through chance she fell in with a group almost as deranged as herself. There is no doubt that she was intelligent, articulate and persuasive, and could have swayed her lesser-ranked followers. Her terrible deeds have become the stuff of myth and legend and, while it is hard to distinguish fact from fiction, it is probable that there has never been a more prolific and depraved serial killer than the Blood Countess of Transylvania.

Catherine II of Russia

Decadent despot, ambitious empress and ruthless reformer

1729–1796

I was very affectionate, and gifted with an appearance which was very attractive. I pleased at first glance without employing any arts or pains to that end.

– Catherine II

Catherine the Great conspired with her followers to remove her brainless, neurotic husband, Peter III of Russia, from the throne.

As Catherine lay wakeful, she heard the movement outside her window that she'd been waiting for. Alexis Orlov climbed into her chamber, whispering that the time for action against her husband, Czar Peter III of Russia, had arrived. Catherine dressed in a simple black gown, as dictated by her state of mourning for her late mother-in-law, and followed Alexis to a carriage concealed in the trees. Under cover of night, the shabby, unadorned carriage hurried toward the headquarters of the Ismailovsky Regiment, where the army was awaiting her. As Catherine stepped down, she looked vulnerable and, without her usual finery, rather less than imperial. Despite her modest appearance, however, she possessed all the skills of an experienced leader. She took a deep breath and announced to the troops gathered round her: 'I have come to ask for your protection. Czar Peter has given orders to arrest me. I fear he intends to kill me'.

Her words had a dramatic effect. The soldiers threw themselves at her feet, kissing her hands and swearing allegiance to their future Empress. Catherine felt the battle was already won as she looked down at the bowed heads, undoubtedly relishing the thought that her husband would pay for the humiliation she had suffered for so many years.

Catherine the Great, a minor German princess who had married Czar
Peter III, became sole ruler of Russia after leading the military coup that
deposed him, claiming sovereignty as if it were her pre-ordained right.
She went on to reign over her unwieldy kingdom with iron resolve,
encouraging its Westernisation, introducing reform of its education and
legal systems, and establishing hospitals. Yet her liberal ideas did not
extend to the serfs, whose situation worsened considerably under her
reign and whose angry resentment eventually posed a serious threat. The
knowledge of what was happening in France, where haughty aristocrats
were mounting the guillotine, left a nervous Catherine keeping a
watchful eye on Russia's own increasingly rebellious masses. At the end of
her reign, Russia had emerged as one of the dominant world powers but
at a huge cost to large numbers of its people, setting the stage for the
eventual emergence of modern Russia. Her megalomaniac tendencies
had become more apparent as her power increased, and found expression
too in what was alleged to have been a voracious sexual appetite.

A German Princess

Catherine the Great was born in the Prussian seaport of Stettin (now
Szczecin in Poland) in 1729, starting life as Princess Sophie Augusta
Frederika, the daughter of the Prince of Anhalt-Zerbst, and his wife,
Johanna Elizabeth of Holstein-Gottorp. As she grew up, the young
Sophie spent many hours examining her family tree and in later life
reflected on these childhood moments. 'The idea of a crown began
running through my head like a tune," she said. But that incessant 'tune'
was probably inspired too by her ambitious mother, whose family had
Russian connections and whose sole aim was to see her daughter
become Empress of Russia. Johanna's brother had almost managed to
marry the Empress Elizabeth of Russia some years before, but the
promise of dynastic power was cruelly snatched away when he died
suddenly from smallpox. Since that day Johanna had been determined to

forge a direct connection with the Russian royal family. She herself was cold, physically abusive, and ruthless in her ambition, and the young Sophie grew up knowing that she must one day be Empress of Russia— or else! In 1744, when the Empress Elizabeth invited Sophie to Russia to meet her adopted heir, the Grand Duke Peter, she was only fifteen. But she knew she must seize her moment.

The Empress was impressed with Sophie, who appeared quick-witted, intelligent and attractive, with bright blue eyes, long black hair and an athletic build. These attributes, together with her noble blood, made her perfect material as a daughter-in-law and a potential Empress. Unfortunately, the Empress could not take much pride in her adopted son, the offspring of her daughter Anne and the Duke of Holstein-Gottorp. (He was in fact Sophie's second cousin.) The future Czar's physical and mental development were all too obviously limited, and he was arrogant, rude and obsessed with practical jokes. Brought up in Prussia until the age of fourteen, he made no secret of the fact that he hated Russia, allying himself with the Lutheran doctrines of Prussia and impressed by the charm of its leader, Prince Frederick. Seeing Peter so ill-equipped for his future role, Sophie determined she would make up for his shortcomings, and began to learn Russian and to study the Orthodox religion. She knew that to rule Russia she must think and live as a Russian, so she widened her reading to include philosophy, state politics and law. Pacing up and down all night, she would repeat what she had learned in the day, exhibiting a dedication beyond her years.

Ironically, the more sophisticated and knowledgeable Sophie became, the more abhorrent Peter seemed. Already lacking in self-confidence, a bout of smallpox now left him almost totally bald, with his skin terribly pitted. He began to drink heavily, becoming more obnoxious toward his future wife. The picture we have of him may be rather biased, however, as Sophie would later paint him in these blackened colours to help justify her own actions. Despite all his efforts, there was no escaping the marriage and after several postponements the wedding took place on

21 August 1745, in the magnificent Cathedral of Kazan. Princess Sophie became the Grand Duchess Ekaterina Alexeyevna, the second highest-ranking woman in Russia. Encased in her wedding finery, Sophie enjoyed this metamorphosis into Ekaterina (Catherine), believing she was on her way to fulfilling her destiny. If only the deeply unattractive, vulgar, boorish figure at her side had not been a necessary means to this end …

Bedroom Battles

The Empress Elizabeth hoped that Catherine would promptly produce an heir, although the teenage bride and groom seemed worryingly ignorant about sexual matters; it began to be believed that Peter was incapable of consummating the marriage. But Catherine at least was up for the challenge, boasting in her youthful diaries: 'I was very boisterous in these days … As soon as I was alone I climbed astride my pillows and galloped in my bed until I was quite worn out'. By contrast, Peter's favourite bedroom activity was playing with toy soldiers. The marital bed became a virtual battlefield, with Peter barking orders at the generals who marched their troops across the covers. Catherine is said to have spent these hours reading.

Six years later, with still no sign of a child, Catherine took the first in a line of lovers, falling madly in love with Sergei Saltykov, a handsome army officer. Almost immediately she became pregnant. When her son Paul was born, no one believed he was Peter's child, although the baby came to strongly resemble him—but an heir had been produced and no questions were asked. Empress Elizabeth immediately took the baby away, declaring herself better equipped to raise him than his parents. Deprived of her son, enduring a soulless, loveless farce of a marriage, Catherine consoled herself with her intellectual and philosophical explorations and, on the lighter side, her enjoyment of the extravagant life of the court.

Perhaps not a great beauty, Catherine the Great was nevertheless said to possess great personal charm, vivacity and intelligence.

No doubt resentful of the assumptions being made about the baby's paternity, Peter now took a lover, parading his new mistress in an attempt to humiliate his erring wife. But Countess Elizabeth Vorontsova hardly seemed competition for Catherine, being described as plain, cross-eyed, lame, scarred by smallpox, and vulgar in her drunken behaviour and foul language. For Peter, the Countess's vulgarity made her the perfect playmate, and he left his wife to find her fun elsewhere. As time passed and Peter's insults multiplied, Catherine felt increasingly insecure. Peter would call her 'Madame Wit' when he needed advice, and allegedly kick her as if she was a dog. Whispers that he was planning to divorce her began to circulate, causing her sleepless nights—she could not bear the thought of losing her position. Soon she was to claim that she was in fear of her life.

Catherine strengthened her connection with her mother-in-law, the Empress Elizabeth, and spent more time with her son, although she found him disappointing. The two women enjoyed a close friendship and when the Empress died in 1762, Catherine was genuinely grief-stricken. At the state funeral, she was careful to observe the strict etiquette of mourning, but to everyone's acute embarrassment her husband pulled faces, interrupted the funeral and generally made a fool of himself.

When Peter was crowned Czar Peter III of Russia, almost seventeen long years after their marriage, Catherine felt certain she would be the target of more of his plots. She was not alone in viewing him with deep distrust. The nobility was concerned about his doltish behaviour and his obvious admiration for Prince Frederick of Prussia and all things Prussian. In one fell swoop, the new Czar managed to alienate the Russian army and the Russian nobles by calling a truce with Prussia over the Seven Years' War, a truce that favoured Prussia over the country he ruled—despite the fact that Russia had been on the verge of winning. When rumours reached Catherine shortly afterward that a plot to have her murdered was in its final stages, it was obviously time to rally her many supporters to her cause.

Empress of all the Russias

With the help of her current lover Gregory Orlov, and his four brothers, Catherine plotted to overthrow her husband, knowing that once she had the support of the army the rest of Russia would flock to her side. On 14 July 1762, under cover of night, she and the Orlov brothers made their way to the Ismailovsky Regiment headquarters to request the army's aid. With the army won over, Catherine rode through the Moscow streets as morning broke. Church bells rang out, and soldiers appeared from every side street to fall into line behind her, forming a huge procession. They stopped at the Cathedral of Kazan, where the clergy and a packed congregation were waiting to bestow their blessing. Finally, Catherine made her way to the Winter Palace where members of the Senate swore allegiance to her. Now attired in military uniform and mounted on a white thoroughbred, she led her troops against her husband. What little support he had soon melted away and Catherine enjoyed a victory that was swift, bloodless and, no doubt, sweet in view of the abuse she had suffered at his hands.

Although Catherine had succeeded in overthrowing her ineffectual and divisive husband, the fact that she had seized power in a coup meant her position would always be vulnerable. Europe was scandalised by her action and by the news that Czar Peter, who had been imprisoned at the Castle of Ropshe, had died from a nasty bout of colic only three days later. It was generally assumed that the Orlov brothers had murdered him with Catherine's connivance. Another claimant to the throne, Czar Ivan VI, long known simply as 'Prisoner Number 1', was murdered in his prison cell in 1764, almost certainly on Catherine's orders, although having been kept in solitary confinement since he was deposed in 1741 he had virtually become a savage and hardly posed a threat. Catherine's son Paul, who admittedly was of a nervous disposition, seemed to believe that his mother was so ruthless that she would eventually kill him too. Despite the outrage expressed in Europe, Catherine was resolute in her determination to rule—she had grown up believing that this was her destiny.

Cathcrine was crowned on 22 September 1762, to the delight of a rapturous crowd, being proclaimed sole ruler and Empress of all the Russias. She thoroughly enjoyed the trappings and privileges that came with power. On the day she became Empress she rewarded Gregory Orlov by making him a count and presenting him with her portrait set in diamonds. Her elaborate court was famed for its extravagance: many of the nobles wore costumes lavishly decorated with precious stones, and Orlov himself had a suit sewn with millions of dollars worth of diamonds. Behind the scenes, however, Orlov behaved like a tyrant, beating Catherine and no doubt reminding her that she owed him for services rendered. He pressed her to marry him but her strong sense of self-preservation meant she always refused. Despite the excesses of her lifestyle, the new Empress took her position and her duties very seriously, working ten hours a day, waking herself up every morning by vigorously rubbing her face with ice and drinking five cups of black coffee.

Messalina of the North

Greatly exaggerated in the reports of foreign ambassadors and official visitors from European countries, Catherine's behaviour was said to be outrageous and utterly decadent. They whispered (so loudly that it became 'fact') that she held orgies during which the guests cross–dressed and she herself became so drunk that her servants had to cut her out of her tight corsets. It is true that she took a number of lovers, the subject of feverish gossip in diplomatic circles, where she was dubbed by some the 'Messalina of the North'. It must be remembered, however, that she greatly valued affection, and was faithful to each of her lovers while she enjoyed his attentions.

While the people of Russia disliked the debauched lifestyle of the court, they found little to complain about in their Empress's politics. When she ascended the throne, she had been shocked by the state of her country's financial and social affairs and by the fact that corruption and injustice were endemic. When she enquired of the Senate how many towns there were in Russia, no one knew; when she demanded a map, none was forthcoming. Catherine quickly identified two of the main targets of her reign. First, she needed to safeguard her position, which meant appeasing the powerful nobles. Second, she would concentrate on acquiring land to increase the country's wealth and to expand the Empire, eventually annexing the Crimea and bringing Ukraine under her rule.

Educated as she was in the principles of the Enlightenment, Catherine was determined to bring its spirit to Russia. She maintained a lifelong friendship and correspondence with the French philosopher Voltaire, and longed to be perceived as an enlightened sovereign, regarding herself as a 'philosopher on the throne'. She was an enthusiastic patron of the arts, and no other Russian ruler provided such a careful written record of their reign. She improved medical conditions, encouraged research into vaccines, and bolstered trade and agriculture. However, there were contradictions in her policies. Despite her talk of bringing light to the darkest regions of her empire, and boasting to her philosopher friends that she was pushing the boundaries of education in Russia, in fact only two per cent of the national income was spent on education; thirteen per cent was spent on improving her palaces.

There was one aspect of Catherine's policies that was to prove a bitter disappointment to those who had hoped she would reduce the privileges of the nobility and improve the plight of the serfs. The pragmatic Empress knew that her position depended on the nobles; rather than disenfranchising them, she exempted them from paying taxes, granted

> DURING WORLD WAR II, German troops invading one of Catherine the Great's palaces reported an extraordinary discovery—four rooms solely devoted to a collection of erotica. Paintings, sculptures, frescoes, chandeliers and furniture were adorned with figurines and motifs engaging in acts that would put the *Karma Sutra* in the shade. The collection, possibly the largest of its kind in the world, mysteriously disappeared after the war. The story was kept alive by the same German soldiers, still recounting their discovery to documentary makers sixty years later.

them greater property rights and gave them even more power over the serfs working for them. She awarded them great tracts of land and with the land came the gift of serfs, who were sold or inherited as slaves. In 1773, the simmering anger against these measures finally erupted in the largest armed revolt the country had ever seen. Catherine was merciless in quelling the rebels and two years later, when the leader was captured, she ordered him to be dismembered and burned. She had seen what had happened in the French Revolution and her early loyalty to French writers quickly melted away when she saw them give their support to the peasants. It seems a terrible indictment of Catherine that by the end of her reign, the number of serfs had doubled and it cost less to buy one than it did to buy a dog.

In 1774, Catherine took a new lover, one who was to have a great impact upon her life. While inspecting a regiment one day, Catherine noticed that the knot of her sword was missing. Out of the ranks stepped the dark, surly Prince Gregory Potemkin, to offer her his. He fell madly in love with her but she reacted by playing a frustrating game of cat and mouse. Dejected, he entered a monastery for a year but Catherine eventually enticed him back to court, promising him the 'greatest of all favours'. An unusual pattern of behaviour later developed between them. Potemkin was often away for months at a time on Imperial duties, but before he left would choose a new young lover to warm Catherine's bed. They were extremely close, and it is thought that they may have secretly married, although there is no convincing proof. But his astute assessment of her nature was to have its reward, for he was the only person to unofficially rule at her side, becoming a key political figure in Europe and eventually Governor of Ukraine.

When Catherine died, apparently of a stroke, on 17 November 1796, lurid rumours circulated about the manner of her death, based solely on the fact that she had been sexually active to the end of her

LAST NIGHT ... THIS incomparable princess finished her brilliant career. – Charles Whitworth, British Ambassador to Russia, 18 November 1796

Catherine the Great allegedly had many lovers throughout her life, right up to her death at age sixty-seven.

life. Her son, who bitterly resented the fact that he had spent his life being ignored by his mother, became the next Czar, and promptly set about dismantling many of her forward-looking policies. It seems surprising that Catherine had made no contingency plans to guard against his accession, because she had always seen him as weak and ineffectual, and believed that Alexander, the eldest of his ten children, would be a better choice.

Catherine had always been a commanding presence, and her political shrewdness and intellectual powers had ensured her survival. She was a woman of startling contradictions, abolishing the death penalty but having no qualms about cutting out gossiping tongues or leaving prisoners to rot in their chains, having no fondness for her son but a great deal for her grandchildren. During her reign, she emerged as a formidable leader who rescued Russia from backwardness and savagery and made it a dominant presence on the world stage. But while in many ways she shared the liberalising spirit of the Age of Enlightenment, in effect she ruled her empire with the single-minded ruthlessness of an old-style despot.

Ranavalona

Proud, cruel, mad monarch of Madagascar
1782–1861

She is certainly one of the proudest and cruel women on the face of the earth, and her whole history is a record of bloodshed and deeds of horror.

– Ida Pfeiffer (explorer)

Ranavalona I, the Queen of Madagascar, established a reign of terror over her island country in the name of preserving its traditions and independence.

The crowd had come from far and wide to witness the annual ceremony of the royal bath. It began with Queen Ranavalona standing on her palace balcony with a crimson cloak draped around her body. Reverently, her attendants carried her behind a decorative screen. Sounds of splashing water filled the air, and faint images could be seen through the screen of the maids who had been honoured by being chosen for the role of bathing their Queen. The lights of the city were extinguished and fires had been smothered, so that all eyes were trained on what might be revealed by the light of the single fire left burning in the Queen's rooms.

At last the Queen stepped out before the screen, now with flushed cheeks and glistening hair. In her hand was an ivory tusk filled with water from her bath, which she sprinkled over the crowd to complete the ritual. As she left, people pressed forward and fought to touch the precious water.

Queen Ranavalona's reign over the island of Madagascar ensured that the traditions and independence of the island were preserved against all attempts at colonial invasion, but it also resulted in the deaths of more than a third of her subjects. Tyrannical, sadistic and eccentric, she signed death warrants as if they were greetings cards; between twenty and thirty thousand people are said to have died annually. She had come from humble origins and only pure chance had brought her to the attention of the ruling king and given her an entrée into the royal family. The saying that 'power corrupts and absolute power corrupts absolutely' seems especially apt when applied to Ranavalona, for she eventually felt herself above all earthly constraints. She savagely persecuted those who had converted to Christianity or challenged her in any way, and hated all Westerners, seeing herself as the chosen defender of the Madagascan gods.

Island Paradise

Ranavalona, daughter of a humble tribesman and servant of the Merina King of Madagascar, spent her childhood far from the intrigues and power struggles that characterised the politics of the court. In the late eighteenth century, the lush island of Madagascar, off the southeastern coast of Africa, attracted the attention of colonial powers, who vied with each other to gain sovereignty over it. For Britain it was an important landing stage on the way to India, while France already owned some neighbouring islands and was anxious to add this jewel to its collection. Although keen to maintain the island's independence, King Andrianampoinimerina, who had united many of the warring tribes and created a centralised state, wanted to learn more from Westerners about the world that lay beyond the Madagascan horizon. However, many of the tribespeople and priests disliked his attempts at modernisation and his own uncle plotted to have him assassinated. Ranavalona's father learned of this conspiracy against the King; when he warned him, the King was so grateful that he offered to adopt his loyal servant's daughter and educate her in the ways of the court.

Ranavalona left her parents' simple dwelling place wearing a shabby dress and carrying her few possessions, and climbed a steep incline in the blistering sun to the palace on the top of the cliff. There it seemed she was to become a princess, or at least enjoy luxuries and a status until now undreamed of. But the realities of a court riddled with intrigue and danger, where executions were commonplace, provided a schooling that was to leave an indelible mark upon her.

The Bloodshed Begins

The King wed his adopted daughter to his favourite son and the heir to the throne, Prince Radama, when she was twenty-two. But although Ranavalona was the highest ranking of his royal harem of twelve wives, Radama paid her little attention. Perhaps this experience introduced a steely element into Ranavalona's nature. As she matured, she became increasingly outspoken, loudly disagreeing with the young prince's policies, which were similar to his father's, and failing to see what 'greedy foreigners' had to offer the island. Prince Radama did not appreciate having his views challenged by a wife with a mind of her own and Ranavalona began to look elsewhere for affection, eventually taking a lover.

In 1810, Radama became king and although Ranavalona's power increased as a result, she was frustrated at being unable to influence her husband's modernising ideas. Keen to Westernise his people's lifestyle, he allowed more foreigners onto the island, particularly Protestant missionaries from Wales, who set up schools and spread the gospel of Christianity. The Queen watched helplessly through the years that followed as the religion that posed such a threat to her gods took root— but at last her opportunity came. In 1828, Radama fell dangerously ill and the island was thrown into turmoil. Who would succeed the King if he died now? Since Ranavalona had not produced an heir, it seemed the crown would go his nephew, Prince Rakotobe. However, according to

Madagascan custom, Ranavalona also had a legitimate claim; additionally, if she were to have a son, even by another man, after her husband died, the child would be the rightful King. The Queen knew she was in deadly peril, for if she did not stake her claim the next ruler would regard her as a threat and quickly dispose of her.

A lucky chance gave Ranavalona the window of opportunity she needed. When the King died, two of his officers decided to keep his death a secret until they could place Prince Rakotobe on the throne. But the Queen's lover, Andriamihaja, overheard their conversation and hurried to tell her the news. As Prince Rakotobe's supporters slept, she mobilised her own followers to carry out a coup. She had previously won support among the priests; their blessing meant she could claim to enjoy the approval of the Madagascan gods. She had also secured the allegiance of two generals from the Merina army who welcomed her traditionalist views and now marshalled their troops and secured the Palace. Ranavalona announced that she was to be crowned as sovereign; if anyone had a problem with that they were to speak up now. Four intrepid officers stepped forward and pledged their allegiance to Prince Rakotobe. Their objections were quickly cut short by a hail of spears.

On 1 August 1828, in an elaborate ceremony, Ranavalona ascended a throne of crimson and gold, surrounded by dignitaries dressed in national costume, and proudly pledged allegiance to her people: 'Never say she is only a feeble and ignorant woman, how can she rule such a vast empire? I will rule here, to the good fortune of my people and the glory of my name! I will worship no gods but those of my ancestors. The ocean shall be the boundary of my realm, and I will not cede the thickness of one hair of my realm!' At forty-six, she was finally queen of her island paradise. But the pledge to rule 'to the good fortune' of her people was soon to be revealed as false, certainly where Prince Rakotobe's supporters were concerned. She subjected them to agonising deaths, systematically wiping out his entire bloodline to ensure no future descendant would dare to lay claim to the throne. The sadistic pleasure she took in watching the killings from her royal balcony was a foretaste of the barbarity to come. In 1829, more than nine months after Radama's death, she gave birth to a son, Prince Rakoto, who by custom was accepted as the late king's heir.

Ruling from her palace perched high on the clifftop with the Village of a Thousand Villages below, Ranavalona's despotic reign began. Crucifixions, beheadings, burnings and skinning people alive became part of the daily business of the new regime. But amid the carnage, she still showed herself vulnerable when it came to her lover, Andriamihaja, whom she promoted to a position of power. Confident of her protection, he foolhardily became outspoken in favour of modernisation and foreign influence. The Queen's political allies, the traditionalists, accused him of treason and demanded that he take the *tanguena*—a trial in which an accused person was forced to eat three pieces of chicken skin rubbed with powder from the poisonous tanguena plant. If they regurgitated the three pieces of skin together they were innocent, but if not, they were guilty and sentenced to death—if, of course, they lived through the ordeal. Sure that her lover would not survive, Ranavalona chose to banish him, proof of her love for him. A few months later, however, when word reached her that he was distracting himself in his exile by sleeping with a younger woman of royal blood, in a frenzy of grief and rage the Queen sentenced him to death. No one would ever trifle with her affections again.

A Gift from France

Ranavalona became ever more staunch in her resolve to resist the attempts of the British and French to colonise the island and destroy—as she saw it—the Madagascan way of life. But the Westerners' sophisticated and superior weaponry and engineering skills were daunting even to the fiercely nationalistic Queen. How could she match them? As if in answer to her prayers to her beloved Madagascan gods, in 1832 the solution was washed up on the island's shores.

Jean Laborde with Queen Ranavalona. When the French weapons maker was washed ashore after a shipwreck, Ranavalona saw a chance for Madagascar to retain its independence.

The son of a blacksmith, Frenchman Jean Laborde's spirit of adventure had inspired him to trawl the Indian Ocean in search of sunken treasure. One night a terrible storm blew up and Laborde's ship was smashed upon the rocks. He awoke to find that by some miracle he had survived and was lying on the glittering sand of a Madagascan beach. Luckily too, he had washed up near land belonging to a French plantation owner called de Lastelle, who looked after him until he was strong enough to work. Keen to curry favour with the Queen, de Lastelle realised that the charming and very able twenty-six-year-old Frenchman might be exactly what she had been looking for, and sent a message to say that Laborde was a skilled weapons maker. Ranavalona was elated. As she had by now severed all ties with Britain and broken off all trade, her supply of weapons had ceased. If she could build up her own arsenal, Madagascar stood a chance of retaining its independence and seeing off the invaders. She sent for Laborde, certain that fate had brought him to her just in time.

Unbeknown to Laborde, his arrival had been foretold by a Malagasy legend which had predicted that a white man would be shipwrecked on the shore, would marry a king's daughter, and rule the island with fairness and wisdom. Laborde was not about to become a ruler but he did have a huge impact on the future of Madagascar. He established factories which not only produced cannons, muskets and gunpowder, but also iron, copper and steel—an industrial complex which helped ensure the island's independence by allowing would-be French and British invaders to be repulsed. He became a favourite with the Queen, his good looks and easy charm seeming to cancel out his background as coming from a colonising nation. Although Laborde was basically regarded as a 'white slave' by the Queen, he was appointed the young Prince Rakoto's personal tutor. The prince's close relationship with Laborde unsettled the traditionalists.

HIGH UP ON A HILL, Laborde built Ravanalona a four-story wooden palace, covered in mirrors, that for many years was the largest wooden building in the world.

The Queen's Bath

Ranavalona delighted in choreographing dramatic scenes intended to show her as ruling a great empire and occupying the same heavenly stratosphere as the Madagascan gods. She loved ancient rites and ceremonies and could make a spectacle out of almost anything. Her greatest *coup de théâtre* was the annual ritual in which she took a bath. People would come from miles around to witness the spectacle and once she had finished, would clamour to touch the bath water. The Queen's Bath was part of a New Year's festival, the Fandroana, in which a number of ancient rituals were celebrated, but itself was not of ancient origin. Based on an earlier custom of washing away the sins of the population in a holy lake, it had been reconfigured by Ranavalona to elevate herself to the status of a goddess. She was referred to by her subjects as Ma Dieu, meaning 'My God'.

Bolstered by her success in thwarting the attempts of the French and British to invade, the Queen turned her attention to slavery, keen to boost the Merina economy by selling slaves from the other ethnic groups in Madagascar (particular those of black African origin) to other countries. When Britain passed the Emancipation Act in 1834, freeing all slaves, Ranavalona was determined her island should not be influenced by such modern ideas, and announced that no one was to follow the Christian religion, which described slavery as barbaric. Her subjects appeared to comply with her decree, publicly recanting but often secretly continuing to practice Christianity. Ranavalona would not tolerate even the suspicion of disobedience, however, and conducted a purge to wipe out the 'traitors' who might ally themselves with her enemies. It is said that her behaviour grew gradually more sadistic and irrational, to the point where disgraced subjects were made to lick her feet, which she covered in a bright pink poisonous powder.

A Sadistic Queen

The Queen's increasingly reluctant lover, Laborde, eventually persuaded Prince Rakoto to write a letter to the French Government imploring them to assume sovereignty over the island and to install Rakoto as ruler. Still smarting from their recent defeat, France chose to ignore the plea and Ranavalona remained unaware of the plot, her obsession with combating Christianity and repelling Western ideas perhaps blinding her to what was going on under her nose.

In 1857 the Queen launched an even more savage persecution of the faithful, first targeting the Europeans living on the island and then turning on her own people. The missionaries had done their work well and despite her previous persecutions there seemed to be an ever-growing number of Christian converts clutching their new Bibles and praising their new god. Ranavalona was having none of it. Her sadistic appetite increased as she encouraged crowds to gather to watch the punishment of those suspected of still clinging to their Christian faith. People were beheaded or thrown from high cliffs onto the sharp volcanic rocks below; some were boiled alive and others were forced to drink a terrible poison which ensured a slow, agonising death. The more the Malagasy people held out, the worse the punishments became. As she went on to annihilate a third of the population, it seems extraordinary that she herself did not meet an untimely end. But throughout her bloody reign, she could count on the support of the traditionalists and the priests of the old religion, who were also determined to ward off change.

But attempted coups left their mark on the Queen, in particular one dreamed up by Laborde and fellow Frenchman Jean-François Lambert. They enlisted the help of a visiting explorer, Ida Pfeiffer, and Laborde's old friend the plantation owner, de Lastelle, who were all keen to install Prince Rakoto upon the throne. Problems in communication meant that their plans never came to fruition—and in the days that followed they lived in dread that the Queen had uncovered their plot and was merely playing a game of cat and mouse before executing some hideous revenge. As time passed they began to relax, because the Queen seemed cheerful, requesting Ida to give piano recitals and carrying on business as usual. But when she demanded that all the Europeans gather together in the marketplace, Laborde and his conspirators broke out in a cold sweat.

Ranavalona had indeed discovered the plot, but instead of indulging in the usual frenzy of killing seemed content to merely banish them. Relieved that the Queen was being uncharacteristically merciful, the Europeans set off on the seven-day journey from the capital city to the port. But instead of seven days, it took the desperate group a total of fifty-three. Deliberately slowed down by the Queen's men, the stricken Europeans died off one by one, victims of Madagascan fever and hunger. Exhausted, de Lastelle, Laborde and Ida Pfeiffer succeeded in reaching the ship. But Ida, the great explorer and adventurer, was to die only a few months later, her body racked by pains from the fever, probably malaria, that she had contracted on that terrible trek. The Queen had shown no

By the end of Ranavalona's barbaric reign, she had eliminated a third of the population of Madagascar.

mercy after all. Instead, she had cunningly devised a way to get rid of the Europeans and teach them a lesson without the foreign powers being able to hold her directly responsible or demand justice for their deaths.

With the Europeans gone, Ranavalona continued to persecute the Christians with what seems even more inhuman savagery. She was once more queen of her domain, hidden from the judgmental eyes of foreign emissaries telling tales of primitive savagery. Now she could do as she pleased and every year became worse than the one before. When she finally died on 15 August 1861, she had wiped out one-third of Madagascar's population and had resisted colonisation for over three decades. Her despotic reign was one of the worst in history, and the madness that characterised her later years might have been present from the moment she took the throne. Six years after her death, her son, now King Rakoto, was assassinated and a new Queen came to power. Ranavalona II was a Christian—a fact that would almost certainly have caused Ranavalona I to turn in her grave.

Some claim that the Queen of Madagascar has been demonised by those who resented the fact she was a strong female ruler with an obsession for power that seemed essentially male. But the facts must speak for themselves, and the reports of explorers such as Ida Pfeiffer support the view that if Ranavalona's reign had lasted longer she might have been responsible for wiping out the entire population of the island. By the time of her death, she was almost certainly insane, which may help to explain, but not excuse, her barbarity. For the thirty-three years of her reign, this diminutive woman succeeded in thwarting the colonial ambitions of France and Britain and maintaining Madagascar's independence. But it was achieved through an act of genocide against the people of the island paradise that she professed to love and whose heritage she claimed to be so loyally defending. In her own head no doubt, with the crazed logic that had driven her on, she persisted right until the end in believing that she was Madagascar's saviour and would be elevated to the status of a god.

Shi Xianggu

The greatest pirate who ever lived

1785–1844

> We pirates are like broken bamboo sticks on the sea, floating and sinking alternately, without enjoying rest.
> – Zhang Baou

Zheng Yi, the powerful leader of the Pirate Confederation of the South China Sea, was keen to celebrate yet another splendid victory against the imperial Chinese navy. Twelve of China's vessels had been destroyed and the remaining twenty-eight seized and added to Zheng Yi's ever-growing pirate fleet. So delighted was he that he decided to celebrate by taking a wife, and ordered twenty of the most beautiful female prostitutes abducted by his crew to be brought before him. One stood out above the others. Her name was Shi Xianggu.

Certain that he had found his bride, Zheng Yi began to loosen the ropes that held her. Shi Xianggu exploded like a wildcat, spitting and clawing at his face. When a henchmen sprang forward to restrain her Zheng Yi held up his hand. Such fiery spirit only made him desire her more, and he tried to entice her by offering clothes and jewels and riches that must surely have seemed beyond the common woman's wildest dreams.

But Shi Xianggu was ambitious. She would only agree to marry him if she received half of everything he owned and they stood together as joint commanders of the Red Flag Fleet. The watching pirates waited for their leader to tell this woman she would be his chattel or nothing. But they were disappointed. Recognising that he had found a woman to match him in bravery and cunning, Zheng Yi agreed. Later that year, in 1801, they were married. The Red Flag Fleet had found its Pirate Queen.

Shi Xianggu eventually led six pirate fleets, which included eight hundred ships and eighty thousand pirates.

This charismatic woman would become the greatest pirate who ever lived, and the one feared above all others by a demoralised Chinese navy. In the early nineteenth century, she commanded the area between Hong Kong and the Vietnamese border on the South China Sea, and maintained a crushing stranglehold on the Guangdong economy. In view of the very rigid oriental attitude toward women at the time, Shi Xianggu's success in instilling order and respect into her lawless gang of pirates is even more extraordinary. She led six pirate fleets that ruled the coast of China's Guangdong province, a squadron of eight hundred ships and up to eighty thousand men. One of the few portraits we have of her shows her vigorously wielding a sabre on a tilting deck, fighting shoulder to shoulder with her buccaneers. The Pirate Queen was also famous for her extraordinary business acumen and set up financial offices along the entire coast, even establishing a tax office in Guangdong. The imperial government of the mid-Qing dynasty seemed powerless to stop her, and most of the time no one even dared to try.

From Poverty to Piracy

Born in 1785 to a poor family living on the coast of Guangdong province, Shi Xianggu discovered from an early age that life was a desperate battle for survival. Beautiful, with a mass of dark curly hair and a lithe figure, she started work as a prostitute on one of the floating brothels of Guangdong, submitting to the often brutal demands of her clients for the few taels that came her way after the brothel-keeper had taken his cut. Together with the poor fishermen also scrabbling for a living, she would gaze longingly at the huge foreign ships sailing past, loaded with a rich variety of supplies destined for wealthy Chinese merchants. The Portuguese and English ships were stocked with fruit, vegetables and meat, and passing trade ships bulged with spices and rare commodities. Shi Xianggu watched and waited, dreaming of another world where she might enjoy such riches. When at last she crossed paths with Zheng Yi, the most notorious pirate of the South China Sea, she knew her moment had come.

When Shi Xianggu found herself dragged aboard the pirate leader's ship with a group of fellow prostitutes, she refused to cower. Well aware of Zheng Yi's gaze falling upon her, she was determined to use every weapon in her sexual armoury to captivate him. In that moment she slipped the chains that held her prisoner and became the partner of the most powerful of men, quickly earning the respect of even the toughest and most bloodthirsty of his buccaneering crew.

Zheng Yi came from a long line of Vietnamese pirate aristocracy who had terrorized the Chinese navy for a century. The shipping lanes around the mouth of the Guangdong River were some of the busiest in the world and it was there that he found rich pickings and his 'prey'. In Shi Xianggu he now had a worthy partner; together they were to prove a lethal and unstoppable force.

Shi Xianggu felt huge pride in her new position and took to life on board ship as if she had been born to it. Female sailors were not uncommon among the lower classes in China at that time, since they weren't subjected to the upper-class tradition of foot-binding and could thus deal with the physical demands of sailing. Women who chose the sea were often tough and aggressive like Shi Xianggu, motivated by the grim alternatives they faced on land. While the risks for those embarking on a life of piracy were huge, with death by hanging the most common penalty, the rewards were plentiful, and most had little to lose. Shi Xianggu showed such aptitude for leadership that eventually even her husband grew to fear her. The relationship had an extra—and possibly exciting—complication. Zheng Yi had kidnapped the son of a poor fisherman, the fifteen-year-old Zhang Baou, whose natural authority and charisma even at that early age led the pirate leader to adopt him as his son. But the boy was also to become his lover—a state of affairs that his wife appeared to accept without a qualm. Certainly it seems she was not impervious to Zhang Baou's charms herself.

By 1804, the two leaders had moved to the supreme levels of piracy. With Zheng Yi at the helm, the couple formed a Confederation of Guangdong's pirate fleets, composed of hundreds of junks and tens of thousands of men. A written agreement was drawn up to bind them together and signed by seven major pirate leaders. For three years the Confederation terrorised the ships entering and leaving China's busiest ports, posing a major problem for the already weak imperial navy. But in 1807 disaster struck, and the future of the Confederation was suddenly in doubt. Zheng Yi died off Vietnam, reportedly hurled overboard by a fierce gale that blew up suddenly. Could Shi Xianggu hold together the pirate fleets with their seventy or eighty thousand opium-smoking, sabre-wielding brigands and their eight hundred ships?

THE RED FLEET CODE

Any pirate who disobeyed an order or stole from the common plunder was beheaded. Deserters had their ears chopped off.
The first time pirates failed to share the goods they had plundered with their fellow pirates, they were flogged. The second time it happened, they were put to death.
If they raped a female captive, they were executed. If the woman had agreed to sex, the man was beheaded, while weights were tied to the woman's legs and she was tossed overboard.

A Stern Mistress

Shi Xianggu, sometimes referred to as Zheng Yi Sao ('wife of Zheng Yi'), acted swiftly. Although some of Zheng Yi's fellow leaders must have had their own eyes upon the Confederation's largest fleet, power passed uncontested into her hands. After all, she had been ruling the Confederation alongside her husband and had proved herself in the heat of battle many times over. The Confederation now consisted of six fleets, each with their own coloured flag—black, white, blue, yellow, green, and red—each with its own area and coastal base in which to operate. Sometimes the pirates worked alone but often they would join forces to overcome larger vessels. To co-ordinate such a force was a huge undertaking, and choosing the right person as her second in command was imperative. The only real contender was her own adopted son, twenty-one-year-old Zhang Baou, whom she appointed her lieutenant. Soon she was binding him to her even more closely, beginning a passionate sexual liaison. At last perhaps, she was able to banish the memory of her servitude on the floating brothels of her youth and revel in being the dominant partner.

Shi Xianggu next slapped a list of conditions on the table. She wanted a charter of rules for life on the sea, accompanied by stern disciplinary action for those who dared to break them. It was the toughest code ever imposed on pirates anywhere in the world, but she was determined it should be adhered to—it was, and it succeeded in cementing the pirates into a more formal, cohesive association. The discipline she imposed was formidable, with punishments much more severe than under the pirate 'articles' of the Caribbean. Shi Xianggu administered the punishments swiftly and cruelly whenever she deemed it necessary. Such severity gave rise to an insurmountable force with an undisputed leader at the helm.

Not only was Shi Xianggu an exceptional military commander but she was also a scrupulous administrator and businesswoman, keeping careful records of all her business dealings. She would take an accountant with her to examine any booty that had been brought back from an 'operation', ensure that it was the complete haul, and see that it was entered into the vessel's ledger. Without so much as a trace of irony, she insisted that the word 'plunder' never crossed the lips of her pirates. Instead, they were trained to use the rather more innocuous phrase 'transhipped goods', which seemed to confer an air of legitimacy on their lawless activities. Clearly, the Pirate Queen was an early mistress of spin.

A Roaring Trade

Shi Xianggu was now determined to capitalise on the continued success of the Confederation and find new commercial avenues for their enterprise. She longed to establish some security for herself and her

From humble beginnings as a prostitute, Shi Xianggu became the world's most successful pirate.

pirates so that they might move away from the hand-to-mouth existence and that overwhelming sense of being, as Zhang Baou aptly described it, 'Bamboo shoots on the sea, floating and sinking … never enjoying rest'. She soon realised that the answer lay in 'protection money'. Since 1805 the pirates had totally dominated the salt trade, with nearly every ship setting sail to Guangdong handing over protection money for their cargo. Sometimes the pirates even provided an escort service, whereby fleets of salt junks would pay two hundred Spanish dollars apiece for the doubtful privilege of a pirate convoy to their destination. It was to prove a hugely lucrative trade-off.

By this time, Shi Xianggu had married Zhang Baou and with his able assistance she extended her protection racket to target traders, merchants, junk owners, fishermen and villagers. By taking monthly collections, she was able to predict incoming funds and build the necessary infrastructure needed for the pirates' survival. She was utterly fearless and showed no hesitation in attacking the European ships, winning ever richer spoils. She took on both the Chinese imperial navy and the Europeans in major sea battles and each time, almost effortlessly, demonstrated her seafaring superiority. The merchant captains, cowed by her daring and enterprise, found themselves offering up supplies and weapons. If any of her pirates broke the 'code' and attacked a ship that had paid its dues, they would be forced to compensate their victims. Shi Xianggu's idea of justice may have been at odds with anything understood in more conventional quarters, but it had an integrity all of its own. Under her leadership the fleet was not only a confederation, it was a booming business model, and its success incensed the Qing imperial rulers.

Chinese officials tried many tactics to bring Shi Xianggu and the Confederation to heel, but every expedition to eradicate the pirates failed. The pirates made sure they had spies all along the coast and any potential threats or targets were quickly reported back to their leader. Under Shi Xianggu's command, the busiest shipping lanes of the East were now totally paralysed. The Chinese navy lost sixty-three ships in the ongoing attacks and every battle would result in the pirate fleet gaining yet more boats. But their attacks weren't limited to the sea alone. Protection money was also collected from poor villagers. If the villagers dared to retaliate, Shi Xianggu's men soon made an example of them. The village would be burned to the ground and the men slaughtered. Shi Xianggu clearly felt no sympathy for the impoverished fishing communities and the oppressed class from which she had come. Perhaps her years at sea had brutalised her, and her love of the power she wielded had become an end in itself.

Shi Xianggu's fleet now also regularly took hostages and held them to ransom, the European captives bringing in the most money. It was during the time of the Confederation that the Red Flag Fleet captured a Mr. Richard Glasspoole, an officer from an East India Company ship, the *Marquis of Ely*, and seven of the ship's crew. They were held captive for eleven weeks, from September to December 1809, when a ransom was finally paid. During his time with the pirates, Glasspoole kept a diary that provides a fascinating and terrifying insight into the conditions on board Shi Xianggu's junks. He describes the living conditions as filthy. Feast or famine was the order of the day—rats were bred as a delicacy, and a diet of rice and caterpillars considered nutritious. Ransom for hostages would include food such as sugar, rice, pigs and chickens. Pirates were only allowed to have women on board if they were married to them—but some of the men had as many as five wives, all crammed into the one tiny cabin. Despite what must have been a terrifying ordeal, Glasspoole couldn't help but be impressed by the steely-eyed efficiency of the Pirate Queen who ruled with a rod of iron.

It was said that Glasspoole became something of a favourite with Shi Xianggu and she would douse him with garlic water to ward off evil spirits before a battle. But it is rather more likely that, if she had any real contact with him at all, she was only interested in the nice fat ransom he would fetch. And despite his special treatment, Glasspoole was still made to witness some of the barbaric events that took place under Shi Xianggu's command. For example, in October 1809, her squadron launched an attack on the villages west of Bocca Tigris ('Tiger's Mouth') in the Pearl River delta. Those not captured for ransom were massacred, the resulting bloodbath highlighting the terrible barbarity of piracy at that time. Women whose feet were hobbled were unable to flee, and were slaughtered or hoisted aboard to suffer the terrible conditions of captivity. Glasspoole's own men were forced to take part and offered money for the head of each villager they slaughtered. Several of them returned to the ship carrying up to six heads apiece. Glasspoole was shocked by how quickly the men adjusted to savagery, by the transformation of supposed Christians into brutal servants of the Pirate Queen.

By now the pirates were completely in control of the coast and their power was further demonstrated by the murder of the provincial commander in chief of Guangdong province. The navy was frightened of the pirates, the atrocities they had committed under Shi Xianggu's command having become the stuff of legend. Many of the Chinese admirals now operated by staying inshore until a favourable wind blew their way, when they might make a quick run for it. By mid-year the pirates had destroyed most of the boats employed for the defence of Guangdong and were boasting that one of their junks was equal to four of the navy's vessels. It was no idle boast. At the time, there were more naval junks in dock awaiting repair than there were at sea. This, combined with the raids on the villages and the naval garrisons, was a huge embarrassment for the imperial government. And the fact that their chief adversary was a woman was a further insult.

Endgame

When a new governor-general arrived with the intention of finally unseating Shi Xianggu from her position of power and putting her pirate hordes to flight, things were about to change drastically. The governor immediately imposed an embargo on coastal trade, preventing all ships from entering port, while he refitted the shattered navy. With sea trade at a record low, the pirates found themselves cheated of their 'prey' and were driven inland to 'raise funds' and raid supplies. Becoming desperate, they decided to attack Guangzhou, the capital of Guangdong province. Reluctantly, the Chinese were forced to ask the British and Portuguese for help. On 15 September 1809, the *Mercury*, belonging to the East India Tea Company, set sail with twenty cannon and fifty volunteers, and was joined by six Portuguese men-o'-war. Together they were to sail with the Chinese navy for six months in the hope of breaking the Confederation.

On 19 November 1809, Shi Xianggu and her men came under attack off Lantau Island, about six miles west of Hong Kong Island, and a barrage of shots tore into their ships. For two weeks the naval alliance held the pirates with a blockade aimed at weakening their spirits and their power. With the pirates starving, it seemed that Shi Xianggu had finally met her match, and the Chinese began to launch fire-ships to defeat her once and for all. But luck was with her that day, and at the last minute the wind changed and the fire-ships ignited the very junks that had launched them. Jubilantly, the Pirate Queen and her lieutenant watched the flames leap into the night sky and the imperial navy and its allies once more retreat in disarray.

The Chinese and the Europeans had failed in their mission but in any event the end of the Confederation was drawing near. With piracy becoming an ever more attractive career option and numbers rising daily, it became impossible for Shi Xianggu to maintain control, and it was internal dissent that finally led to the demise of the Confederation. The Commander of the Black Flag Squadron, Cheung Po-tsai, was jealous of the power enjoyed by Zhang Baou and in the midst of a fierce battle refused to come to his assistance. Zhang Baou survived but, furious at Cheung Po-tsai's betrayal, took their two fleets head to head. Hundreds of men were killed and boats destroyed. Zhang Baou, eventually admitting defeat, withdrew. But Cheung Po-tsai recognised that the battle signalled the end for the Confederation, and surrendered to the authorities. Hearing that he had been pardoned and given a position in

Life on board a Chinese pirate junk was often far from luxurious, and in lean times rats and caterpillars were served up as food.

the imperial navy, Shi Xianggu knew she had to move quickly if she was to win an equally attractive offer for her beloved Zhang Baou, and ensure a comfortable retirement for herself. The golden era of piracy was at an end and it was time for the Pirate Queen to come in to harbour at last. But she was determined to do it in style.

Again, Shi Xianggu proved herself to be an astute and intelligent leader. In April 1810, still only twenty-five years of age, she entered into negotiation with Bai Ling, a powerful imperial official, confident that she was still in a strong position and could force him to meet her demands. On 20 April, Shi Xianggu, Zhang Baou and the pirate fleets formally surrendered, the pirate flags were run down the masts, and Bai Ling and the imperial government breathed a huge sigh of relief. As a result of her negotiations, fewer than four hundred pirates suffered any form of punishment—sixty were banished for two years, 151 were exiled and 126 executed. In an amazing coup, the remaining 17 318 pirates surrendered their weapons and junks, but were allowed to retain their plunder and received official pardons. Zhang Baou and many of the pirate leaders were offered commissions in the navy and in a remarkable about-face became the scourge of any pirates still intrepid enough to sail the South China Sea.

Zhang Baou died at the age of thirty-six, and Shi Xianggu lived out the rest of her days in Guangzhou. Never one for the quiet life, and always interested in financial gain, as Madame Zhang she ran a gambling house, a brothel and, it is rumoured, a smuggling ring. She died peacefully in her bed in 1844, at fifty-nine—which was almost certainly a ripe old age for the period. There is no doubt that Shi Xianggu was quick-witted, an excellent strategist, ruthless, cruel and a brilliant negotiator. Her ambitious nature ensured that she escaped from what could have been a life of destitution spent on the floating brothels of Guangdong. Instead, she led the largest pirate armada the world has ever seen and is viewed by many as the most successful, powerful—and certainly the most notorious—pirate of all time.

Mary Ann Cotton

The Black Widow with a predilection for arsenic and infanticide

1832–1873

Mary Ann Cotton murdered up to twenty people, including eight of her own children.

Wearing a starched apron, her dark hair coiled beneath a cap, Mary Ann scrubbed the iron bedsteads in a ward in Sunderland Infirmary with an arsenic-impregnated soap to kill off bedbugs, and smiled coyly at the patient whom she knew was watching her every move. It was backbreaking work, but no doubt it would pay dividends in the end. Nursing was even better than housekeeping in bringing her close to those most in need of her services—eligible and vulnerable men. The patient smiled back, clearly captivated by the 'delicate and prepossessing' Mary Ann, who seemed at that moment full of all the womanly virtues, including compassion.

Mary Ann Cotton was one of Britain's first serial killers, and the first woman to be given the sobriquet 'Black Widow' after a spider that devours its mate after consummation. By conservative estimates, she is believed to have murdered twenty people, including her mother, three husbands, a sister-in-law, a lover, eight of her children and seven stepchildren. Using arsenic administered through cups of tea, or potions that she claimed were for medicinal purposes, she dispatched her 'loved ones' with a breathtaking callousness, almost as if they were flies which had to be swatted to ensure they didn't get in the way of her personal comfort. She regarded her victims not as human beings but as useful commodities on which she could collect insurance. For an extraordinary twenty years she maintained a murderous spree, flitting from place to place and husband to husband, hoping to finally unearth the pot of gold which would maintain her in the style she felt she so richly deserved. An overweening arrogance was to be her undoing. Aged forty-two, after giving birth to her final child, she died at the end of a hangman's rope in Durham Prison in northeast England.

Early Lessons in Hardship

Born in the quiet north country English village of Low Moorsley, County Durham, Mary Ann Robson, the daughter of a miner, had a strict Christian upbringing, quickly learning that she was expected to be grateful for the smallest of mercies and the thinnest of gruels for her supper. Her father died when Mary Ann was eight, in a fall down a mineshaft, and the family's poverty-stricken state became even more desperate. Mary Ann had always lived in terror of the workhouse, learning about its horrors in the schoolyard where many had already found themselves rudely incarcerated behind its walls. Money, or rather the appalling lack of it, was to dominate Mary Ann's early years and leave a permanent mark on her attitude. Perhaps she promised herself that one day she would never again suffer the indignities poverty imposed. She found sporadic work in the kitchens of the more affluent, there no doubt coming to understand the truth of the simple adage that money invariably equals power.

As she matured, Mary Ann realised that her looks and engaging manner were her chief assets, and began to experiment to see whether she could use them to snare herself a comfortable life. An apprenticeship in dressmaking gave her a trade, which also meant that she could run up a dress or trim a bonnet that would guarantee she got noticed. And she was, by a timekeeper called William Mowbray. Mary Ann quickly became pregnant, perhaps calculating that the besotted William would not let her down. Indulging in premarital sex and entrapping the man who thought he was taking advantage of her became a pattern she was to repeat throughout her life. She married William secretly and left home in disgrace, no doubt relieved to escape the tittle-tattle of the small community and, she hoped, begin a new and more prosperous life in faraway Plymouth in the southwest.

But Mary Ann's next five years were to be dominated by child-bearing, with five babies arriving in quick succession. William Mowbray got a job on a steamboat, which meant long periods of time away from home, and Mary Ann found herself oppressed by the struggle to survive. Her strong practical streak may have been behind her eagerness to make sure all her children and William were insured with the Prudential Insurance Company (the 'Pru'), the premiums seeming a small price to pay for peace of mind. Her babies seemed excessively sickly though, even in a period when the infant mortality rate was so high that a quarter of infants did not live to see their first birthday. By the time that she and William moved back north to Sunderland, after he'd injured his foot on the steamboat, four of the children were dead and the fifth soon followed. During their marriage the couple produced nine children, seven of whom died. Soon after the death of the seventh child, William was seized with gastric pains and himself passed away. The grieving widow visited the Pru and collected the princely sum of £35. When the mourning period was over (some say even before it ended), Mary Ann treated herself to a smart new dress. She had discovered a reliable source of income.

A Chilling New Career

In the nineteenth century, arsenic was readily available, being combined with soap for disinfecting purposes, mixed with paste to hang wallpaper, and used to rid households of vermin. Mary Ann had discovered another use for it, and had slipped it into husband William's tea, confident that it would go undetected since it was odour-free. A gastric upset was so common in Victorian England that no eyebrows were raised at William's unexpected demise. But more shocking is the fact that her children probably went the same way. Mary Ann must have decided on this as the solution for ridding herself of unwanted children who stood in the way of her comfort and ambitions while simultaneously, by insuring their lives, treating them as commodities capable of bringing her in an income. The fact that she could murder her own babies without a qualm marks her as extremely mentally disturbed or, in the language of the time, a 'monster'.

Mary Ann was now on course with her terrible new profession, the dark secrets of which she hid behind her somewhat fragile appearance and winning smile. After moving to Seaham Harbour on the coast, she spied another potential victim, Joseph Nattrass, at the time inconveniently engaged to another woman. Joseph eluded Mary Ann, however, and she may have blamed this on the fact that she still had two children who were proving serious obstacles to flirtation. Before leaving Seaham she buried one and sent the other, her daughter Isabella, to live with her parents. Returning to Sunderland, she found herself a job as a nurse at the Sunderland Infirmary where arsenic, used as a disinfectant, was readily available. She quickly made herself popular with the patients, her bedside manner carefully honed. George Sand was especially taken with her, grateful to the woman who had nursed him back to health. He was to pay a heavy price for such gratitude, for his joy when she agreed to marry him was to be short-lived. Mary Ann bided her time and then slipped him some arsenic—but not before she had checked that George was properly insured with the Pru and that she was the main beneficiary of his will.

After this murder Mary Ann's confidence grew. And now another hapless victim wandered into her web. James Robinson, who worked as a foreman in the local shipbuilding yard, was still heartbroken from the recent death of his wife, Hannah. He desperately needed a housekeeper to help look after his four children and when he met Mary Ann, no longer working at the infirmary, he thought he'd found the perfect candidate. But not long after she had begun work as his housekeeper in 1866, his family began to shrink. The first to die was the ten-month-old baby, struck down, it appeared, by gastric fever. Devastated by this loss, Robinson turned to his kindly housekeeper. Mary Ann had scored yet another 'success'—in taking away a child who mattered so much to the distraught James, she had been certain he would turn to her for comfort.

In March 1867, Mary Ann's widowed mother fell ill. Playing the role of dutiful daughter, Mary Ann hurried home to look after her, apparently also eager to spend some time with the daughter she had left in her mother's care. Her mother was clearly cheered to hear that her daughter was doing so well for herself and was engaged to a wealthy foreman. But the mother's health suddenly took a turn for the worse and she was struck down by gastric fever, to die nine days after her daughter's arrival. Unfortunately, there was no insurance to cash in, so Mary Ann made do with the furniture, which she sold. No sentiment or natural affection appeared to cloud her vision at the murder of her mother and the destruction of what had been her childhood home.

The Black Widow

With scarcely a backward glance, Mary Ann took her daughter back to Sunderland and prepared for marriage to the hapless James. In June 1867, the wedding took place, no doubt the congregation fondly imagining that poor James had found someone to take care of him at last. However, the gastric fever that appeared to follow Mary Ann around soon struck down not only Isabella, but two more of Robinson's children. By the following March, the first of the couple's two children together had also succumbed to the illness, and James was beginning to have doubts about his new wife. Each time a child died, she seemed to rush with unbecoming haste to collect the insurance money from the Pru. When James began to receive bills for debts that Mary Ann had incurred, he began to piece the story together. Although he could not bear to face the appalling possibility that his wife was a murderess, he did throw Mary Ann out—leaving her free to kill again.

Mary Ann took their surviving child, a daughter, with her, perhaps hoping this would make her a more pitiable sight and that Robinson would have a change of heart. When this ploy failed, she dumped the little girl on a friend, who returned her to Robinson. In later days, this child must have counted her blessings for this lucky escape.

As always, Mary Ann knew the secret was to keep moving and now she travelled north and set herself up in Walbottle, Northumberland. There her friend Margaret Cotton kept house for her brother, Frederick, who had just lost his wife and two of his four children. Not long after Mary Ann's arrival, he found himself also in mourning for his sister, who had been struck down by a sudden gastric attack. Like the Black Widow spider, Mary Ann inched closer to her prey. Her comforting words and soft looks worked their magic on Frederick and in September 1870, aged thirty-eight, Mary Ann Robinson went through a bigamous wedding ceremony at St Andrews Church, Newcastle-upon-Tyne. A year later, Frederick presumably felt his happiness was complete when she gave birth to a son.

However, always on the lookout for a man who could provide her with a better lifestyle, Mary Ann discovered that her old flame Joseph Nattrass was living in the area—and he didn't have a wife. Did she love Nattrass or was he merely a fly that had escaped from her web? Whatever the case, she pursued him with single-minded zeal and began a relationship. Frederick Cotton was now an irritating obstacle, and she quickly disposed of him in the usual way. This time it was she who played the part of the grief-stricken mourner, and the kind-hearted Nattrass moved in as a lodger to provide comfort and to ease her financial problems. But for Mary Ann there was never enough money for her needs, especially since she enjoyed being able to pay people to do her shopping and housework.

At this time she took a job as a nurse to John Quick-Manning, a cut above Nattrass on the social scale, and who was recovering from smallpox. Mary Ann summarily dumped Nattrass and became pregnant by Quick-Manning. Within a month, two more children and Nattrass were dead and she had collected the insurance on them. Only one child, seven-year-old Charlie Cotton, remained—and she had plans for him too.

It is tempting to think that Mary Ann might have felt some twinge of compassion for poor little Charlie, since she took him to the local workhouse rather than choosing to dispatch him immediately. But serial killers are not known for feelings of remorse, and it was now that Mary Ann, no doubt puffed up with confidence at her success in hoodwinking people, made a mistake. When the workhouse administrator, Thomas Riley, refused to take the boy in unless Mary Ann came with him, she was reported to have said, 'I could have married again but for the child. But there, he will not live long and will go the way of all the Cotton family'. Soon afterward, little Charlie was sent to the apothecary to buy some arsenic—which he was refused because he was obviously not twenty-one. It was only to be a brief respite, however, for by July of that year he was dead.

Mary Ann's luck had run out. The suspicions of the local doctor and of Thomas Riley, who remembered Mary Ann's strange prophecy, were

MARY ANN COTTON—
She's dead and she's rotten!
She lies in her bed
With her eyes wide open
Sing, sing, oh what can I sing?
Mary Ann Cotton is tied up
with string
Where, where? Up in the air—
Selling black puddings a
penny a pair.
– Children's rhyme

aroused and they demanded an inquest before the death certificate was signed. For once Mary Ann was unsuccessful in her ritual visit to the Pru—no death certificate. The doctor had saved some cells from Charlie's stomach which on examination were found to have traces of arsenic. The bodies of several others with whom Mary Ann had been connected were then exhumed, and all were found to be contaminated by arsenic. Despite Mary Ann's vigorous protestations of innocence, the evidence was overwhelming. On 24 March 1873, after a trial in which she was convicted of the murder of Charlie and five other victims, the Black Widow was condemned to death. She suffered horribly at the hands of the hangman, who bungled the execution so that she dangled from the rope for three minutes before dying.

IN ONE OF THE EARLIEST cases of 'airbrushing', the newspaper artists of the day deliberately toned down Mary Ann Cotton's 'delicate and prepossessing appearance', choosing to coarsen her features and make her appear more like the monster she was believed to be.

There have been other murderesses in history who have done away with their husbands with poison, but Mary Ann's combined predilection for infanticide places her in a category of her own. It seems extraordinary today, in view of the massive trail of death she left behind her, that she succeeded in escaping justice for twenty years. But her constant moves around the country, her frequent changes of name, and the ready availability of arsenic, together with the fact that gastric fever was endemic at the time, probably help to explain why the secret of her comforting cups of tea remained hidden for so long.

The ruthlessly ambitious Cixi ruled a quarter of the world's population for over fifty years.

Cixi

Qing Dynasty dragon empress—vain, manipulative and power crazy

1835–1908

I have often thought that I am the most clever woman that ever lived, and others cannot compare with me ... I have 400 million people dependent on my judgment.

– Cixi

The young concubine Cixi waited patiently night after night, hoping that soon it would be her turn to spend the night with the Emperor. Each evening a tablet carved from jade was turned over to reveal the name of the chosen concubine. Cixi drew in her breath sharply as she saw that tonight's tablet belonged to her. The court eunuchs stripped her naked to ensure she could not smuggle a weapon into the imperial bedchamber, and wrapped her in a red rug. She was then carried to the bedroom and placed at the foot of the Emperor's bed. That night, Cixi used all her considerable sexual skills in order to captivate the Emperor and ensure that there would be many such nights to follow.

Empress Dowager Cixi (Tzu Hsi) ruled over a quarter of the world's population for more than fifty years, competing in this respect with her English contemporary, Queen Victoria, whom she came to admire. Although politically astute, once Cixi had tasted power she became increasingly autocratic. Ruthless, inconsistent, but all the while bent on self-advancement, her stubborn resistance to change combined with her mistrust of foreigners meant that China was held back from industrialisation and plunged into futile foreign wars. By the time the Dragon Empress realised her mistake and hastily began to introduce Western innovations such as railroads and schools, China was in the grip of terrible poverty and the Qing dynasty was rapidly crumbling.

Cixi was never formally installed as Empress but reigned unofficially, instructing two child Emperors in turn through a bamboo screen and being closer to the Imperial throne than any woman in China's long history.

Early Ambition

Yehonala (or Yehenara) was born in 1835, the eldest daughter of a low-ranking official of the Manchu Yehonala clan. She spent her early life in Anhui province before moving with her family to Beijing, the stronghold of the ruling Qing dynasty. It was not a happy childhood for Yehonala; she later spoke of being constantly pitted against her siblings, continually having to assert herself to win favours.

Her father died when she was fourteen and the family's income shrank. Soon afterward, her natural opportunistic tendencies having been strengthened by this misfortune, Yehonala found a potential rescuer in the form of Ronglu, a young garrison commander. It is said that she planned to marry him, until a public announcement that the Emperor wished to increase the number of his royal concubines caught her eye. Ronglu was forgotten while Yehonala explored this interesting option. Perhaps her destiny lay within the walls of the Emperor's home, the Forbidden City.

The Empress Dowager Kangci drew up a list of sixty Manchu women deemed worthy of her son, with beauty as the main criterion. Yehonala's winning attributes of jet-black hair, liquid dark eyes, high cheek bones and warm smile, combined with a sensuous voice and mercurial personality, meant that she soon came to the Empress Dowager's attention. At sixteen, she was selected to begin her two-year concubine training. As Yehonala entered the Forbidden City, with its outer and inner palaces and maze of ceremonial halls and courtyards where the concubines lived, she knew that she would need all her wits to survive; the Emperor's court was one of the most dangerous political arenas that ever existed.

A Concubine of Feminine Virtue

AT THIS TIME China was under the rule of the Qing dynasty, established by Manchu invaders in 1644. With a population divide of five million Manchus compared with four hundred million Chinese, the Manchus viewed themselves as superior, and were determined to maintain the purity of the Manchu bloodline.

At court Yehonala had to rely on her own resources, the survival skills she honed serving her well. She rose quickly through the ranks of the concubines, astutely cultivating influential people along the way, including the Empress Dowager and the court eunuchs, as always in Imperial China a very powerful group of officials. At eighteen, she finally became a fully-fledged royal concubine and was given the name Cixi, meaning 'Kindly and Virtuous'. Now all she needed was for Emperor Xianfeng to notice her.

Night after night a different concubine was laid naked at the foot of his bed, and at last Cixi's turn came. Making use of all her bedroom skills and charm, she soon became his favourite. When she gave birth to the first royal son, she found herself occupying a position second only to the Emperor's primary wife, Ci'an, who happened to be Cixi's cousin. As the baby uttered his first cries, he was whisked away and placed in the care of the Empress Dowager Kangci. If Cixi had any maternal feelings at that

moment, she was forced to suppress them and prepare herself for what was to be a long waiting game.

Cixi remained on good terms with Ci'an and was an ever-watchful presence in the background as her son, Tongzhi, grew to boyhood. She excelled at the power games being played out at court, increasingly determined that one day her boy would become Emperor and she would be the Empress Dowager. But five years later, in 1861, as the Emperor lay dying, her ambitions were threatened when a group of nobles and imperial advisors—later known as the 'Gang of Eight'—proclaimed themselves the official regents of the kingdom.

Cixi had not clawed her way up the ladder to have her dream suddenly snatched away from her, so she stormed into the Emperor's bedroom, demanding that he recognise her son as the next Emperor. In front of witnesses, the dying Emperor decreed that Tongzhi should succeed him and that Cixi and Ci'an should be his regents and share the title of Empress Dowager. But the Gang of Eight had also been appointed regents, and together the unlikely group attempted to govern. Power sharing, however, did not fit into Cixi's game plan.

Cixi set about gathering support, procuring the help of the dead Emperor's brother, Prince Gong, and of her first love, Ronglu, by now military commander of the garrison guarding the Forbidden City. Together they staged a military coup that resulted in the two Empress Dowagers seizing control of the government and becoming sole co-regents of the empire. The members of the Gang of Eight received short shrift, being summarily convicted of treason. Some of them were beheaded while those who were of royal blood were invited to commit suicide. 'Kindly and Virtuous' began to seem a most ironic misnomer for the young Empress Dowager as Cixi ruthlessly removed the opposition and dominated the more reserved Ci'an, who having been primary wife was still superior in rank.

Although known as Yehonala while she was a young concubine, Cixi's actual birthname is unknown.

The Dragon Empress

Cixi loved the power that came with her new position and is said to have begun to display a disturbing sadistic streak, sometimes amusing herself by ordering two maids to slap each other's faces while she watched. People within the court were murdered for the most trivial of reasons, hurled down a convenient well by her executioners—the eunuchs. She was extraordinarily vain and was said to have been furious with a servant for pulling out two hairs on her head, demanding that the girl put them back. Revelling in the fashion of her times, she became ever more startling in appearance, plastering on her pale make-up as if to wall herself in, growing her fingernails until they curled like talons and became weapons,

SINCE HER DEATH, biographers have recounted stories of Cixi's outrageous behaviour and hunger for power. The story of the concubine down the well was originally told in a biography by a palace insider, then retold in numerous accounts of her life. In *Dragon Lady: The Life and Legend of the Last Empress of China*, biographer Sterling Seagrave disputes the famous tale. Although he admits that Cixi was temperamental and quick to anger, he claims she was the unwitting dupe of powerful men in the palace, who manipulated the ignorant and powerless Empress Dowager to rule China.

used for lashing out at some hapless servant. It was now that she began to be known as the 'Dragon Empress'. Barely five feet tall and famous for her sudden rages, she inspired awe in counsellors and courtiers alike.

Cixi's irritability was made worse by insomnia. At night she lay in bed surrounded by clocks, as if anxious to mark each second she was in power. As sleep eluded her, she would gaze in fascination at a portrait of her English contemporary, Queen Victoria, a short stout woman dressed in widow's weeds, hair tucked into a lace cap. At least it must have helped pass a few hours of those long sleepless nights.

Cixi thoroughly appreciated the luxuries of her position, ordering lavish banquets at which she ate with a pair of gold chopsticks and drank from a jade cup. She did not hesitate to plunder the national purse to build a beautiful summer palace, even though the money she siphoned off meant that the military and the navy were ill-equipped for battle. Corruption was the everyday currency of the Forbidden City and Cixi turned a blind eye as conniving, self-serving eunuchs charged extortionate prices for food, knowing it was crucial to keep them on side. She enjoyed their company and rewarded them handsomely for their favours. When her favourite was executed for financial extortion, her grief was better understood when it was discovered that, as she put it, 'his teapot had a spout'.

The Puppet Mistresses

For years, Cixi and Ci'an ruled 'through a bamboo curtain' placed behind the throne, instructing the young Emperor Tongzhi in what he should and should not do. Ci'an was not particularly interested in matters of government so much of the politics was left to Cixi—a state of affairs which delighted her. When Tongzhi reached manhood at the age of seventeen, his 'mothers' were forced to step down. But watching her weak-willed son take the throne, Cixi was confident she would not be sidelined for long.

Tongzhi seemed more interested in trawling the city walls in search of prostitutes—of both sexes—than ruling China. When he took a wife, a headstrong Mongol woman called Alute, Cixi was worried that she would easily dominate him. She made it her business to surround him with concubines to keep him distracted while she unofficially made government decisions. Not yet nineteen, Tongzhi died in 1874 of a lethal combination of venereal disease and smallpox; his wife was said to be so devastated that a few months later she took her own life with a massive dose of opium. Rumours quickly spread that the Dragon Empress had used her powers of persuasion on the grieving widow. No doubt believing that power was hers once more, to Cixi's dismay she discovered that her son's favourite concubine was pregnant. If the child were a boy, he would be the new Emperor, and the concubine would become Dowager Empress, just like Cixi all those years ago. But the concubine died mysteriously before giving birth, allegedly poisoned by one of the loyal eunuchs. The Dragon Empress remained in control.

By now, she was so adept at manipulation that she felt she could defy rigid imperial tradition by deciding who the next Emperor should be. In 1875, not long after Tongzhi's death, Cixi nominated a successor, her own three-year-old nephew Guangxu, who was not in direct line to the throne. By adopting him, she maintained her position and ensured that she would rule through the bamboo curtain for another thirteen years. When Cixi fell ill in 1880, however, it became clear that Ci'an, despite never showing great interest in government, was herself astute and well versed in the running of the country. As tension between the two powerful women mounted, Ci'an decided to show Cixi an Imperial document which she had concealed for twenty years. Cixi was shocked at what it said, realising that it could serve as her own death warrant. Emperor Xianfeng had apparently taken the measure of her character long ago, for the document stated that if Cixi started to meddle in state affairs, the Grand Council had his permission to 'assist her suicide'.

Despite Ci'an's assurances, Cixi did not believe that she had only shown her this 'time bomb' to demonstrate how loyal she had always been in not revealing its contents. She was certain that Ci'an could and would use it to destroy her. Appearing outwardly grateful and affectionate, Cixi quietly began to plot. Ci'an died the next year, allegedly having 'choked on spit' after eating some milk cakes delivered to her by one of Cixi's faithful eunuchs. Without a qualm, the Dragon Empress had successfully defused the time bomb, sealing the fate of the woman who had been her trusted companion for so long. All that mattered was that Cixi was now sole regent of the Middle Kingdom.

SIX-INCH HEELS

At the age of sixty-nine, while on a tour of the Summer Palace Opera House with the painter Katherine Carl, Carl commented that the Dowager Empress 'mounted the steep and difficult steps with as much ease and lightness as I did, and I had on comfortable European shoes, while she wears the six-inch-high Manchu sole in the middle of her foot, and must really walk as if on stilts'.

Cixi pictured in the centre of a royal procession, 1903, when the Dowager Empress was aged sixty-eight.

The Worm Turns

Like his predecessor, the young Emperor was told what to say through the bamboo screen and parroted Cixi's instructions. But as he grew older, Guangxu started to develop his own beliefs and ideologies; in 1889, when he came of age, he forced a furious Cixi into retirement. She hated the way he experimented with Western gadgets, read books on science and the law, and studied the ways of the Western world. Desperately opposed to change, Cixi ignored the fact that the dynasty was in decay. Great tracts of land were being leased to the European powers who were invading many of the countries in Asia. Then, in 1894, with the Imperial court still indulging in banquets of more than a hundred different dishes, the Chinese army, ill-equipped and badly resourced, buckled in the face of invading Japanese forces and China was forced to cede control of the Korean peninsula and Taiwan.

Emperor Guangxu and his irascible aunt were now locked in a fierce power struggle. The Emperor believed that it was imperative for China to embrace Western civilisation, and announced the Hundred Days of Reform. He ordered railroads to be built, the military to be modernised and the legal system reformed, declaring that the empire must banish 'bigoted conservatism and unpractical customs' and learn from Western countries if it was to lead the world. Cixi's entire power base was, of course, 'bigoted conservatism', and she was horrified by her nephew's revolutionary plans. When the ever-faithful Ronglu told her that he had uncovered a plot to have her thrown into prison until the reforms were over, she was incensed. In September 1898, with Ronglu's help, she staged a successful coup against the Emperor and soon had him begging her forgiveness—but she imprisoned him on an artificial island within the Forbidden City. Although he retained the title of Emperor, Cixi was back in power and calmly cancelled all the planned reforms.

The Boxer Rebellion

But the experience gained from thirty-seven long years in power did not save Cixi now from making a huge miscalculation. There was one rebellious faction which she failed to quell. The Boxer Rebellion was started by a society made up mainly of farmers and peasants who blamed foreigners and imperialism for the abject poverty in which they lived. They were recklessly brave, believing that a type of boxing which they practised protected them from bullets. Cixi empathised with their hatred of Westerners who, at the time, seemed to be attempting to stamp their mark upon China, indifferent to a way of life steeped in centuries of tradition. Businessmen from America, Britain, Japan and Russia saw the country as a lucrative new market, obtaining favourable trading rights which helped to fuel the Boxers' anger and resentment.

Cixi may have covertly encouraged the rebellion. In 1900 the Boxers rampaged through northeast China, murdering not only foreigners but also those of their Chinese countrymen who had become Christians. As they marched on Beijing, she assured anxious foreign diplomats that she would put a stop to the rebellion—but when the Boxers entered the Chinese capital, uttering their bloodcurdling battle cry of 'Burn, Burn, Burn! Kill, Kill, Kill!' Imperial troops were nowhere to be seen. But while Cixi quietly applauded the rebels, who had targeted the section of the city occupied by Westerners, a huge force of allied troops was being marshalled to eradicate the Boxers. Beijing was captured and a humiliating peace treaty imposed upon the Chinese.

According to legend, as the victorious allied troops entered Beijing, Cixi was busy having her hair combed. Removing her layers of pale make-up and dressing in a peasant outfit, she hid her jewels and fled the city with the Emperor and his wife. When his favourite concubine begged to be allowed to accompany him, it is said that Cixi ordered her eunuchs to throw her down a well—or give her the option of jumping. Age had not softened the Dragon Empress. But as they travelled toward the city of Xi'an, southwest of Beijing, she was to see the depths of poverty into which the country had been plunged and to which she had previously been oblivious, safe behind the walls of the Forbidden City. It is said that it was only at this point that she finally realised that reform was necessary; perhaps because of this change of heart, Cixi was called back to rule once more.

Weeks later, the Imperial party returned to the Forbidden City under the wary eyes of the foreigners, who climbed the walls to watch the Dragon Empress approach. Cixi had carefully orchestrated the moment. Seeing them lining the city walls, out of place in their Western clothing, Cixi looked up and executed a series of little bows. The foreigners were delighted at what they saw as her humility, and any lingering concern that she was a tyrant was quickly dispelled as she assured them of her horror at the atrocities committed by the Boxer rebels.

But the humiliating Peace of Peking, which resulted in Western nations gaining in power, acquiring lucrative trading rights and even being able to station troops in the capital city, fuelled the anger of the Chinese people against their Manchu rulers. The dictatorial power Cixi had enjoyed for so long was ebbing away. In 1908, she was struck down by a serious liver complaint and Guangxu also fell ill. On 13 November with Guangxu's life hanging by a thread, Cixi appointed a successor, again only three years old—Puyi, the son of Prince Cu'un and the grandson of her early love, Ronglu. The Emperor conveniently died that night. Although she must have known that she herself was terminally ill, Cixi could not give up the power games—but even she had no control over her own mortality. On 15 November 1908, as she finished telling the three-year-old Puyi that he must obey her in all matters, she was near death.

Following tradition on the impending death of a sovereign, Cixi's loyal eunuchs laid her in her bed facing south and surrounded her with her jewels. The last words she uttered were: 'Never again allow a woman to hold the supreme power in the State. It is against the house-laws of our dynasty and should be forbidden'. Perhaps she felt genuine remorse. But the more sceptical might suspect that even at the end she was driven by one all-consuming desire—that she, Cixi, 'Kindly and Virtuous', should be the only woman able to lay claim to such an extraordinary achievement.

Cixi had ruled China for fifty years and until her change of heart after the Boxer Rebellion had seemed more concerned with power for its own sake than with the welfare of her millions of subjects. Protected by the walls of the Forbidden City, she had lacked any insight into their suffering, and the long years of her anti-foreign policies were to result in China's downfall. At seventy-three, the Dragon Empress left China in total chaos with a three-year-old boy at the head of the Qing dynasty—a boy who would become known to the world as 'the Last Emperor' and would end his days as an ordinary citizen of Communist China.

A funeral procession carries the body of the Dowager Empress Cixi on its way to be interred in the Eastern Qing Tombs in 1908.

Belle Starr

Gun-toting, horse-rustling Southern temptress
1848–1889

I am a friend to any brave and gallant outlaw.
– Belle Starr

Belle scrubbed the floors of the little cabin, beat the mats and hung them out to dry. She had just spent nine months in prison for horse stealing, and was enjoying her return to freedom. But while Belle was languishing in her cell, her bad reputation had flourished in the outside world. Everyone now knew that this ordinary woman with the tired, drawn face was the leader of a wild gang of outlaws, that she could shoot and fight and curse better than any man. They had found a six-gun hidden in her skirt when she was arrested and two derringers in her blouse— and she had consorted with Jesse James and Cole Younger and other wild, gun-toting men. Belle heard the whispers as she bought her provisions in the local store, and knew it was crazy to think she could ever escape her past.

So Belle decided to give the gossipmongers a run for their money and play up to the infamous role they had created for her. In the following weeks the little community nodded in smug satisfaction as they watched Belle parade down the street on her black mare, Venus, dressed in black velvet and riding sidesaddle. On her head was a man's sombrero, golden earrings jangled at her collar, and strapped to her hip was her 'baby'—a Colt 45.

Belle Starr in her customary tight-laced, velvet riding habit, sitting sidesaddle on her black mare.

Belle Starr at twenty-two in 1870, during the time she was married to Jim Reed, who introduced her to the Starr gang and the world of crime.

Countless wild tales have inflated the legend of Belle Starr, one of the most notorious of female outlaws, famed for taking on the men at their own game, allegedly leading a band of horse rustlers, and surviving at a time when the Wild West lived up to its name in every respect. In the dime novels and yellow newspapers that recounted her exploits with relish and with scant regard for the facts, she is celebrated as an

Amazonian woman of the prairies, a female Jesse James, a temptress in a tightly-laced velvet riding habit who galloped through town, guns blazing. She is admired for her recklessness, her ability to make a mockery of sheriffs and judges, and her habit of marrying her Cherokee lovers in order to keep their land. Her name, of course, caught the imagination— 'Belle Starr' being a wonderful source of inspiration for the balladeers who celebrated her exploits. But beneath the hype and the romantic embellishments that turned Belle into a legend is a more fascinating figure—feisty, independent and flawed, breaking all the rules that were intended to keep a woman in her place in the nineteenth century, defying every challenge that inhospitable terrain could throw at her, but in the end a woman hardened by circumstance leading a far from glamorous life.

A Southern Belle

Belle was born Myra Maybelle Shirley on 5 February 1848 near Carthage, Missouri, the daughter of wealthy innkeeper and slave-owner John Shirley, the black sheep of his family, and Elizabeth Pennington, closely related to the Hatfields notorious for their involvement in an infamous and very bloody feud with the McCoy family. Perhaps the young Belle listened to tales of the wild adventures of the Hatfields and McCoys in place of regular bedtime stories and felt a thrill of excitement. In any event, there is a tale that at the tender age of ten, she rode through town, two guns clamped in her chubby fists, and proceeded to open fire to the amusement of onlookers. That spectators were amused at seeing a small girl with a gun must tell us a great deal about the times.

But for the moment Belle, like any well-brought-up Southern girl, was engaged in her studies, her father's wealth making it possible for her to attend the prestigious Carthage Female Academy. Here she excelled, having a natural flair for languages, learning Latin, Greek and Hebrew, and showing considerable talent on the piano. In another age and place she might have remained plain Myra Shirley and become a high-flying academic. But while she shone in class, she was disliked by the other students. Her sharp tongue often got her into trouble and the fact that her family was well-to-do made her think she was a cut above the others. But Belle didn't care what her classmates thought of her, having never been much interested in the company of girls. From an early age she had loved the camaraderie of men.

A natural tomboy, Belle spent long, happy hours with her dashing, handsome older brother, John 'Bud' Shirley, whom she adored. With Bud, Belle rode deep into the wilds, hunting, fishing and shooting, and learning respect for the tracking skills of the Native Americans as she followed a trail or caught fish in the rivers. Bud provided her with the sort of finishing school that made his sister a very different Southern belle to her easily shocked contemporaries. And while he gave her lessons in firearms that made her the equal of any man, he also inspired in her a confidence in her own powers and a determination never to turn her back on a challenge.

These idyllic years were to be cut short when the Civil War broke out in 1861 and Missouri disintegrated, its people torn apart by their divided allegiance to either the Union of the North (the United States of America) or the Southern Confederacy. Bud, a natural scout with his knowledge of Native American lore, became a daring bushwhacker for the South and quickly attained the rank of captain. The intrepid Belle longed to ride out at his side and, to her delight, was given a role by the Confederacy. She was employed to carry intelligence across the lines, reporting the whereabouts of the Union troops, ducking and weaving her way on horseback but playing the tremulous Southern belle whenever she attracted suspicion. She was breaking all the rules relating to a woman's place—and loving every minute of it. But tragedy was about to strike. Bud was killed in action and Belle was heartbroken. It is said that in a frenzy of rage and grief she reacted in a way which was to become a pattern in her life—strapping on a gun and arming herself with two revolvers as well, hell-bent on exacting her revenge.

But as Confederate guer[...]
packed his family, including a pr[...]
burning city for Texas, taking up [...]
kilometres southeast of Dallas. The los[...]
the precipitous flight was to prove a turning[...]
she wrote, 'My life is a wreck. A great necessity[...]
drift high upon the waves of notoriety, or sink in[...]
life. The latter I can never do'.

Saddled with Poverty

In those days Texas was a refuge for drifters and the down and out [...]
as for people made destitute by the war. John Shirley was angry at findi[...]
himself among them. No longer the wealthy slave-owner, and mourning
the loss of his son, he worked his land himself, growing crops and raising
horses. Without the family wealth to bolster her, Belle became more of a
rebel, relishing her role as misfit. A fellow schoolmate claimed that Belle
would fight anyone who crossed her, boy or girl.

The Shirley farm appears to have become a breeding ground for
disaffection and resentment. When the fugitives Jesse James, his brother
Frank, Cole Younger and other members of their group came calling, Belle's
father welcomed them in—for they too had been betrayed by the Union.
They had fought as bushwhackers, like Bud, and after the war, were
planning on making society pay what they reckoned was their due.

Belle was infected by the rebellious mood and excited by the visitors,
particularly the good-looking Cole Younger. She enjoyed keeping a
lookout to ensure the forces of law and order didn't descend on the
Shirley farm, perhaps feeling closer to Bud, since he had known the James
brothers and fought alongside them. But keeping watch soon wasn't
enough and before long she took to occasionally riding out with the
men. Striking up a relationship with Cole, she apparently hit the outlaw
trail for a couple of months. Belle was developing a taste for dangerous

ntier guerilla, Jim
e impressive gun-

l of desperados and
back with a gang
et Jim he wasn't a
atch. He shared the
oting father to their
le Pearl'. But while
he restless and started
ing, leaving Belle to
y with the Cherokee
g.

s churchgoing dutiful
ntroduced her to the
ey'd carried out a raid
d of their takings. But

pilfering and cattle raids soon led to more seri rimes, and in 1871 Jim
was charged with being involved in the assassination of the man who had
murdered his brother. Jim and Belle had no choice but to hightail it to
California, where Belle gave birth to their second child, James Edwin. The
Federal officials weren't about to give up, and Jim was forced to flee again
as they followed his trail. Left to fend for herself with two small children,
Belle headed back to the Shirley farm in Scyene. Married life had proved
rather more eventful than she could ever have imagined.

Taking the Reins

John Shirley gave his fugitive daughter a small patch of land. When Jim
rejoined her, they tried to make a living from its often barren soil. But the
meager returns to be earned from honest toil didn't impress Jim, who was
soon on the lookout for richer rewards. In 1873, he took part in the

notorious robbery of a Cherokee called Grayson, who was known to have access to a substantial sum of money. Grayson's attackers hung him from a tree until he revealed his secret, and then rode off to find the 'pot of gold'. Jim was now completely off the rails, and Belle moved into her parents' house as he went into hiding yet again. But he was not to evade the law for long; Belle found herself having to identity his body after a deputy sheriff finally caught up with him. Perhaps she even breathed a small sigh of relief—Jim had been nothing but trouble. She might be better off on her own.

And for a brief period after her husband's death, Belle managed to steer clear of wild men. But when her father died in 1876 and her mother moved to Dallas, taking Pearl with her so she could go to school, Belle was left with an increasingly troublesome and troubled small son, Eddie. He took after his father in all the most worrying ways, and mother and son had a stormy relationship. When he left home at the age of twelve, Belle decided to sell the farm and move on.

She met yet another 'Mr Wrong'. Bruce Younger, half-brother of Cole Younger's father, whom Belle had known long ago on the Shirley farm, became her new beau. They lived together in the Evans Hotel in Galena, Kansas, where the owner remembered her as 'mighty good-looking … not tough like the newspapers made out'. Here we get one of those rare glimpses of the woman behind the legend, as she defied the saloon bar talk and those who sat in disapproving judgment on her, keeping up appearances even as she broke all the rules.

But in 1880, as if set on a downward spiral, Belle gravitated back to the notorious Starr gang, now operating in Arkansas and Oklahoma. Sam Starr had all the recklessness and the skills with a gun and a horse that Belle had always admired in a man, together with the proud heritage of the Cherokee Nation. When she married him, she lopped five years off her age and began calling herself Belle instead of Myra, which she felt had never suited her. Perhaps her new name, meaning 'beautiful star', offered a way to forge a new and more romantic identity. She and Sam were

BUCKING BRONCO by Belle Starr, Indian Territory

My love is a rider, wild broncos he breaks,
Though he's promised to quit it, just for my sake.
He ties up one foot, the saddle put on,
With a swing and a jump, he is mounted and gone.

The first time I met him, 't was nearly one spring,
Riding a bronco, a high-spirited thing.
He tipped me a wink as he gayly did go,
For he wished me to look at his bucking bronco.

The next time I saw him, 't was late in the fall,
Swinging the girls at Tomlinson's ball:
He laughed and he talked as we danced to and fro,
Promised never to ride another bronco.

He made me some presents, among them a ring:
The return that I made him was a far better thing:
'T was a young maiden's heart, I'd have you all know.
He'd won it by riding his bucking bronco.

Now, all you young maidens, where'er you reside,
Beware of the cowboy who swings the rawhide,
He'll court you and pet you and leave you and go
In the spring up the trail on his bucking bronco.

from Jack Thorp's collection,
Songs of the Cowboys, 1921

given an allotment on the banks of the Canadian River by the Cherokee Nation, where they built a cabin and established a farm. Belle tried her very best to live quietly there but, as usual, it was an act she could not keep up for long. The little community busily gossiped about the infamous woman in their midst and Belle didn't help things by sheltering her old friend, Jesse James, for a month. Almost without her lifting a finger, Belle ensured that her notoriety continued to grow in leaps and bounds.

The Hanging Judge

Belle and Sam Starr's relatively peaceful few years came to an abrupt end in 1883 when they were arrested for stealing a horse, a serious crime in those days. Belle's reputation as a gun-toting bandit was enhanced by the fact that when she was arrested, she had a six-gun in the pocket of her skirt and two derringers in her blouse. By this time, any concern for the facts had gone out of the window and the courtroom was packed with spectators, all waiting with bated breath to see the woman who they believed was the unopposed 'queen' of a gang of wild horse thieves. Belle seemed to play to the gallery and even Judge Isaac Parker, famous as a 'hanging judge', was impressed by her haughty air of disdain. Taking into account that, despite Belle's reputation, this was in fact her first offence, he gave her two sentences of six months and Sam got one year. After nine months, both were released for good behaviour and headed home for Christmas, on the way picking up Pearl, now finished with school and foisted on long-suffering friends.

The spell in prison and the nickname 'Queen of the Outlaws' combined to ensure that the legend of Belle Starr would career headlong down the tracks. It was now that she seemed to give in and play up to her reputation, donning the sombrero and velvet riding habit, inventing an image to inspire the fevered imaginations of those whose lives must have seemed dourly uneventful in comparison. Perhaps we can detect now a wilder, more perverse streak in her. Certainly, she made another foolish mistake when she provided a haven for John Middleton, a man accused of murder. She and Sam helped him escape by swimming a horse across the Poteau River. When Middleton drowned, Belle was arrested and accused of stealing the half-blind animal on which he had tried to make his escape. Whatever Belle did now, it seemed a sheriff or marshal was at her heels. A photograph taken with the convicted Cherokee murderer, Blue Duck, which appeared in a local newspaper, added yet more fuel to the flames. Furious when she saw the photograph, Belle is said to have taken a whip to the reporter whom she felt had tricked her. But she must have known it was a losing battle. Society had passed judgment on the outlaw queen, and there was no turning back.

Belle stuck by Sam, who now seemed engaged in a running battle with a Native American police officer, Frank West, who perhaps felt that Belle's husband was a poor advertisement for the Cherokee Nation. Sam spent his time in hiding or in court appearances as West kept on his trail. Then on 18 December 1886, a Christmas party attended by Belle, Sam, Pearl, and Eddie, briefly intent on playing happy families for once, ended in tragedy. Sam was gunned down by his old enemy Frank West, who had

From well-heeled beginnings as a Southern belle, Myra Maybelle Shirley evolved into Belle Starr, often called the 'female Jesse James'.

arrived unannounced to arrest him once again. Probably high on Christmas spirit and bootleg whiskey, Sam drew his gun first. But as the fatally wounded Frank fell to the floor, he managed one last shot. Exactly five minutes from the moment the two men set eyes on each other across the room, both lay dead.

For an increasingly hardened Belle, it was just one more hard knock, and she tried not to allow herself the luxury of grief. Sam's death meant that she had lost her legitimate claim to the land on which they had lived, and to rectify this she needed to move quickly. She began a relationship with the much younger Cherokee bandit, Jim July. The Indian Council agreed she could have the land, but only on condition that she never harbour any fugitive. And to cement the union that was never to be formalised in church, Belle insisted that Jim should take the name of Starr. It seems that in this 'marriage', based on tough practicalities rather than romance, Belle was determined that she was in charge.

But the relationship appears to have been doomed from the start. Belle's son, Eddie, at fifteen only seven years younger than Jim July, bitterly resented the presence of the intruder. Belle's only response to Eddie's troublemaking was the whip. When she gave him a beating in public, Eddie was humiliated and stormed off. She also rode roughshod over Pearl, refusing to let her marry the man she loved and throwing her out when she became pregnant by him. Belle treated her children to the summary rough justice she felt would keep them in line but the end result was that she alienated both of them. She drove Pearl to make a living on the streets, and in Eddie, who resembled his hell-raising father Jim Reed more with each month that passed, she had lit a dangerous fuse.

July, as if to live up to his Starr credentials, was getting himself into all kinds of trouble too. When he was arrested in the summer of 1887 for stealing horses, Belle refused to stand bail, arousing his fury. After one of their many quarrels, he was reported to have offered someone $200 to kill her. When the man refused, July was heard to say, 'Hell, I'll kill the old hag myself and spend the money for whiskey!' Or was this just one of the many fictions invented by the dime novelists to give colour to their stories? Whatever the case, there was little love lost between the warring pair. About the same time, Belle entered into a fierce dispute with her neighbour Edgar Watson, to whom she had rented some land. She had discovered Watson was wanted in Florida and, conscious she could be turned off her own land if she harboured a criminal, she told him to leave, threatening to tell the Florida authorities. Watson packed his bags, infuriated no doubt by the fact he had been given his marching orders by a woman. Belle had made yet another dangerous enemy.

Biting the Bullet

Nemesis was now to catch up with Belle. On 2 February 1889, she rode to a nearby settlement to shop and spend the night with friends while Jim July went on to Fort Smith to answer a charge of horse stealing. As she rode home along the river bank next afternoon, not far from the Watsons' place a shot rang out, hitting her in the back and throwing her from her horse. As she tried to raise herself from the ground to confront her killer, a second shot took her in the face and shoulder. Belle Starr died in the dirt, two days short of her forty-first birthday.

For her funeral, Belle was dressed in her finest black velvet riding habit, a pearl-handled Colt 45 cradled in her hands. She was buried in front of her ranch house in a full Cherokee funeral ceremony. On her headstone were engraved images of her favourite horse, Venus, a bell and a star. Her daughter, Pearl, wrote the epitaph:

Shed not for her the bitter tear,
Nor give the heart to vain regret;
'Tis but the casket that lies here,
The gem that filled it sparkles yet.

Although the main suspect was the man she had evicted from her land, Edgar Watson, there was not enough evidence to convict him. Suspicion fell also on Jim July and on her firebrand son, Eddie, whom she had humiliated with her horsewhip not long before. In the end, the killer of Belle Starr was never brought to justice. We can only surmise that whoever murdered her must have known that Belle never forgot the lesson taught her by her brother, Bud, all those years ago—never turn your back on a challenge. For it is certain that the assassin must have been aware that the only way to stop the legendary Belle Starr in her tracks was to shoot her in the back.

In the period that Belle Starr lived, the West was a new frontier for women, a place where they had to take on the work of men and make

The controversial photograph of Belle Starr with murderer Blue Duck, which appeared in the newspaper and caused Belle to go after the reporter with a horsewhip.

new lives for themselves. The lawless nature of the territories meant they often encountered difficult conditions and it was only a strong breed of non-conforming women who survived; tough, independent and prepared to write their own rules. Belle Starr had all the attributes needed to make it in that uncharted country, a bright, strong-minded woman who rejected the traditional female roles—but she was fatally attracted to men who lived outside the law. Perhaps they reminded her of her long-lost brother.

Over the years, she has been romanticised in comics, cartoons and movies and, in those first dime novels that were published soon after her death, as a wild-eyed temptress always ready to take another man's horse or another woman's man. The line between fact and fiction was soon lost in the sand. Cult status has meant that her legend is discovered anew by every generation, all eager to learn more about Belle Starr.

Amy Bock dressed as her male alter-ego, Percival Redwood, in 1909, the year of her ambitious 'wedding scam'.

Amy Bock

New Zealand's cross-dressing conwoman
1859–1943

It's in my blood ... The malady I suffer from has been with me since childhood, and no one but God and myself knows the fearful horror I have had to face the consequences of my crimes.

– Amy Bock

As Percy Redwood, a small, dapper figure in a morning suit, stood at the altar waiting for his bride to arrive, an unmistakable air of curiosity rippled through the church. Surreptitiously studying the groom behind the convenient safety-screens of their prayer books, the assembled wedding guests harboured a suspicion they dared not voice. It was 21 April 1909, and the biggest society wedding New Zealand's South Otago region had ever seen was about to take place. Agnes Ottaway, the thirty-two-year-old daughter of one of the wealthiest local families, was finally getting married, having been swept off her feet by this newcomer to the area. Charming, witty and apparently wealthy, Redwood seemed to be perfect husband material. Generous to a fault and a natural raconteur, he had quickly been accepted by the community— although his unusually effeminate appearance had attracted some notice.

The church was packed. The Ottaways, sparing no expense for their daughter's wedding, had invited hundreds of guests, including the press and the local Member of Parliament. A nervous-looking Agnes finally arrived, escorted down the aisle by her father, and the couple exchanged their vows.

As the wedding party and guests attended the reception afterward, the celebratory music was accompanied by a fugue of conspiratorial whispers. Why had the bride and groom hardly been near each other all evening? Agnes was looking decidedly miserable, although Percy was clearly enjoying himself, chatting with the guests, dancing, and playing the piano. But as the reception came to a close, and the guests drifted away, the Ottaway family had a quiet word with Agnes's new husband, making the odd suggestion that it would be better if he slept in the groomsman's hotel room that night.

The gossip had been building about Redwood's financial status, particularly since the previous day, when debt collectors had turned up demanding payment for moneys loaned for the engagement ring. Not only that, but Redwood had recently touched several of his new acquaintances for money to pay for his honeymoon. Difficult questions were being asked, although Redwood had confidently assured everyone that his wealthy mother would be arriving within the week with funds. His new family was starting to feel very wary, however. And there was another, more worrying issue regarding Redwood's identity—not that he might not be who he said he was, but that he was, in fact, a 'she'.

Several people had commented on Redwood's slight figure, rather high-pitched voice and hairless face, but since no one had the courage to make the accusation that he might be a woman they had focused criticism on his financial problems instead. The day after the wedding, the Ottaways belatedly began to dig into Percy's background. Enquiries made about his mother revealed that no such person as 'Mrs Redwood' existed.

A visit to Redwood's old boarding house in Dunedin by a man already doubtful of his identity uncovered a basket of clothes he had left there,

The Tainui Boarding House in Mokau, New Zealand, 1900, where Amy Bock (possibly pictured in the group) was living at the time, by now already well into her life of crime.

clothes supposedly belonging to an elderly aunt. Along with garments made for a woman of exactly Redwood's small build, the basket contained unevenly cut longish hair that appeared to be that of a woman. The doubter took his finds to the police and described Redwood to them. The description seemed uncannily familiar to Detective Hunt. He started to put the pieces of the puzzle together and realised that the description—although of the wrong gender—matched that of a well-known trickster whose trail he was now following over the matter of a fraudulent bill of sale—a forty-five-year-old woman named Amy Bock.

Amy Maud Bock was one of New Zealand's most notorious conwomen and a habitual criminal. Primarily a petty thief and a fraudster, she spent much of her life imprisoned for a long series of misdemeanours. She specialised in adopting different personas and devising elaborate schemes to embezzle funds from unsuspecting dupes. For all the guises she assumed, however, the scam that she is remembered for above all

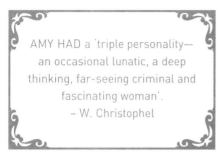

AMY HAD a 'triple personality—
an occasional lunatic, a deep
thinking, far-seeing criminal and
fascinating woman'.
– W. Christophel

others was not as a conwoman, but as a conman. Her greatest performance was playing the part of Percy Redwood, the bridegroom of the unfortunate Agnes Ottaway.

A Restless Life

Born in Tasmania, Australia on 18 May 1859, and moving to Victoria in 1867, Amy had an unsettled childhood. Her mother was mentally unstable, believing for the greater part of her life that she was Shakespeare's Lady Macbeth. She died in an asylum when Amy was only fifteen, leaving her daughter under the protection of her father. Like her mother, Amy grew up exhibiting an inconsistency of personality. One moment she would be extroverted, focused and full of high spirits, the next introverted, absent-minded and eccentric. Although Amy was never as unstable as her mother, these conflicting character traits contributed to an overall sense of restlessness which apparently could only be satisfied by the role-playing that was to become a way of life.

In the early 1880s, Amy took up a post as governess in Melbourne, Victoria. On the outside the well-educated young woman seemed hard-working, morally astute and a pillar of the community. On the inside, however, her natural penchant for duplicity was beginning to surface. In late 1884, at the age of twenty-five, she found herself facing minor charges for acquiring goods using false credit. Hoping for a fresh start, she left Australia and moved to New Zealand with her father and his second wife. But for Amy there was to be no new beginning—instead, she embarked on a lifelong relationship with the New Zealand judiciary. Having excelled in amateur dramatics as a child, she dreamed up the most brazen of scams, assuming a variety of differing identities and spinning the tallest of tales. She was an excellent con-artist and an expert at entrapment. Her setups were always meticulously planned and totally convincing. But once she had hoodwinked her victim she always lost interest, apparently more addicted to the thrill of the chase than to the financial gain the con might yield. Before she had properly tied up the loose ends and any incriminating evidence from one scam, she was already excitedly hatching the next. As a result, her past continually caught up with her.

The Casket Scam

The strength of Amy's success at grifting lay in her charismatic personality, her impressive powers of persuasion, and a certain compulsive, almost foolish, boldness. Getting caught time after time did nothing to quash her inventiveness. Quite the contrary, in fact.

Amy even chose a member of the judiciary as the victim of one of her scams. In Christchurch, going under the name of Miss Lang, Amy visited a draper's store and ordered a large quantity of household goods on credit. She informed the store owner that she worked as a governess for Mr Caleb Whiteford, the magistrate at the nearby town of Kaiapoi, and that the goods would be paid for when they were delivered to his house. As usual, Amy's natural acting talent served her well and the draper wasn't at all suspicious. The goods were duly despatched and Amy boldly intercepted them at the local train station—but the game was soon up, and she was apprehended and sentenced to one month's hard labour.

Between 1887 and 1904, Amy Bock was arrested and charged at least ten times and served a total of approximately seven years in prison. Between these stints in gaol she gained work as a music teacher and governess, but she never remained in these positions for long, her compulsion to commit fraud increasing, her cons becoming more frequent and fantastic.

She seemed to delight in a sense of the ridiculous. On one occasion she visited each of the funeral directors in the area and purchased their most expensive casket for her 'dead mother', who naturally deserved only the best. She paid by cheque for each casket, managing to scam some change from each transaction. Weeks later, a large number of caskets turned up at the train station, addressed to a local family—all of whom, of course, were fit and healthy.

Amy had a unique gift for the unusual and unexpected, many of her confidence tricks almost edging on the foolhardy. Whether her next trick was foolish or masterful is subject for debate.

The Wedding Scam

Moving to a small community in South Otago, Amy decided on a new venture which, although highly risky, if successful would really pay off. Her first move was to adopt men's clothing and introduce herself to the community as Percival Redwood, son of an affluent sheep-farming family in the north. Having a somewhat masculine appearance, it wasn't a huge stretch to pass herself off as a man. Stepping out in his sharpest suit, smoking a pipe and assuming a dandified air, 'Percy Redwood' introduced himself to his wealthy landlord's daughter, Agnes Ottaway. Finding him to be naturally amusing and charming, Agnes quickly became besotted with the gentleman.

Having managed to maintain his false identity in this small community for three months, 'Percy' proclaimed his love for Agnes, and requested her hand in marriage. At this stage the Ottaway family had no suspicions and the proposal was immediately accepted.

Amy's confidence in her acting ability allowed her to act in much the same way as any prospective groom, being fitted for a new suit for the wedding, even making a visit to the barber's. Her self-assurance was apparently well founded since the barber, on being questioned later, although referring to Percy as a 'curious lookin' little cuss', commented that at the time he hadn't noticed anything particularly untoward.

This wedding scam was no quickly executed con, and Amy was going to need all her wits about her if she was going to pull it off. Not only was she pretending to be a man, but she was pretending to be an extremely

The grand family house of Agnes Ottaway, Percival's (Amy's) hapless fiancée, South Otago, New Zealand.

wealthy man, and she had to keep up the masquerade at least until the wedding had taken place.

However, Amy had been too cocksure. Just when it looked like the scam might work, Percy Redwood's story started to unravel. In her attempts to prove that Percy was a man of means, Amy became entangled in a web of lies, borrowing money from numerous sources with no hope of repaying it—the typical compulsive lies which were the trademark of her scams. She also realised that the Ottaways were starting to get suspicious that Percy might not be quite as he appeared, and had to find a way of allaying their fears. In a forged letter, Percy's 'dear mother, Mrs Redwood', assured the Ottaways of her son's financial status. 'Mrs Redwood' wrote at length, telling the family how delighted she was about the forthcoming match. She even went so far as to confide that she had feared her son would never again find love, for 'poor Percy' had been so devastated when the love of his life had drowned twelve years earlier that she had thought his heart would be broken forever. She signed off by offering to buy a new house for the happy couple.

The Ottaways were suitably impressed. With Agnes having reached the ripe old age of thirty-two, the family was keen for the wedding to go ahead. The last thing they wanted was for their daughter to remain a

A table set with a lavish banquet in readiness for Percival's marriage to Agnes, 21 April 1909.

spinster. In the weeks following, the engagement received much media coverage, since the wealthy match made for a good local story. But for Amy it became another problematic layer in an already overly-complicated con.

With all the wedding preparations to be paid for, and no income, Percy's cash was running low. A number of debtors began to show up demanding money, but he managed to wheedle his way out of the situation, promising that his mother would be arriving with funds very soon. Just a little longer, and the wedding march would be playing! But of course there was no mother. The Ottaways once again became suspicious when they received a letter informing them that Mrs Redwood would be unable to attend the wedding, due to another family commitment on the same day. Every time an obstacle appeared, Amy managed to cover it with yet another lie. One wonders what future she had in mind. Was her plan to abscond with funds once the wedding vows were exchanged, or did she really see herself playing the role of the wealthy husband, at the age of forty-five, in an unconsummated marriage?

On the wedding day, like any good actor, Amy hid her nerves, but under the surface she must have been seriously rattled. Behind the scenes things were getting tense—lawyers had arrived prior to the wedding and questioned Percy about several incidents. Suspicion hung in the air. Percy's financial independence was appearing dubious, and an unspeakable suspicion had arisen that he might actually be a woman. But what could the Ottaways do? There was no solid proof. The wedding was a runaway train and they were keen to avoid a public scandal.

Amy must have known she was in trouble, yet there was no obvious escape route. The day after the wedding, the Ottaways held a family conference to which Percy was summoned from his hotel room. As no one had the courage to accuse him of being a woman, his monetary status was again called into question. Percy played for time, once again invoking his wealthy mother, and the Ottaways agreed to wait another week. But they were adamant that Percy was to stay away from Agnes until Mrs Redwood arrived.

The following day, the Ottaways set about finding out all they could about Percy's elusive mother. After the discovery of the basket of woman's clothes and hair in the boarding house in Dunedin, the game was up.

The Bridegroom Who Was a Woman

That was really the end for Amy Bock. Her most audacious confidence trick of all had finally been exposed. As she meticulously prepared for yet another day of deception as Redwood, there came a thunderous knocking on the door. Amy gave herself up to the police with a mixture of apprehension and relief. It appears she had been so busy concentrating on her current scam that she had failed to cover the tracks of her previous misdemeanours. Once again this failing proved her downfall.

Later, as Amy approached the court, reporters noted that she did so with a natural air of masculinity, 'walking with hands thrust deep into the pockets of a stylish grey overcoat in the way of a man when the wind is

Amy Bock, photographed in 1914 in Mokau, New Plymouth, by an unidentified photographer.

raw and his underclothes are thin'. Her admission of guilt meant the case never went to trial, much to the disappointment of the New Zealand public and press. Amy Bock was charged with false pretences and making a false statement under the Marriage Act of 1908, declared a habitual criminal, and sentenced to two years in jail. The press still had a field day. The 'Bridegroom Who Was a Woman' became the talk of the country. The Ottaways were disgraced and the marriage was annulled. Agnes later married but would never truly get over her role in Amy's legendary scam.

As with all her crimes, Amy was sorry to have caused distress, but it seemed she just couldn't help herself. 'It's in my blood', she once confessed to a policeman. 'The malady I suffer from has been with me since childhood, and no one but God and myself knows the fearful horror I have had to face the consequences of my crimes'. Why she had chosen this particular swindle is anyone's guess. Following an earlier conviction, Amy had reportedly told police that she was 'tired of defrauding men; they are too soft and easy to work on', and it has been suggested that this is why she set her sights on a woman.

Released from prison yet again in 1911, Amy married Charles Christofferson in 1914, but the marriage lasted less than a year. With her masculine traits and a tendency toward cross-dressing, it seems a fair assumption that Amy Bock may have been a lesbian. Perhaps Amy's most notorious swindle was not about money after all, but rather a desperate attempt by a woman who had always felt like an outsider to step into a role in which she would genuinely feel comfortable. She was known in New Zealand as 'the Masquerader', and it is possible that Amy Bock's final and greatest concealment was her own sexuality.

SHE BORROWED MONEY from almost everyone in Mokau but paid very little of it back and used it mostly in buying presents, as she was extremely generous, using very little herself.
– W. Christophel

Over a period of twenty-two years, Amy served a total of sixteen years and two months in prison. In 1931, aged seventy-two, she made her final court appearance. The cheeky young trickster was long gone and in her place stood 'a faded old lady in a dove grey alpaca cloth costume, with a drooping hat of lace straw, grey gloves and supporting herself on a walking stick'. She died twelve years later, on 29 August 1943. During her lifetime Amy Bock had travelled under many names but, ironically, her final resting place was an unmarked grave.

According to Amy's biographer, R. W. Robson, while in prison Amy would sit for long periods of time, no doubt busily devising her next ingenious scam. Deep in thought, she would throw her head back in laughter. 'What is it, Amy?' someone would ask. 'Oh, nothing', she'd reply, still laughing. 'I was just thinking.'

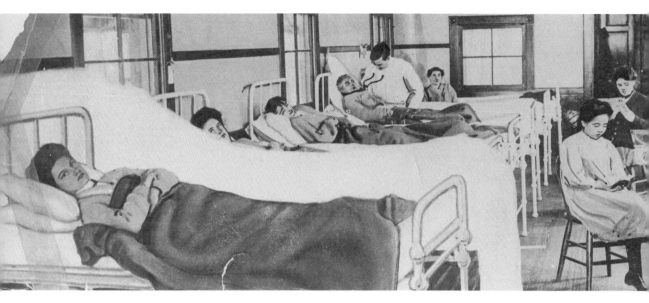

'Typhoid' Mary Mallon in quarantine at Riverside Hospital, New York.

Mary Mallon

Typhoid Mary—a one-woman epidemic

1869–1938

I never had typhoid in my life, and have always been healthy. Why should I be banished like a leper and compelled to live in solitary confinement with only a dog for a companion?
– Mary Mallon

Mary stared out of the kitchen window at the ambulance arriving outside. Had someone else in the house been taken ill? A smart-looking woman came through the gate, followed by several policemen. Her heart beat faster at the knock on the door. Opening it, she peered out. The smart-looking woman gave her a stiff smile. 'I am Dr Josephine Baker, an inspector from New York City's Department of Health', she said. 'It is our obligation to take you in.' Mary was outraged. Not again! Hadn't she already told that rude man Soper there was nothing wrong with her! Why wouldn't they leave her alone?

Mary Mallon became a figure steeped in controversy in early twentieth-century New York when early in 1907 it was established that she was a 'healthy carrier' of deadly typhoid bacteria. Already responsible for at least forty-seven cases of the disease and three deaths, Mary was dubbed 'Typhoid Mary' by the press and even described as 'the most dangerous woman in America'. She was to be banned for life from the only profession she knew—that of cooking—and held in quarantine on an island in the East River, where she was constantly tested for typhoid and treated like a leper. Mary protested vigorously and in 1910 was allowed to return to the city on the condition that she swore never to work as a cook again. Up to this point, she might have been regarded as an innocent victim rather than a cold-hearted murderer. But she continued in her conviction that she had never had typhoid fever and thus her cooking could not be a danger to others. Quietly flouting the authorities for many years, she finally came to grief when she obtained employment as a cook at a New York maternity hospital. Disaster followed.

A Comfortable Niche

Born in 1869 into an impoverished family in County Tyrone, one of the poorest regions of Ireland, for Mary Mallon life was a struggle from the beginning. Those who survived the crippling poverty of the time developed a natural resilience to all that life threw at them. In 1884, when Mary was just fifteen, she joined the large numbers of Irish immigrants sailing for the United States in search of the American Dream. She lived for a while with an aunt and uncle in New York, but had to fend for herself when they died. Because she was Irish, Mary found herself the target for prejudice and bigotry. Everything that was negative was heaped upon the Irish immigrant community, a group generally regarded as ignorant, filthy drunks; not only that but Catholic, in a city where Protestants held the power. Anger at this attitude could help to explain Mary's legendary temper.

Mary herself was bright and well read, enjoying the novels of Dickens in particular, perhaps moved by his sympathy for the outsider. But she was also tough and resourceful and coped well with the awful conditions of the slums on New York's East Side. Described as tall and Amazonian in stature, with blonde hair and blue eyes, Mary was one of a new breed of independent Irishwomen who prided themselves on their ability to survive without a man to support them. She seemed one of the toughest, fighting with her fists if necessary and giving as good as she got. Dissatisfied with the poorly-paid position of maidservant, Mary took every chance to learn the techniques of cooking, and discovered a natural talent. Soon her skills were in high demand and she rarely found herself out of work, unlike many of her contemporaries. A cook had real status in a household and was paid relatively high wages. Although she might not be making a fortune, Mary had found a comfortable niche.

Mary grew less combative as she found herself appreciated by the well-to-do and let loose in their well-equipped kitchens. Over the next twenty years she seemed to go from strength to strength and, with a steady flow of work coming her way, could pick and choose her employment. As her reputation grew, most of her time was spent in the mansions of rich New York folk, catering for dinner parties and working in a privileged, well-heeled environment. But all this was to change in a moment.

Ice-cream and Peaches

In 1906, Mary Mallon took a short-term position with Charles Warren, banker to the Vanderbilts, who was holidaying with his family in a luxurious home in the Oyster Bay resort on Long Island. Mary was cooking for an appreciative household, often preparing their favourite dessert of ice-cream topped with fresh peaches. But on August 27 one of the Warren daughters was struck down by a serious illness, which was diagnosed as typhoid fever. Soon another six of the eleven occupants of the house fell ill.

More often than not, typhoid could be linked to bacteria found in the water supply and to unhygienic conditions. In New York itself, with its poor neighbourhoods and teeming slums, there were four thousand cases a year. But Oyster Bay was a world away, a place beloved of the rich and powerful, including Theodore Roosevelt himself. How could a disease of the slums have made its way there? The owner of the house in which the Warrens had holidayed moved quickly to uncover the source, afraid he would never be able to rent out the house again. Experts checked the water and milk supplies and, as panic spread among the wealthy community, examined the local shellfish to see if the bay was polluted by sewage. But they drew a blank. By this time Mary, who'd helped nurse the sufferers back to health, had moved on.

George Soper, a sanitary engineer and a specialist in typhoid outbreaks, was now brought in to investigate. Soper reviewed the findings, and turned his attention to the housekeeping staff. Aware that there is an incubation period of three weeks before typhoid develops, he asked the Warrens who had worked for them recently. Busy on her next assignment, Mary was unaware that a net was closing around her, for when Soper looked at her employment records, he found an ominous pattern. Over the preceding ten years, Mary had worked for eight families, in six of which cases of typhoid fever had developed shortly after she joined them. The diligent Soper learned too of the Warren family's fondness for the ice-cream and peaches dessert. Since it was uncooked, ice-cream would have acted as the perfect incubator for the typhoid bacteria, which is destroyed by cooking. Mary's American Dream was about to be cruelly shattered.

George Soper became a man obsessed, determined to track Mary down and confirm his suspicions. It was probable that she had suffered a mild and unrecognised attack of typhoid in the past and her immune system had failed to totally destroy the bacteria in her body, turning her into a 'symptomless' or 'healthy' carrier. Mary was working for a family on exclusive Park Avenue in Manhattan when Soper came knocking at the kitchen door. When he accused her of spreading the disease, she was outraged, interpreting it as a personal attack. She had probably never even set foot in a doctor's surgery and here was a complete stranger asking for samples of her urine, faeces and blood. According to Soper, who may have exaggerated Mary's violence in order to save face, she seized a carving fork and chased him from the premises. Soper's approach had been tactless and ill-judged, to say the least, and the tug-of-war that now developed was to have fateful consequences.

Further investigations led Soper to discover that Mary was spending time at a rooming house on 3rd Avenue with a man called Breihof. Following Breihof to a bar, Soper bribed him to arrange a time when he could be sure of finding Mary at the rooming house. Days later, Soper pounced. Mary was enraged by this second intrusion—and smart enough to realise that Breihof must have tipped Soper off. She turned on the tormentor who was once more accusing her of spreading typhoid, and forced him to beat a hasty retreat. From the moment Soper burst into her life, Mary felt that she was the innocent victim of a stalker. His belief in the rightness of his powers of detection appeared to blind him to the fact that Mary felt violated. She could not, would not, believe him. Unfortunately, Soper was right—excellent cook though she was, Mary's personal hygiene left a lot to be desired.

Soper was a man of dogged determination. Realising that he did not have the power to get the samples he wanted, he passed his information to Hermann Biggs, the Commissioner of the recently founded New York City Health Department. Biggs was waging a crusade to wipe out the infectious diseases that were plaguing the city, wielding his power to vaccinate and confine people if they posed a threat to public safety, and using force if necessary. There was no doubt that Soper's evidence implicated Mary in the typhoid outbreak at Oyster Bay—and a daughter of the household where she was now working had recently died of typhoid fever. Mary could no longer be allowed to remain at large. Biggs decided to send an expert to reason with her. Dr Josephine Baker, a pioneer in the area of preventative diseases, set out to explain to Mary Mallon the implications of being a healthy typhoid carrier.

When Mary opened the door to yet another 'busybody', it was the last straw. She had never felt so healthy. Why couldn't they leave her alone? Grabbing a fork, she threatened the doctor and made a run for it. When at last she was discovered, cowering in a cupboard like a trapped animal, her humiliation seemed complete. Dr Baker ordered police officers to carry her into the waiting ambulance. Mary fought every inch of the way. Being taken to the Willard Parker Hospital, which specialised in infectious diseases among the poor, must have added insult to injury.

A Peep Show

Mary's world had been turned upside down for reasons that seemed to her totally inexplicable. She was probed by doctors as if she were no more than an interesting medical specimen; all her protests were ignored. When the test results from the new bacteriology laboratory proved she was a typhoid carrier, she refused to believe it. She had never had typhoid! And she was further enraged by a visit from Soper, eager to write a book about her, wanting to know more details of her work history, promising that she would have all the proceeds. Mary slammed the door in his face.

The health experts were faced with a dilemma. It was felt that since Mary worked as a cook she should not be released into the community, for fear of further infection. Some argue that being a woman rather than a male bread-winner, an Irish immigrant, and a Catholic to boot, may have combined to tip the scales against her. Without legal representation or trial, Mary was deprived of her liberty and taken to a cottage in the grounds of Riverside Hospital, New York's biggest quarantine facility, on North Brother Island in the East River. She realised to her horror that she was to be confined there with no prospect of release. To Mary, who had loved the bustle and excitement of life in New York, it was like being sentenced to a living death.

Day after day, Mary sat in a shabby room in the cottage that looked across to the city, so close yet so far away. Visiting practitioners and students examined her whenever they chose; she felt that she was looked on as nothing more than an exotic exhibit. The head of the hospital described her as intelligent but with 'an almost pathological anger'. In view of the treatment she was subjected to, such a level of anger seems entirely understandable. She hated the invisible enemy they told her was inside her, and detested those who confirmed week after week that it was still present. She spent all her time pleading her case to the local newspapers and writing to the Health Department, describing the awful injustice of her predicament: 'I have been in fact a peep show for everybody. Even the interns had to come to see me and ask about the facts already known to the whole wide world. The tuberculosis men would say, "There she is, the kidnapped woman!"'

The Department of Health seemed determined to use Mary as some sort of guinea pig, experimenting on her with new drugs that they thought might cure her and suggesting she have her gall bladder removed, since they believed that might be the seat of the infection. Appalled at the idea of being cut open, Mary refused the operation, deaf to what the medical team and the Health Department termed 'reason'. Making everything more unfair, in her opinion, was that the samples she managed to send to a private laboratory always came back clear. Her predicament fuelled a furious public debate. Should a woman who had done no conscious wrong and who had not undergone a legal trial be incarcerated like a common prisoner? Her case began to attract more attention, and Mary sensed that public opinion was starting to turn in her favour.

> THIS CONTENTION that I am a perpetual menace ... is not true. My own doctors say I have no typhoid germs ... I have committed no crime and I am treated like an outcast— a criminal. It is unjust, outrageous, uncivilised.
> – Mary Mallon

Despite all that had happened, Mary was still putting up a spirited fight. She began to court the press with even greater vigour, sending endless letters and pleas for help. She even attracted the attention of the newspaper magnate Randolph Hearst, who must have seen that he could use her to up his sales—a middle-aged woman facing life imprisonment for doing nothing more that carrying germs. Her case had implications for anyone suffering from a potentially life-threatening disease, and even wider implications in terms of individual freedom. Finally, George O'Neill, a young Irish lawyer, offered to defend her and on 29 June 1909, in the New York Supreme Court, he put forward the case for Mary's release. He pointed out that there were many other typhoid carriers in New York City, and none of them had been imprisoned. At the most, they had been detained for a few weeks. The fact that Mary worked as a cook seemed to be the main sticking point. Surely that was a problem that could be overcome. For the first time in two years, Mary dared to hope.

In the trial that followed, too much attention was paid to Mary's violent temper, her lack of co-operation and the difficulties the authorities had encountered in apprehending her. The real issue was often lost in what seemed like a character assassination. One witness claimed that 'if she should be set to work in a milk store tomorrow in three months she could accomplish as much as a hostile army'. The judge was sympathetic but failed to order her release. He directed that she be taken back to North Brother Island, but he wanted her living conditions re-examined and demanded that the Health Department present evidence to prove she was still infected. Yet again the tests proved positive. Mary was certain that the Health Department just wanted credit for protecting the rich. Bleakly, she contemplated the future, convinced now she would never be free.

But Mary's luck was to change when a new Health Commissioner, Ernst Lederle, replaced the uncompromising Hermann Biggs. Lederle had monitored the case and like many people felt that it reflected badly on the work of his department. He made a public statement explaining that although Mary was still a carrier, she had now been properly educated in matters of hygiene and was no longer a threat to society. In 1910 she was released, on condition that she never work as a cook again. She leaped at the chance to escape, agreeing to anything and everything they demanded. But back in New York City, she found herself at the very bottom of the heap. Lederle had managed to get her a job as a laundress but it was soul-destroying work that paid practically nothing. Now living in a squalid rooming house with Breihof, Mary felt herself being dragged down into a life as poverty-stricken as the one she had known as a child. Anger raged in her.

Mary was now in her early forties and had to weigh up her options. She still would not believe she was the carrier of a deadly disease. Not all the tests had come back positive. And hadn't she nursed the sick in many of the households where she had worked before the hateful Soper came knocking, and actually helped them recover? As she toiled in the steamy laundry, she asked herself again and again why she should be forced to sacrifice the profession she loved. Her freedom seemed to have been bought at a terrible price.

Revenge is Sweet

It was at this time that Breihof died from a heart condition, and Mary was to describe herself poignantly as being once more 'alone in America'. Perhaps feeling that she had no one left to embarrass other than herself, she decided to take the risk and covertly return to cooking. Her strength, as always, lay in the skills that produced dishes too tempting to resist. Mary disappeared into the labyrinth of New York's kitchens, where she remained undetected for the next five years.

In 1915 there was a typhoid outbreak at the Sloane Maternity Hospital in Manhattan that resulted in twenty-five people contracting typhoid, and two deaths. The health inspectors descended and soon began to focus on a mysterious 'Mrs Brown', an Irish kitchenhand who had recently failed to turn up to work. It was not long before they established that Mrs Brown was none other than Mary Mallon. George Soper and Dr

Josephine Baker were now on her trail again. When they finally tracked her down, both tried to take the glory. But this time there would be no public support. Mary had sunk to unforgivable depths by consciously putting mothers and babies at risk.

Mary was returned to the cottage on North Brother Island, where she was forced to live alone for the rest of her life. No one knew what else to do with her. She had alienated her few supporters by what seemed like a callous indifference to those she could infect. In any case, the fight had drained out of her and the fiery-tempered Amazon was replaced by an empty-eyed, slatternly woman resigned to her fate. As the years passed she was allowed to go to the mainland once a week but she never spoke about where she went or who she visited. The staff at the hospital were kind to her and she assisted them with various jobs, sometimes helping in the laboratory. In December 1932 Mary suffered a severe stroke and was hospitalised for the last years of her life. When she died, she had been on the island for almost twenty-six years.

Only three deaths were positively attributed to Typhoid Mary, but the number of people she infected was put as high as fifty. If George Soper and the Health Department had treated her as a human being rather than a 'culture tube', the outcome might have been very different. This treatment, which seemed to Mary to be persecution, stirred up the furious resistance that led her to make the fateful decision to return to the kitchen. Referred to in the press as a 'one woman epidemic' and a 'mass murderer', Mary Mallon will be forever remembered as Typhoid Mary, but her tragic case must still inspire debate. The fact that she was denied any respect once she had been identified as a carrier must be taken into account. Certainly, it should help us to empathise with a woman who felt herself singled out from other carriers of the deadly disease, to be extraordinarily vilified and, quarantined on North Brother Island, to suffer the loneliest of fates.

Chicago May

International queen of crooks
1871–1929

I enjoyed living.

– Mary Duignan

May claimed it was the greatest night of her life, a moment when everything could have changed and she might have become the toast of the town. She had captivated so many of the dignitaries and the upper crust of Rio's high society already. They seemed to enjoy hearing the pretty Irish brogue which she could make sound as if she came from the upper echelons of society rather than from a poor farming background in rural County Longford. She had certainly impressed the Consul-General of Argentina, who had invited her to accompany him to a ball. He seemed the perfect gentleman, perhaps a little bit too polite and stiff-backed for May's tastes—but then, she had come to grief so many times when she had thrown in her lot with gangsters and rebel-rousers. The Consul-General might be just the meal ticket she needed. May smiled up at him, roguishly tossing her auburn curls and flashing her eyes.

Days later, for reasons never revealed, the Consul-General shot himself and a crestfallen May was left feeling it was typical of her sort of luck. What on earth was the matter with the man? She was going to have to start all over again.

The red-haired, blue-eyed May Duignan was an expert at duping unsuspecting men out of their money through a scam known as 'badgering'.

Chicago May, or Mary Duignan as she was christened, rebelled against the smothering Catholic ethos of the small village in Ireland where she was born and headed for a new life on the bustling streets of New York, taking with her the family savings. She expected to make her fortune but in fact became an international criminal, blackmailer and prostitute, pulling off scams in Chicago, Cairo, London and Paris, and even assisting in a bank robbery. Her choice of men and her lifestyle led to her spending half her adult life behind bars but, amazingly, as she approached her sixties and was still living off the streets, the prospect of fame and fortune came knocking. Thinking it might be time to go straight, May concentrated her efforts on writing her autobiography, a long, lurid and no doubt partly fictional tome. However, disappointed that the life of a writer was not as lucrative as she had imagined and that offers from Hollywood did not come flooding in, May went back to the streets, unable to abandon the only trade she knew.

First Class Only

Mary Duignan, known as May to her family, grew up on a poor farm outside the little village of Edenmore in County Longford in Ireland at a time when the Catholic Church and the English aristocracy were all-powerful. The young May, with her bright auburn hair and sparkling blue eyes, turned heads in the community, and no doubt a few young men came knocking on the door. But the high-spirited girl aspired to something better, knowing too well the gruelling life of domestic drudgery and childbearing in store for her. In 1890, her mother was about to give birth yet again and nineteen-year-old May knew that, just as had happened with the rest, she would be expected to play her part in rearing this new baby. The prospect must suddenly have been unbearable. The diseases that were rife where such poverty as theirs was concerned might keep family numbers down, but May was not about to leave things to chance.

While her mother was noisily giving birth, May came to a sudden decision. She pocketed the entire family savings, a painfully hard-earned sixty sovereigns, and rushed away, heart pounding. She planned to get a boat to Liverpool in England and use the stolen money to book passage to New York. Finally reaching Liverpool and deciding not to do things by halves, she bought herself some smart new outfits and a cabin-class ticket. She spent her ill-gotten gains with abandon, refusing to think of the backbreaking work that had gone into earning each gold coin—and the heartbreak she had left behind.

Ten days later and dressed to the nines, May waited excitedly as the ship docked at Castle Garden, on an island off the tip of New York's Manhattan. Bright, attractive and vivacious, she had little reason for self-doubt, imagining that her remaining haul would soon buy her a piece of the action. But the money quickly ran low and the tough realities of city life began to dawn on her. She had already realised that there were rich pickings to be had on the streets but she had also seen the ravages a life of prostitution inflicted on even the prettiest of girls. So she took the train to Nebraska to stay with an uncle, brazen enough, it would seem, to expect a warm welcome even after what she had done to her family. Or perhaps she knew she could rely on her parents being too embarrassed to brand her a thief. Either way, May's conscience does not seem to have caused her many sleepless nights.

Nebraska did not hold the same appeal as the bright lights of New York but before long May met and fell in love with a man named Dal Churchill. She brags in her autobiography that Dal could do just about everything, being 'a robber, highwayman, safe-cracker, cattle rustler and general all round crook'. Not only that, but he was 'strong, muscular and as quick as a panther'. Dal taught May all the tricks of his trade and she seemed a natural, discovering skills of her own. Most of the time, Dal worked with a gang but between jobs he would team up with May, robbing banks and pilfering. May, a born rebel herself, felt that she had found a kindred spirit, and when Dal proposed marriage she heartily accepted. But life on the edges of society was fraught with danger. When Dal went on one of his many jobs, May headed for Chicago to wait for him there. She was never to see him again. While trying to rob a train, Dal had been lynched by an angry mob of locals. May was devastated at the loss of her first love, the realities of the life she had chosen finally hitting home.

The Badger

With her funds gone, May decided that prostitution would be the easiest way to make a living. It was 1892 and Chicago was an exciting place to be. The building of the White City of the World's Fair and Columbian Exposition had begun, and Chicago was teeming with work-weary, sex-starved men. May and her friend, Dora Donegan, began to work a double act, with one of them having sex with some unsuspecting, drink-befuddled john while the other rifled his pockets. May would also get a male accomplice to pose as her husband—he would erupt into the room where she was about to entertain a client and demand money to keep quiet. This was referred to as 'badgering', and May always preferred to call herself a badger rather than a prostitute—as if pickpocketing and blackmail were a superior trade. She lived for the moment, never saving what she earned, confident with the optimism of youth that the future would take care of itself.

May was drawn like a moth to the flame to the criminal underworld of the city and a punishing lifestyle that would eventually take its toll on her health. It was later estimated by the Chicago Vice Commission, set up in 1910, that an average night at a brothel would see each woman service twenty-six men at twenty-five cents a time. Often the women were drunk or drugged—how else could they get through? May soon carved out her niche and became known as one of the toughest. She was loud and aggressive and would not hesitate to knock out a punter's teeth or brandish a hot poker at an over-zealous pimp. She became part of the Chicago criminal fraternity and one of its leading lights, known as 'Chicago May'. Although she liked to re-invent herself and created a number of aliases in the years to come, this was the name that would stick with her for the rest of her life.

In time, May moved on to New York, to the Tenderloin district of Manhattan. As she dabbled in a heady cocktail of crime and prostitution, her natural talents as an actor came in useful. She seems to have got pickpocketing down to a fine art, able to put on an extravagant show of affection for a customer while niftily biting the precious stones from his tie-pin. But when one of her close friends accused her of stealing from him in this way, she claims in her autobiography to have been so devastated that she went home and downed a dose of cockroach poison. This does not quite square with the character revealed by a girl who could steal her parents' life savings without turning a hair—and it is also unlikely that she would have survived relatively unscathed. Perhaps she added this colourful detail to make herself seem more sympathetic, poetic licence yet another stock in trade.

New York Belle

As America's cities became more heavily populated and the number of women on the streets increased, May needed to find a new way of earning a living. When an opportunity presented itself to audition for a Broadway musical, she leaped at the chance. Tall for a woman in those days of often inadequate nutrition, at five feet six inches she stood out from the other hopefuls and managed to secure a part as a Salvation Army girl in the chorus of *New York Belle*. She loved this new role, which got her off the streets and showed her an exciting new side of life. Perhaps the backstage camaraderie—as well as the regular pay cheque—awoke a hankering for a little more stability. But still she could not seem to help herself—she always had an eye out for a quick scam or a regular customer to bring in some extra cash.

When she stole a wallet from a church minister, however, May faced her first prison sentence and thought the game was temporarily up. To her surprise, however, a man called Jim Sharpe, who was only a vague acquaintance, approached the District Attorney, offering to marry May and remove her from the streets. The District Attorney released her to marry Jim. As May later relates, 'I had visions of escaping from the life I was leading'. As she headed off with her new husband to the salubrious Manhattan suburb of Belleview, New Jersey, it might have appeared that she was about to discover the joys of a stable family life.

But May soon found that the man she had so impulsively married had some disturbing traits, one of the more obvious being that he was obsessed with trying to murder his brother. Jim still lived with his mother, who not surprisingly welcomed May with open arms, perhaps hoping that this feisty Irishwoman would lay down the law and sort out her troubled son. May liked Jim's mother and the warmth she exuded was a relief after her experiences walking the streets. For a year May put up with Jim's mental state, but finally she decided the trade-off she had made was too much. She wanted to put as much space between herself and her psychotic husband as she could.

Night Train to Paris

May loved travelling—perhaps both as a way of covering her tracks and of finding a new clientele—and was pleased to discover her particular trade was one of the few that had international appeal. She sold her wares in the gambling dens of Cairo, and flirted with important dignitaries in Rio de Janeiro, putting on a performance that would have graced a Broadway stage. It was at this time that she attended the ball with the Consul-General and thought her fortune was made—until he disappointed her by shooting himself. But she soon picked herself up again, with South America, Egypt and London all on her hit list. Despite some setbacks, May considered herself to be one of the best badgers around, adapting with ease to whatever country she was in. In 1900, with the World's Fair attracting people from all over the world to Paris, she decided to head across the Channel to London and make that city her home base.

It was in London that May fell in love with Eddie Guerin, an Irish-born gangster who had just spent ten years in a French prison. As usual May seemed drawn to the danger she sensed, and she and Eddie embarked on a passionate affair. When Eddie was asked to assist in an ambitious heist on the American Express office in Paris, May was sure they were about to hit the big time and willingly agreed to be an accomplice. Catching the night boat-train with him from London to the Gare du Nord in April 1901, May must have imagined that she was about to enter a world where she would no longer need to sell her body to strangers. She describes how she hid in a back room of the bank and, when the last workers left, opened the doors for Eddie and his accomplices. May then kept watch as the others blew open the safe. They had pulled off a daring robbery and Eddie felt it was sweet revenge on the French gendarmerie who had 'stolen' ten years of his life. But the gang had made some fatal errors and, to May's horror, Eddie was taken into custody as he tried to board the return boat-train to London.

Eddie was potentially a big earner and May felt it was in her best interests to help him as much as she could. Risking arrest, she returned to

Paris and pleaded his case with the American Consul. But the Consul tipped off the French police that Eddie's mistress was in town, and May was also thrown into prison. It was a year before the case finally came to trial and May had plenty of time to review her options. She wanted to plead guilty in order to get a lighter sentence, but Eddie told her to say that they had been together in a hotel room all night and to deny that she had received stolen money from him while she was in Paris. May's performance on the witness stand was clearly not a *tour de force*, however, because in June 1902 the jury found them both guilty. Eddie was given a life sentence and shipped off to Devil's Island—a harsh penal settlement off the coast of French Guyana—while May was sentenced to five years' hard labour in Montpellier Prison in the south of France. Her visions of living the high life were replaced with the grim realities of a prison cell and a postage-stamp of sky viewed through the bars.

But ever resourceful, May gained the support of some female prison visitor 'patrons' on the lookout for prisoners keen to change their ways. She was delighted when she was released in 1905 after four years, but resented having to put up with one of her patrons accompanying her on the boat back to London, talking incessantly of the need to reform. When someone asked who her companion was, May quietly told them the woman was her maid.

The Prodigal Daughter

It was not long before May went back to her life of petty pilfering and prostitution, but this time not all of the funds were for her own personal needs. She was trying to raise money for Eddie's escape plan, although by this time she was fearful of Eddie for she knew he suspected her of betraying him. On impulse perhaps, she decided to return home to Ireland. She was thirty-four. Perhaps it was time to make her peace.

Life in Ireland had not changed very much since May had left all those years ago. It was still a country frozen in time, where the subject of women's sexuality was taboo and certainly sex outside marriage brought unspeakable shame upon a family. The return of the prodigal daughter who had made off with the family savings, whose reputation as a loose woman had no doubt traveled before her, sent shockwaves through Edenmore. On the surface everyone accepted her and at least she still had her Longford brogue, but it was a God-fearing community and the staunchly Catholic citizenry despised everything she had become. Her family found it in their hearts to forgive her but must have been embarrassed by her reputation. It was hardly a warm welcome home and, realizing that she had been judged and found wanting, May caught the boat back to London, vowing never to return.

Betrayed by a Woman!

The last person May wanted to see at this time was Eddie, but as she was sinking a few ales in the local bar in early 1906, in he walked, having miraculously escaped from Devil's Island a few months before. May must have had to look twice, for the good-looking adventurer had long gone, and in his place stood an embittered man, cold, hard and controlling. He demanded that May team up with him so they could travel together, looking for opportunities and scams. May felt she had no choice, and later recounted, 'I was always afraid of him, even when we were friends." He seemed volatile and threatened to disfigure her face if she were ever to leave him. With May still working as a prostitute for extra cash, Eddie's jealousy was soon out of control. Convinced that he planned to kill her, she decided to make the first move and later that year boarded a ship bound for Argentina, disguised as a nurse. Days later the headlines in the *News of the World* read 'Betrayed by a Woman'. Eddie had been picked up by the British police, who examined his case before extraditing him to France. May was to be terrified of Eddie's vengeance for the rest of her life.

May was right to be scared, for even in a French prison Eddie had ways of reaching her. He became friendly with a young American burglar,

Chicago May and Charley Smith at their trial in London for attempted murder, 1907.

Charley Smith, and arranged for him to maim May as soon as he was released. But despite his mission and their age difference, when Charley met May he fell in love with her and changed his allegiance. He was kind and full of youthful energy and just what May needed at a time in her life when she felt she had lost direction.

She would soon be in desperate need of Charley's protection because, against all the odds, in 1907 Eddie was released from prison— and finding the ex-mistress he saw as his arch-betrayer was top of his list. What happened next is unclear, but within twenty-four hours Eddie had been shot in the foot and Charley and May charged with attempted murder. After a sensational trial, Charley was sentenced to life imprisonment and threatened with deportation while May was cast in the role of temptress in this ugly *ménage à trois* and received fifteen years' hard labour. As she stood in the dock, she was sure that Eddie, her nemesis, had finally won.

A World of Books

As May sat and waited for the time to pass in Aylesbury Prison in England, she was to experience what seemed like a moment of epiphany. For the first time she understood the joys of reading and once she had started she could not stop. Shakespeare, Dickens and the Irish poets were her favourites, and she would often imagine that she was an actor playing the parts in a Shakespearean play. Outside the prison walls, men were signing up to fight and being shipped off to the horrors of the trenches in war-torn France. May's pickings would have been rather lean anyway had she been free. In 1917, after ten long years and now aged forty-six, May was released and deported to America—she had become a US citizen after marrying Jim Sharpe—never to set foot on British soil again.

May might have gained an education but she did not seem to have learned any lessons when it came to men. Returning to Manhattan, she picked up with some low-life who was young, like Charley, but lacked Charley's kindness. She set him up with a shebeen, a drinking booth, where he fraternised with his customers, lied about being married, slept with other women, and after an eight-year relationship absconded with May's money and her furs. Never one to take things lying down, May hired a detective to track him down so she could shoot him but he had managed to successfully vanish into thin air.

Now at her lowest ebb, May moved to Detroit, where she trawled the streets with insufficient clothing to keep her warm during the bleak winter months. She was ill, her kidneys seemed to be failing, yet she was still on the game. But as she lay near death in hospital, August Vollmer, a much-respected social reformer who worked for police departments throughout America, walked into her ward and by chance found out who she was. Vollmer encouraged May to write her life story, and the project gave her a new lease of life. For the whole of 1928, she worked on her autobiography which, after many rejections, was finally published as *Chicago May, Her Story: A Human Documentary by the Queen of Crooks*. The book was fiction as much as fact, but May had high hopes for it. It earned good reviews, but the money that came in was not enough to keep her, so despite her earlier protestations of intending to go straight, May went back to the streets.

With the rigours of her tough life catching up with her, within the year, at the age of fifty-eight, May was forced into hospital in Philadelphia. Just as she was nearing the end, an old flame appeared. It was Charley who, having served his sentence, came back to be by her side. They planned to marry—but May died on the day the ceremony was to take place. She was buried in Philadelphia, and no one she knew attended the funeral. Even Charley disappeared, sending a nun to represent him. The funeral home later tried to get payment from him, but he had long gone.

Chicago May's autobiography is the main source of information on a woman whose chequered career as a criminal ensured that the book was full of colourful anecdotes and a certain degree of wish fulfillment. A natural rebel with a vivid imagination, May was attracted right to the end by those who stood outside society. No matter what hand fate dealt her, she was always drawn back to life on the streets. She seemed to see burglary, pickpocketing, blackmailing, badgering and prostitution as being justified whenever her money ran out, and was proud to proclaim herself 'The Queen of Crooks'. It will always be difficult to separate myth from reality, for Chicago May was as skilled at inventing new personas and covering her tracks in print as she had been in a life that turned out to be a roller-coaster ride, never for a moment lacking in incident. And we may imagine thast even on her deathbed she saw Eddie behind Charley's shoulder, waiting to exact his revenge.

Mata Hari

The stripper who might have been a spy

1876–1917

I am a woman who enjoys herself very much; sometimes I lose, sometimes I win.
– Mata Hari

Margaretha Zelle studied her face in the mirror as she smudged the black kohl under her eyes, hardly recognising the woman who stared back. As she wound the diaphanous veils around herself, Dutch-born Margaretha completed her metamorphosis into the exotic, mysterious and smouldering 'Mata Hari'. She was about to introduce a new dance—one with a definite twist. Taking a deep breath, she stepped onto the stage.

The audience in the Musée Guimet could hardly believe their eyes. This tall, dark-haired woman of exotic oriental appearance was dancing seductively for the Hindu god Shiva. One by one, she removed seven transparent veils. Stripping down to nothing but a body-stocking and ornamental breast cups, the routine climaxed with the dancer surrendering to a rhythmic beat invoking sexual passion. At last, totally spent, she slid to the floor. There was a moment's stunned silence before the audience burst into rapturous applause, knowing it had witnessed the birth of a star. By the next day Mata Hari was the talk of Paris.

Mata Hari dressed in her full exotic dance regalia, including the famous jewelled breast cups.

Twelve years later, during her trial at the Palais de Justice in July 1917, Mata Hari was to be described as one of the most dangerous spies who had ever lived. She was portrayed as the ultimate femme fatale, a wanton woman who had betrayed her country to the Germans and caused the deaths of thousands. So what had turned the young, sweetly naive Dutch girl, Margaretha Zelle, first into Mata Hari, the exotic dancer, and then into the notorious spy? Two tragedies had torn her early life apart, and it may have been these which drove her to play the dangerous game that was to end in front of a firing squad, where all the 'veils' she had used so effectively to captivate an adoring audience were finally to fall away.

An Orchid Among Buttercups

The daughter of Adam Zelle, a wealthy hat maker, Margaretha was born in Leeuwarden in the Netherlands in 1876. Her father adored her, calling her 'an orchid among buttercups', her dark eyes and olive skin making her stand out against the blond hair and blue eyes of her family and playmates. Her childhood was idyllic but when she was thirteen, on the brink of adolescence, her world was turned upside down. Her father went bankrupt and Margaretha woke one morning to find him packing his bags. It was to be a bitter blow, this sudden fall from grace, and an early lesson in abandonment she was never to forget.

Sent to live with her godfather in Amsterdam, Margaretha leaped at a chance to better herself and began training as a teacher. But the proprietor of the college had taken a fancy to her and, perhaps craving a father figure, Margaretha was flattered. When the liaison was discovered, she was forced to leave the college in disgrace, her hopes of entering the teaching profession well and truly quashed. Marriage now seemed her only option. Her attention was caught by an advertisement in a local newspaper placed by a Dutch army captain seeking a wife. Carefully she composed a letter extolling her charms and sent it off with her most flattering photograph. A reply came winging back.

Captain Rudolph MacLeod, a Dutchman despite his Scottish name, was much older than Margaretha—forty to her eighteen—but she was captivated by tales of his dashing military exploits and eagerly accepted his proposal of marriage, sure she had found her longed-for protector. She was soon to realise her mistake, for MacLeod was an alcoholic who regularly abused his terrified young wife. But with the birth of her son Norman in 1987 Margaretha found new purpose in life, and her husband's posting to Java seemed to offer a fresh start. She was fascinated by the culture and, having a natural ear for languages, soon learned Malay.

Her daughter, Jeanne Louise, born there in 1898, was known affectionately by the Malay name, Non.

As the wife of the garrison commander, Margaretha was expected to entertain on a grand scale and MacLeod was proud of her, although he hated the attention she received from the junior officers. They buzzed around her excitedly, like bees to the honeypot, attracted to the striking young woman who 'played the piano most musically' and 'danced with unusual grace'.

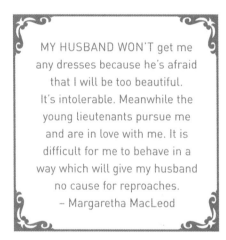

MY HUSBAND WON'T get me any dresses because he's afraid that I will be too beautiful. It's intolerable. Meanwhile the young lieutenants pursue me and are in love with me. It is difficult for me to behave in a way which will give my husband no cause for reproaches.
– Margaretha MacLeod

One dreadful night in June 1899, woken by screams from the children's bedroom, Margaretha ran to investigate and found them writhing in agony. She flung herself down beside them, screaming for her husband to fetch a doctor. But for her small son it was too late. His body went limp even as she tried to hold him. What could possibly have caused this? Gradually the chilling realisation that they had been deliberately poisoned began to emerge, and suspicion fell on their nanny. It was thought that a soldier with a grudge against MacLeod had persuaded the besotted girl to do the deed. Non survived but Margaretha was traumatised by the death of her son, a loss that was to haunt her for the rest of her life.

Margaretha longed to escape from this place of horrors and was relieved when MacLeod was posted back to Europe. Within days of their return he walked out, taking Non with him and administering a final violent beating to Margaretha, who found herself abandoned once more, and more alone than she had ever been. Although it was almost unheard of at the time, she decided to divorce her husband and, to her delight, was awarded custody of Non. But MacLeod ignored the court ruling that he should support them, and Margaretha was forced to make an agonising decision. She gave Non back to her husband but promised the child, who was looking at her with the sorrow of abandonment that Margaretha recognised only too well, that one day, when she was rich, she would return.

'Mata Hari' the Striptease Artist

In 1905, with only five centimes in her pocket, Margaretha arrived in Paris, having decided that the French capital, with its reputation for culture, glamour and fast living, was the perfect place to start a new life. Working in the bohemian Montmartre district as an artist's model, she soon realised she needed a more lucrative source of income if she were to keep herself in style and get Non back. As she sat at a pavement café watching the *haut monde* pass by, she was struck by a daring idea. She remembered the applause that she had received for her dancing in Java and how she had thrilled to the sight of the erotic dances of the locals. At this moment Mata Hari— from a Malay term meaning 'eye of the dawn'—was born.

The success of her first appearances on stage inspired Margaretha to become ever more adventurous. She found herself free to express the sexuality that had been so brutally suppressed by her husband. Her routine involved the simulation of an Indian dance, and a slow striptease as she removed the seven colourful veils until she was almost naked. She would look over her mask at her captivated audience, flashing her dark eyes provocatively, wearing just a body-stocking and ornamental breast cups generously augmented with stuffing.

The Dance of the Seven Veils was one of Mata Hari's most popular numbers, where she would strip down to just a bodystocking and breast cups.

Mata Hari was an overnight sensation and audiences flocked to see her in the most famous Parisian venues. Her costumes became more and more daring and her performances ever more sensational as she gained in confidence, but always she retained the air of mystery which was the most potent aphrodisiac of all. One enamoured writer commented that she was 'so feline, extremely feminine, majestically tragic, the thousand curves and movements of her body trembling in a thousand rhythms'. Her luck had turned just in time. When asked later what she would have done had her gamble not paid off she replied quietly, 'I had a gun ready and my decision was taken'. Her desperation was such that she had considered suicide.

For almost ten years, Margaretha in her role as the exotic dancer Mata Hari was enormously successful. She cast her net wider than Paris, accepting engagements in most of Europe's capital cities and attracting devoted followings there too. She was now commanding huge fees and earning quite enough to support her daughter ... but a child would never have fitted into this lifestyle. Intoxicated by the heady excitement of her performances, and by the gifts and flattery of her adoring lovers, she tried to stifle the guilt she felt about breaking her promise to Non.

But the storm clouds were gathering. By the time war broke out in 1914, European society was changing. Margaretha's erotic dancing and decadent ways, once so celebrated, were beginning to be regarded with distaste; her theatre bookings declined. She clung to the role of exotic dancer, but her audience was fickle. Now almost forty, she no longer had the stamina she once had, and knew her body was losing the suppleness to sustain her performances. She looked around for new ways to make the money she needed to keep herself in the style she had come to expect.

Margaretha's many lovers were to provide her with the answer. They at least were still adoring, and happy to pay for the pleasure of her company. The lifestyle of celebrated performer was exchanged for that of high-class courtesan, Mata Hari's sexually charged performances now playing behind bedroom doors. In return, Margaretha demanded money, or property in the more salubrious areas of Paris. She still wrote to Non, but her letters were returned unopened—and as her dreams of being with her daughter faded, her motives became more mercenary and self-serving. If a man wasn't rich and important, she simply wasn't interested. For a while she seemed content with the rewards of her new profession. But there was a far more exciting and dangerous role still to play, one that Margaretha would fall into by accident rather than design.

MARGARETHA LONGED to see her daughter and at one time plotted with a close friend, Anna Lintjen, to kidnap her. Anna waited outside Non's school near Amsterdam, ready to seize her and take her to Paris. But MacLeod chanced to meet Non after school that day and the plan was foiled.

Pillow Talk

Although her bookings as an exotic dancer were now few and far between, early in 1916 Margaretha was delighted, despite the dangers of wartime, to be asked to do a six-month season at the Metropole in Berlin. Keen to fill in the empty hours between performances, she bestowed her favours on a number of high-ranking German officers, one of whom, it appears, was the head of German espionage, Traugott von Jagow. Was this the moment when she was recruited to spy for Germany or was she just being fatally naive? It was later alleged that von Jagow persuaded her to join a training course on which she learnt sophisticated spying techniques and was given the code name H21. Whatever the truth of that story, Margaretha had never confined herself to German officers—already renowned for her preference for lovers of the highest possible rank, she had partied in the most influential of circles and formed liaisons with officers of all nationalities. She once said, 'To me, the officer forms a race apart … I never noticed whether they were German, Italian or French'.

In many senses, Margaretha with her liberated views about sex, and her feisty independence, seems to have been born before her time. It was unfortunate for her that, just at that moment, Europe was in the grip of 'spy paranoia'. Anyone could be considered suspect, particularly women, who were looked upon as naturally manipulative and adept at secrecy and thus easily coerced into espionage. A woman such as Margaretha, who failed to conform in any way with the stereotyped role assigned to women during war—working to support the men on the home front, sewing, cooking, working on the land—was almost bound to be viewed with distrust.

When her Berlin engagement ended, Margaretha decided to return to neutral Holland. But her activities in Berlin had attracted the attention of the French Secret Service. With so many military lovers, who knew what secrets might have been revealed across the pillow? Her journey to Holland took her via England, and at Folkestone she was stopped by officials and interviewed. Reportedly, while she gave two differing stories

After ten years of dancing, and aged forty when World War I broke out and theatre bookings declined, Margaretha began to look for new ways of funding her luxurious lifestyle, including consorting with rich lovers.

as to why she had recently been in Berlin, she remained calm and appeared intelligent in her responses. Ironically, this only served to fuel suspicions that she was a spy. After all, they reasoned, no normal woman would have appeared so composed in such circumstances. She must be hiding something. But this time the English officials let her pass.

So why was Margaretha Zelle undertaking a reckless journey through Europe at such a volatile time? Was she just pretending to herself nothing had changed or could she have been capitalising on the conflict in order to make money? There is no doubt that had she wanted to be a spy, she was ideally suited to the role—she had the contacts and the dramatic skills, and her lack of allegiance to a particular country would have been an advantage in assuaging any guilty conscience. But perhaps any conventional notions of home and loyalty to family, friends and country had long vanished. Her husband had brutalised and deserted her, her son had been murdered, and her daughter was achingly close yet so far away.

In the spring of 1916, a restless Margaretha decided to revisit her old haunts in Paris. But the British intelligence service, MI5, had tipped off their French counterparts about their suspicions and she was refused entry into France. Undeterred, Margaretha used some of her influential contacts to charm her way in. On her arrival in Paris, however, Captain Georges Ladoux, a specialist in military and counter espionage who had developed a keen interest in the activities of the one-time exotic dancer, had her followed by two detectives. They told Ladoux that Margaretha Zelle was receiving an inordinately high number of male guests, many of them French and Belgian officers. This 'debauched' behaviour would later be used as evidence against her.

But now Margaretha, who for so long had viewed men in terms of their financial assets and military status, fell madly in love. The object of this sudden passion was Vladimir de Masloff, a handsome twenty-one-year-old Russian pilot flying for the French. Vladimir was about the age her son would have been, and one can speculate that he inspired in her some long-buried maternal instinct. Her happiness was to be short-lived. Vladimir had to return to the front, leaving her in an agony of suspense as she waited for his letters to arrive. Then news came that he had been seriously injured in a mustard gas attack that left him blind in one eye. Desperate to be with him, she applied for a visa to access the military zone in which he was stationed. Captain Ladoux intercepted the papers, sure that she had a secret agenda. He requested a meeting immediately.

Ladoux told her of the suspicions she had aroused both in France and in England, and asked her point-blank if she were a German spy. Margaretha stared at him incredulously. Why on earth would she side with Germany? Wasn't her lover fighting for the Allies? As usual she was calm, composed and charming, and by the end of the meeting Ladoux had made her an extraordinary offer. Her contacts meant she could be useful to them. They would pay her one million francs if she would consider an espionage mission for France. Margaretha couldn't resist. This seemed to her the perfect role, and she came up with a daring idea. She told Ladoux that if she could get to Brussels, she had the necessary contacts to engineer a meeting with the Crown Prince of Germany, from whom she might elicit information. Ladoux seemed impressed. If she hadn't been a spy prior to the meeting, she was now.

Out in the Cold

Getting to the Belgian capital involved a complicated journey which included crossing to England. Once again Margaretha was detained by suspicious officials, this time because MI5 was convinced she was the German spy, Clara Benedix. Margaretha was almost amused at the mistake. With the air of a magician plucking an ace from her sleeve, she shared her exciting secret—she was in fact a French spy. When the English checked out her story, however, Ladoux failed to support her. In fact, to her horror he denied that he knew her and merely suggested that MI5 send her to Spain, from where she could make her way back to Paris and he could interview her further. It seems certain that Ladoux was covering his own back here. What if MI5 was right and Margaretha was a German spy? He didn't want anyone to think he had been duped—and certainly not by a woman. The British released her, but MI5 now firmly believed that she was lying and was working for the Germans.

Margaretha was unnerved by the experience but not about to give up on her mission or, more importantly, on the money promised by Captain Ladoux. She had no instructions and little money but, ever resourceful, took matters into her own hands and by January 1917 had got herself to Madrid, where she managed to get an appointment with the German military attaché, Major Arnold Kalle. Seducing him, she encouraged him into indiscretions as she lay in his arms. It seemed even easier than she had imagined—but Kalle wasn't the sort of man to make mistakes. He 'let it slip' that German submarines would soon be dropping German and Turkish officers onto the coast of Morocco, a French military zone. Excited that she was proving to be such an accomplished spy, Margaretha sent the information to Ladoux. She was puzzled to receive no reply.

Margaretha reached Paris in February, eager to receive the generous payment she had been promised. She couldn't wait to be reunited with Vladimir and to return to her former luxurious lifestyle. Booking herself into one of the most expensive hotels in the city, she managed to contact the elusive Ladoux. She was stunned when he told her that her information was worthless. Margaretha was an accomplished lover but apparently a transparent spy. Major Kalle had given her false information, simply to see how long it would take to get back to the French, and sent a message to Berlin in a code that the Germans knew the French had already cracked, identifying her as the German spy H21 and saying that she had proved invaluable. This message was to seal Margaretha's fate.

Dupe or Double Agent?

On 13 February 1917, Margaretha was arrested and brought in for questioning by French military prosecutor, Captain Pierre Bouchardon. She was accused of 'espionage, complicity, and intelligence with the enemy', and incarcerated in Saint-Lazare Prison. The arrest was kept secret. In a state of nervous exhaustion she was subjected to lengthy interrogations by Bouchardon, during which it was established that she had many lovers across the Continent—a fact she'd never tried to hide. One has to wonder whether she was being tried as a spy or merely as a scarlet woman. After being interrogated no less than seventeen times, she finally made a fatal error.

On May 21 she admitted that a German diplomat had once paid her 20 000 francs to spy on France and she had been directed to act under the code name H21. However, she claimed, she had never carried out a mission. She had kept the money only because she felt it was fair recompense for the loss of her luggage after she had been peremptorily removed from a train by German guards on an earlier occasion. But to Bouchardon this, together with the fact that they had discovered she was carrying 'invisible ink' upon her person, was damning evidence of her guilt. Her protests that the invisible ink was nothing more than a contraceptive douche fell on deaf ears.

On 24 July 1917, Margaretha was brought to the Palais de Justice to be tried before a military tribunal. Excited crowds gathered outside, hoping to catch a glimpse of the legendary dancer. The tribunal was told that French intelligence services had intercepted radio messages from the German military base in Madrid, which spoke of agent H21, a code they claimed to know for a fact referred to Margaretha Zelle. With the Allied forces struggling against their German enemy, the idea of using pillow talk to procure secrets served to inflame public opinion against this traitorous femme fatale. In his opening statement, the chief prosecutor portrayed her 'as a sort of Messalina, dragging a horde of admirers behind her chariot'.

It seemed that Margaretha's guilt had already been decided. All that remained was for the tribunal to be swayed by the eloquence of the prosecutor who claimed, despite some rather shaky evidence, that she was one of the greatest spies of all time. He summed up by saying, 'The ease with which she expresses herself in several languages, especially French, her numerous relations, her subtle ways, her aplomb, her remarkable intelligence, her immorality, congenital or acquired, all contributed to make her a suspect'. The tribunal took forty-five minutes to decide her fate. Death by firing squad. She cried out in disbelief, 'It's impossible! It's impossible!'

IN THE COURSE of his enquiries Bouchardon had interviewed Margaretha's lover, Vladimir Masloff, when he returned to Paris intending to end their relationship. Her failure to answer his letters, coupled with the shame of her trial, was too much for him.

On 15 October 1917, Margaretha walked out to meet her end. An officer stepped forward and offered her a white blindfold but she chose not to wear it, preferring instead to look the firing squad in the eyes. A performer to the end, Margaretha smiled and blew them one last kiss as they took aim. The officer dropped his sword as a signal and the bullets rang out. Three found their mark and she fell to the ground. A soldier stepped forward and placed his gun to her temple, firing one last shot, just to be sure.

Not Enough Evidence to Swing a Cat

The trial judge claimed that Margaretha had 'caused the death perhaps of 50 000 of our men, without counting those who perished at sea through her information'. But the prosecutor, André Morat, was later to confess that 'there was not enough evidence to swing a cat', and that although she was not totally innocent, 'she wasn't guilty enough to deserve to die'. In 1999, MI5 reopened their original Mata Hari files and decided that the hard evidence needed to convict her had never existed. Although there is certainly some suspicion surrounding her activities, the British and French secret services were under pressure for results, and the Germans were bent on teaching her a lesson for taking off with 20 000 francs.

TWO YEARS AFTER the execution, another stunning young woman, tall, with jet-black hair, had completed her teacher training and was excitedly preparing for a new life in the Dutch West Indies. Sadly, Non was never to make the trip, dying suddenly from a brain haemorrhage. She would have had little to remember her mother by, for after Margaretha's death all her possessions were auctioned off to pay for the cost of the trial.

Throughout her life, Margaretha seemed addicted to the various attentions she received. When she was no longer bringing down the house with her dance performances she turned to her sensational life as a courtesan; if that were not enough, the fantasy of masquerading as a master spy must surely have been the ultimate thrill. But she was to be haunted to the end by thoughts of the daughter she had lost almost as surely as she had her baby son. Just before her execution, it is claimed she wrote to Non—a letter that Captain Bouchardon never forwarded, simply clipping it into his file.

Margaretha's life was overshadowed by personal tragedy, and her choices often dictated by the desperate financial circumstances in which she found herself. Perhaps the roles of exotic dancer, actress and spy were naturally appealing to someone intent on escaping the realities of a difficult life. Despite increasing evidence that would seem to support her claim that she was innocent, Mata Hari for now seems destined to remain our favorite femme fatale and a byword for betrayal. No doubt she would have been delighted by the afterglow surrounding her dramatic demise.

Tilly Devine

Rough, tough, tea-sipping, street-fighting madam

1900–1970

On 2 June 1953, as the newly crowned Queen Elizabeth II walked out onto the steps of Westminster Abbey to be greeted by cheering crowds, one of her enthusiastic subjects seemed to be cheering more loudly than the rest. Tilly Devine, dressed in all her finery, diamonds flashing to almost outshine those in the royal crown, had travelled all the way from Australia to be present at this great ceremonial occasion. She watched misty-eyed as the slim royal figure adjusted her ermine robes. Tilly smiled now over the heads of the cheering crowds, feeling for a second on a par with the Queen, bedecked with jewellery just as she was. Then an over-eager spectator trod on her heel and Tilly let fly with a curse. As always, she could keep up the pretence of graciousness for only so long.

Not a true monarch like Elizabeth, Tilly was queen of a rather different kingdom back home in Sydney, New South Wales. Known as the 'Queen of the Night', Tilly was the madam of forty brothels and years earlier, in the late 1920s, had been a key player in the Razor Wars, the bloodiest gang warfare that Australia had ever seen.

Police records, including mug shots taken of Matilda 'Tilly' Devine after her arrest for the razor attack in the barber's shop, 1925.

No. *659*

Name... *Matilda Devine*

State Reformatory   Date when Portrait was taken... *27~5~* 192*5*

Native Place *London, England*

Year of Birth *81 Sept. 1900*

Arrived in State { Ship.........
{ Year.........

Trade or occupation } *Domestic Duties*
previous to conviction }

Religion ...... *Roman Cath*

Education, degree of ...... *Read & Write*

Height, without shoes... *5* feet *4* ins.

Weight in lbs. { On committal *11st 4lbs*
{ On discharge ....

Colour of hair... *Fair*

Colour of eyes... *Blue*

Marks or special features ......
Scar over R. eye.
" " " face"
" over L. eye.
" on Chest.

(Nos. of previous Portraits ....

CONVICTIONS

Where and When	Offence	Sentence
Sixty one Convictions	*per Police Report*	

Early Years

Born in England in 1900, as the Victorian age creaked to a close, Tilly (Matilda Mary) was the daughter of Edward Twiss, an impoverished bricklayer from Camberwell in South London. From the beginning, her life was a struggle for survival. She felt trapped in the grim streets with their back-to-back houses, where everyone knew everyone else's business and passed judgment on girls like Tilly—beautiful and just a little too bold for someone of her lowly station. The young Tilly loved the theatre and would beg, borrow and steal to buy a ticket to the latest play or music hall extravaganza. For a few hours she would be transported to a glamorous world, where showgirls were applauded and showered with gifts. She frequented art galleries too, standing before glowing oil paintings of women covered with jewels, their heaving bosoms tightly encased in silken bodices, feathered hats pinned to elaborate coiffures, and imagining herself encased in such finery. How could she make her dream come true? She could see only one way.

Tilly began taking to the dingy Camberwell streets after nightfall and selling her body—the only asset she had. There were many willing takers and she was soon dressing in the style that she so admired in the showgirls. But her new profession had its downsides—by the age of fifteen, she had made her first appearance in Bow Street Court, charged with soliciting. Not only that, she couldn't help but notice the terrible toll the lifestyle had taken on the older prostitutes. Beauty was a short-lived commodity on the streets. How she longed for the heady excitement of being centre stage, for the swell of that rapturous applause. As she stood on street corners, displaying a shapely ankle, Tilly dreamed of escape.

Escape of a sort was to arrive in the form of a sapper in the 4th Tunnelling Company of the Australian Imperial Forces, a former sheep-shearer who went by the name of 'Big Jim' Devine. Devine had a chequered army career, having gone AWOL and been imprisoned on several occasions. However, his larger-than-life personality and tall tales of the Australian outback were attractive to Tilly, who persuaded herself she was madly in love. It was rumoured that Big Jim had spun her a tale of being well off and owning a kangaroo farm but, if that were true, she was a willing victim. Here was the fresh start she craved in an exciting new country. In 1917 they were married; Tilly fell pregnant almost immediately but the baby girl died soon after she was born. A second child, a son, survived but by that time Big Jim had gone back to Australia. Tilly, desperate to follow him, left the boy with her parents. Her idea of a fresh start did not include giving up the only trade that she knew.

Tilly secured passage on the *Waimana*, full of young war-brides following their Australian husbands home to a new way of life. In 1920 she arrived at Circular Quay in Sydney to join up with Jim, waiting only a few days to recover from her marathon voyage before starting 'work'. Demobbed troops, happy, sex-starved and keen to celebrate, thronged the streets of Sydney and provided easy pickings. It seemed that with Jim at her side Tilly was ready to take on all comers and whatever fortune life saw fit to throw at her. She might work as a prostitute, but she was not victim material. Jim bought a Cadillac and operating out of its backseat seemed to Tilly preferable to standing on windy street corners. It was not the luxury to which she aspired, but at least it seemed a step in the right direction.

The Worst Woman in Sydney

By now the marriage had erupted into violence, with Jim administering regular beatings. But Tilly always sprang back. The tough lessons she had learned in the streets of Camberwell stood her in good stead. The small son she'd left behind in England might have softened her, but without him Tilly developed a skin of the proverbial leather and drank even her most hardened clients under the table, matching them curse for curse. She and Jim were soon recognised as major players in the Sydney underworld. Tilly established her own little empire and saw off all comers while Jim drove the getaway car for the local thugs. But the police were soon pulling Tilly in on a regular basis—in the five years following her arrival she was arrested seventy-five times for whoring, obscene language, offensive behaviour and fighting. If Tilly were to survive, things had to change.

A slum cottage on Palmer Street provided the warring Devines with a solution and the opportunity to move off the streets. It was here that Tilly—deciding at the ripe old age of twenty-five that her own whoring days were more or less over—opened her first brothel. She had spotted a loophole in the law and seized it: while the law stated quite clearly that men weren't allowed to run brothels, there was no specific mention of women. Soon Palmer Street was doing a booming trade and Tilly decided to cast her net wider. By the 1930s she had become a successful entrepreneur, operating between twenty and thirty bordellos throughout East Sydney. Each bordello had a room which was 'let', so that if anyone asked what her business was, Tilly could claim to be nothing more than an innocent landlady. Of course everyone knew that Tilly Devine was anything but innocent—but woe betide anyone who said so to her face.

By now Tilly had developed a distinctive style, inspired perhaps by the girls she had seen parading on her long-ago visits to those East End music halls. She was almost impossible to miss, epitomising the vulgarity of the *nouveau riche*. With furs draped round her shoulders, fingers encrusted with diamond rings, she chain-smoked and drank, boasting a capacity that would have put most men to shame. Beauty had long ago fled, and police mug shots of the time show her as a rather heavy-jowled woman with defiant eyes, her short-cut hair crammed under a toque. Her personality became louder, more aggressive and more temperamental over the years. Physically fit, despite a hacking cough, she was good with her fists and was frequently caught brawling with men and women on the streets.

When Tilly wasn't fighting, she was throwing parties, and the more outrageous they were the better. Often, when they were in full swing, she would belt out music hall hits from her past. At last she had her audience, and she revelled in being centre stage. They were decadent, wild parties at which violence could break out at any moment—particularly if the hostess was involved. At one such event, a guest made a pass at Tilly. At first it was nothing more than harmless flirting, but when he made a playful grab the game was over. Spotting a pair of tailor's shears, she stabbed him in the face. Blood sprayed everywhere but the party continued. The hostess had shown in no uncertain fashion that she was the boss.

If Tilly didn't resort to open violence, she'd turn to profanity. She was regularly arrested for letting fly with torrents of abuse, and seemed to enjoy her position as the 'number one swearer in Sydney'. Hauled up in court on one occasion for hurling abuse at a fish seller who had sold her a bad oyster, the magistrate shook his head in amazement and remarked that they were the 'worst words he'd ever heard!'

On the streets Tilly was the roughest woman you could meet, but behind the closed doors of genteel parlours she aspired to mingle with Sydney's elite. With her successful business ventures, she now had the money and the material possessions she had longed for. But despite sipping tea from bone china teacups and hiring musicians from the Conservatorium of Music to play for her, there was no hiding her true character and her dangerous underworld connections. The soft strains of chamber music could suddenly give way to outbursts of violence and the sound of gunshots. Tilly was a strange mixture, riding roughshod over anyone who tried to stand in her way, deftly crooking her little finger to lift a teacup as she listened to Mozart, and playing Lady Bountiful when Christmas parties were held for the deprived children of the Sydney slums, paying for an elaborately decorated Christmas tree and lavish gifts.

Tilly had a keen instinct for making money and her business flourished under a three-tier system. The top prostitutes worked in furnished terraced houses and bedded the likes of senior police and businessmen. The second class entertained factory workers and tradesmen—and then there was the third class, crudely referred to as 'the boat squad'. This group was made up of the older, hardened women and poor factory girls, who lay in squalid rooms with merchant seamen. When the women weren't working at night, Tilly pushed them onto the streets in the daytime to try their hands as pick-pockets. They trawled department stores, sports stadiums, and public swimming pools looking for an easy wallet. Tilly was a hard taskmaster, driving her girls without as much as a nod in the direction of female solidarity. The suffragette movement might have been carrying all before it elsewhere in Australia, but Tilly gave its feminist ideals short shrift.

Most of the time the police turned a blind eye to the brothels, for many were customers themselves. Occasionally an opportunistic new recruit would drop by, thinking he could make some easy cash if he promised to keep quiet about Tilly's business. But Tilly had no fear of the law and wasn't about to let some rookie constable tell her what to do. As one would-be entrepreneur waited in a pre-arranged toilet cubicle, gleefully anticipating some easy cash, Tilly's thugs had been given different orders. They doused the man with petrol and set him alight. It was a brutal warning from the Queen of the Night to think twice before trying to blackmail her.

However many times she appeared in court, and no matter whether she lost or won, Tilly always attracted an audience and gave a bravura performance. On one occasion when Big Jim was in the dock, Tilly started hurling abuse at the judge, forcing him to have her removed. Outside, she fell to the floor, screaming and waving her legs in the air. The Chief Prosecutor was understandably shocked at the spectacle, for Tilly wore no underwear. When he tried to pull her dress down to restore her 'modesty', she grabbed him between her legs and held him in a vice-like grip. As he scrambled to his feet, he found he was covered from head to toe in a white powder. Tilly had planned the whole spectacle and dusted herself with lavish amounts of talcum powder beforehand. The Chief Prosecutor went back into court, distinctly rattled and smelling of violets. But in 1925, Tilly overstepped the mark. She walked into a barber's shop and slashed a man with a cut-throat razor. This time, no amount of play-acting would avail. She was sentenced to two years in prison and hailed by the press as 'the worst woman in Sydney'. It is often said that Tilly holds the record among Australian women for the most court appearances—possibly as many as two hundred and four.

Rival Queens

Around this time Tilly acquired a rival in the notoriety stakes. A woman called Kate Leigh had spotted an opportunity to trade in illegal liquor following the State government's introduction of a law prohibiting the sale of alcohol after six o'clock. This inevitably heralded what was referred to as the 'six o'clock swill," when customers tried to down as many drinks as possible between the end of the working day and closing time. The law, which stayed in place until 1955, resulted in a thirsty public seeking alcohol elsewhere. Kate Leigh seized her moment and set up a chain of 'sly grog' shops where customers could drink through the night. Like Tilly, Kate was a colourful personality, one who was ideally suited to the liquor industry. She carried a gun and was said 'to have a punch like a mule'. Kate's business became hugely lucrative and her well-refreshed customers would often leave the scene of her hospitality and stumble across to the bordellos provided by Tilly.

In theory, the two entrepreneurs, each with her own empire, could have operated their businesses peacefully within the same city. Tilly was known as Queen of the Night and Kate was hailed as Queen of the Underworld. But peaceful cooperation just wasn't in their natures. They despised each other and a furious battle of one-upmanship ensued. Inevitably the two would come across each other in the street from time to time, and when this happened all hell broke loose. A young policewoman of the period, Maggie Baker, describes a typical meeting: 'Tilly could handle herself, no fear … I saw her and Kate have a 'blue' on Oxford Street one day. Kate was a big woman, very fat. Tilly had Kate's hat off and was pummelling her on the ground. Kate got much the worst of it'.

The violent rivalry between the women infected their respective gangs and resulted in constant street brawls. These brawls were containable, but in 1927 a law was passed which inadvertently led to the most terrible bloodshed. The pistol licensing laws decreed that anyone carrying a gun could be subjected to heavy jail terms—and as a result the thugs of Sydney took to carrying the blades of cut-throat razors, usually jammed into a short, solid piece of wood. More terrifying even than a gun, these razors could cause all sorts of painful damage and were easily hidden. When a Melbourne crime boss attempted to stake a claim in Sydney, he was murdered, leaving the coast clear for Tilly and Kate. It was to be all-out war between them for the next two years as rival gangs went head to head in Sydney's 'Razor Gang Wars'.

The battles were bloody, messy and vindictive. Cocaine was Sydney's drug of choice at the time and pharmacists, doctors and dentists sold it illegally. The majority of Tilly's girls were hooked. Kate traded in cocaine as well as liquor and would send girls out onto the streets dressed as prostitutes, selling the drug. Tilly didn't want Kate's prostitutes on the street and sent her men after them, ordering them, with callous indifference, to disfigure the girls' faces with their blades. In a similar fashion, Kate would send her men after Tilly's girls with the intention of disfiguring them and forcing them out of business. It was a dirty business and many people died when they were dragged into the vicious vendetta.

On 9 August 1929, Sydney saw its worst mob violence ever. The rival gangs fought for over an hour, leaving many with terrible slash wounds and the streets running with blood. This forced the government to push through new laws under which anyone seen talking to someone with a police record could be arrested. In 1936, the new Police Commissioner, William Mackay, called Tilly and Kate into police headquarters to try to effect a truce. He was clear in his demands. He would leave the women alone to operate their respective businesses, but he would not put up with any more bloodshed on the streets of Sydney. The women agreed, probably having tired of it themselves. By now, Tilly was a very worn thirty, and Kate was nearing her fifties. The spark had gone out of it for them both. Now they were to engage in a war of a very different kind.

Tilly and Kate embarked on furious propaganda campaigns, each slandering the other and extolling their own virtues. Tilly famously accused Kate of being a 'white slaver' and 'dope pusher'. They both gave interviews in which they tried to present themselves as being essentially good-hearted and benevolent, but journalists soon got their measure. Tilly was portrayed as mean-natured, whereas Kate was seen as a bit of a laugh, a woman providing harmless grog to the thirsty troops. No one would openly support Tilly's prostitution racket for fear of being thought to be one of her customers. Alcohol was an acceptable vice. Illicit sex was not.

God Rest the Old Bitch's Soul

In 1943, Tilly divorced Jim Devine, tired of his violence and his womanising ways, and later married Eric Parsons, a merchant seaman. With Eric, Tilly seemed to enjoy a measure of domestic happiness and relative peace. Eric threw a lavish party for her fiftieth birthday, one celebration which did not descend into brawling and bloodshed. Tilly's trip to England for the coronation of Queen Elizabeth II was the high point of this period. Unfortunately for Tilly, the Taxation Department was now hard on her heels and in 1955 caught up with her. Once regarded as the wealthiest woman in Sydney, Tilly was forced to sell her brothels and her most treasured pieces of jewellery to pay £20 000 in taxes and fines. Two years later, Eric died of cancer, leaving Tilly feeling isolated and bereft. It was the beginning of the end for the Queen of the Night.

In 1964 Kate Leigh died and Tilly, along with seven hundred other people, attended her funeral. Detective Jack Aldridge read the eulogy and spoke of her fondly. Kate might have been a criminal, but she was well liked and popular. It was thought by some that she would have given up the war with Tilly far earlier than she did, but that Tilly had been too selfish and proud to accept any offer of peace. In later years, however, the two developed a grudging respect for each other. Perhaps they recognised their similarities and understood that in another time and place they might have been friends—although neither would ever have admitted such a possibility. On Kate's death, Tilly remarked, 'God rest the old bitch's soul'. Who knows whether that was said with affection, respect or relief.

In later life, with most of her friends and contemporaries dead, few remembered Tilly Devine. Life had come full circle and Tilly was trapped once more in the soul-destroying poverty she had so longed to escape. She had once boasted, 'There's lots in Sydney who will miss me—even the coppers'. She was proved wrong. Her audience had melted away and she died in lonely obscurity. When she succumbed to cancer in 1970, only a handful of mourners attended her funeral. The *Daily Telegraph*'s headline on her obituary read, 'They'll Shed only Crocodile Tears for Tilly Devine'.

Georgia Tann

Tennessee's stealer and seller of babies
1891–1950

Madge is five years old, and awful lonesome.
– Advertising campaign instigated by Georgia Tann

Georgia Tann drove along the bumpy roads of Jasper County, enjoying the warm spring sunshine, convinced she was on a mission of mercy. The woman she was going to see was sick, widowed, already burdened with two small children, and pregnant. How could people get themselves into such terrible messes? She had seen the most pitiful cases come before her father, Judge Tann, in the Mississippi Court. Not that she'd felt much pity. Pity was not part of her nature.

Georgia pulled up outside the ramshackle cabin and through the windshield watched a small boy playing in the dust. He was filthy, of course, but looked the picture of health—a perfect candidate for what she had in mind. Quietly entering the cabin, she saw the woman asleep in a back room in grubby sheets, the place showing signs of dire neglect. Georgia went back outside and called quietly to the boy, who came running. No doubt he was glad to have someone show an interest in him.

Georgia lured the boy into the car and closed the door. The sound must have woken his mother, for she appeared on the back porch. She stared in horror as Georgia let in the clutch and took off. The little boy stood up on the seat, fists hammering at the window: 'Mommy, Mommy!' he wept as the car accelerated away.

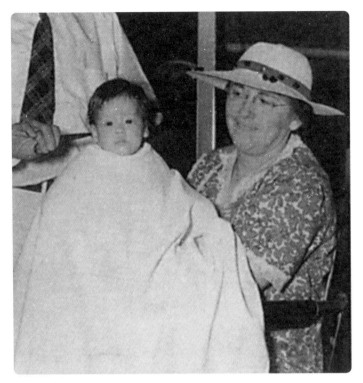

Despite her abhorrent black-market techniques, Georgia Tann is still considered the founder of modern-day adoption in the United States.

Between 1924 and 1950, Georgia Tann made an estimated $1 million from selling more than five thousand babies and small children on the black market, most stolen from vulnerable single mothers and poverty-stricken families. She showed scant regard for the children in her charge, many of whom were sexually abused and some of whom died. All who survived were sent to unscreened adoptive parents, wealth being the only criterion by which their suitability was judged. On the outside, Georgia appeared the concerned professional, offering friendly words of advice to those whose children she was about to remove and managing to convince most of them that she was acting in their children's best interests. On the inside she was a heartless predator who seemed to thoroughly enjoy the power she wielded over the vulnerable parents she so cruelly deceived. This woman's baby-trafficking activities were to remain one of America's blackest secrets for over half a century.

The Turning Point

Georgia Beulah Tann was born in 1891 and grew up in the small town of Hickory, Mississippi. Her mother, Beulah, came from a prominent Mississippi family and her father, George, was Judge of the Mississippi Second Chancery Court. From an early age, Georgia was anxious to win her father's approval, all too aware that her rather sickly older brother, Rob, was her mother's favourite. Unfortunately, Judge Tann was hardly an exemplary role model. Highly intelligent, he was also egotistical, obsessed with power, aggressive, arrogant and an incorrigible womaniser. Georgia's mother meekly put up with his philandering, and Georgia followed him about like a shadow. While her brother stayed home to be cosseted, she attended court, watching proceedings from the public gallery. Perhaps it was while observing her father deal with the most pathetic cases that Georgia began to develop the ability to be chillingly objective.

Destitute children who had been made wards of court would stand in front of Judge Tann awaiting a ruling on their future. Despite feeling little empathy with them, he was frustrated by a system which offered the poorhouse or the asylum as the only solutions, and sometimes brought them home until he could make other arrangements. Growing up in an environment in which orphans were given temporary refuge with her family, at fifteen Georgia first took the initiative to help children herself. Visiting her father's court one day, she found a brother and sister clinging to each other after being placed in the Mississippi Children's Home Society. Through sheer chutzpah she managed to organise their adoption by a wealthy Mississippi couple. This was an amazing coup, for at the time adoption was virtually non-existent. In later years, Georgia would refer to it as a turning point in her life.

One case in particular seems to have had a lasting effect on the young Georgia. A woman had been taken into custody for being a morphine addict, with the result that she and her children were immediately institutionalised. In moments of lucidity, the woman kept calling out for her 'other child'. When Judge Tann got a call in the middle of the night suggesting that the welfare authorities might have left a child behind, he had no option but to drive to the woman's home to check it out. Georgia accompanied him and they set about searching for any signs of life. Under a pile of oily rags they found the missing baby, alive but very weak. With no immediate placement available, the child's care fell to Georgia, who nursed it until a home was found. No doubt she had learned by then not to get too attached to the children who passed through the house.

As Georgia grew older, her relationship with her father became increasingly fraught. She inherited his intellect and looks but, although close in some ways, their similarities and fiery temperaments often drove them apart. The independent nature he valued in himself and might have appreciated in his son he hated in Georgia. To correct what seemed to him her 'rather male' tendencies, he insisted that her musical abilities meant she must become a concert pianist. From the age of five she had been forced to practise for hours every day. But Georgia had one burning ambition. Witnessing the power her father wielded, she set her sights on becoming a lawyer, despite the fact that it was a totally male-dominated profession. Her determination seemed to have paid off, for her father said he would allow her to sit the State bar exam. But at the last minute he had a change of heart, claiming the law was 'too masculine'. The frustration of being denied the opportunity to follow her dream career must have left deep scars.

Although Georgia obediently attended Martha Washington College in Virginia to study music, she was not about to turn submissive. In the conservative early twentieth century South, she stood out from the crowd with her cropped hair and flannel trousers, her lesbianism dawning on her. When she graduated in 1913, at the age of twenty-two, she made the bold decision to strike out on her own, and enrolled at Columbia University to study the relatively new profession of social work, specialising in adoption. Her early experiences in her father's court provided a perfect grounding. There is no reason to think that Georgia's motives were anything but admirable at the outset, but she had one fatal flaw—she failed to manifest any real feelings of empathy for the children she was dealing with. It seems her heart had hardened long ago.

Playing God

Taking up a position as field agent for Mississippi's Home Finding Society, Georgia returned home to Hickory and joined other social workers in placing children in the poorhouse. She began to pass harsh judgments on the lower classes, which she regarded as feckless and irresponsible. Why did poor women insist on having a brood of children when they knew they could not support them? In Georgia's mind the middle classes and the wealthy occupied the moral high ground. Soon she began to dabble in adoption, matching lower-class children with childless middle-class parents who deserved to be 'rewarded'. On the surface this solution seemed a good one, but the power to change lives was to prove intoxicating. Soon Georgia could not resist the temptation to play God.

In 1922, driven by what she saw as her 'mission', Georgia stole two children from an impoverished local woman who was ill and pregnant with her third child. She'd lured one boy into her car while the woman slept, later returning to collect his three-year-old brother, then persuaded her father to rule that the woman was an unfit mother and have the two boys put up for adoption. The people of Hickory were outraged when news of what amounted to a kidnapping spread, and Georgia was driven out of town.

Shaken but apparently undeterred, Georgia applied for and gained the position of Branch Director of the Tennessee Children's Home Society, a non-profit orphanage of high repute amongst the citizens of Memphis. In the 1920s the concept of adoption was particularly fraught due to the current scaremongering by the eugenicists, who claimed the 'mixing of blood' would have catastrophic results. They encouraged a belief that the sins of the parents would be visited upon the children, and consequently members of the middle class, though desperate to adopt, were too frightened to take the risk of adopting lower-class children. Georgia quickly became aware of the number of children from the lower classes that were potentially 'available' for adoption. Confident that her knowledge of the law and her legal contacts would help her, she knew she had a valuable 'commodity' to trade if only she could combat the fear sown by the eugenicists.

Georgia decided that what the customers didn't know wouldn't hurt them. Birth certificates were forged and children born as the result of incest or to impoverished single women had their identities changed overnight. With the flick of a pen, the children of the orphanage were transformed into the genetically desirable offspring of irreproachable, middle-class Christian professionals who had been forced to give them up through an unfortunate change in circumstances. Georgia became known for her pioneering work in the field of adoption, hailed by one Memphis magazine as 'the guardian angel of Tennessee's homeless, dependent children'. She made it seem not only acceptable, but expected, that it was in a child's best interests to be given to 'worthy' parents who were able to offer them a fine future.

GEORGIA TANN ADOPTED her life partner Anne Hollinsworth as her sister, because that was the only way Anne could be recognised as her official heir. Anne died at the age of ninety-six, still proclaiming undying love for the woman whom everyone else described as a demon.

Home Life

By this time, Georgia was living with her long-term partner, Anne Atwood Hollinsworth, who kept her record books and tried to provide a stable family life. But they were living together at a time when lesbians were considered inverts and sexual deviants, and Georgia tried to keep this part of her life secret. She would sometimes disappear for weeks, locking herself away with Anne, suffering from bouts of depression. Anne already had a son and when Georgia herself adopted a baby, whom she called June, her reputation as a woman of great compassion was no doubt enhanced. Under Mississippi laws, adopted children had no legal rights as heirs, so Georgia adopted June as a sister rather than a daughter. By all accounts she was a difficult mother, and June later referred to her as a 'cold fish'. Her behaviour at important moments in her daughter's life does suggest that she was self-absorbed and manipulative. She refused to attend June's wedding and even burned the girl's clothes while she was on her honeymoon. Anne Hollinsworth seems to have been alone in seeing a softer side to Georgia, referring to her as the most generous woman who ever lived.

A Lucrative Black Market

In the early years, Georgia's reputation was exemplary. She placed orphans with good Memphis families who often occupied highly influential positions in society and were eternally grateful to her for what she had done. Within a year of her arrival in Memphis, amazingly, she had control over every available adoptee in the State. By forging their birth certificates, she overcame the problem posed by the eugenicists and removed the final barriers surrounding adoption. She was seen as a trailblazer for her work with adoption. Georgia virtually had the 'keys to the city' through a lifelong friendship with the mayor of Memphis, E. H. Crump, who was influential throughout Tennessee, and had close ties with the County Family Court judge, Camille Kelley.

The non-profit Tennessee Children's Home Society charged $7 to adopting couples within the State, and $750 to couples in adjoining States. 'Contributions' were encouraged at all times. By the late 1940s, however, eighty per cent of adoptees were 'privately' placed out of state, and their adopting parents charged upwards of $5000 for Georgia's 'services'. Both Crump and Kelley played a large part in the operation and benefited financially. While Georgia appeared a committed professional, caring and law abiding, she was becoming increasingly egotistical and

'Mommie Dearest' Joan Crawford with Christina, one of her adopted daughters, both of whom were sold to the actress by Georgia Tann.

power hungry. She became obsessed with extending her operation, dreaming of setting up offices throughout the country and embarking on an emotive advertising campaign that tugged unashamedly at the heartstrings. Sad, doe-eyed children looked up at the camera under the heading of 'Wants Home'. The captions provided extra colour, declaring, for instance, that 'Madge is five years old, and awful lonesome'.

In what was virtually a mail order system, social workers from the orphanage boarded airplanes with babies under their arms, bound for parents who had undergone no screening as to their suitability and who had been chosen merely on financial grounds. Children were sold throughout the United States and as far afield as Canada, Panama, Mexico, and England.

Georgia's advertising campaign reached Hollywood, where a number of people in the movie industry adopted children; Joan Crawford adopted five, including twin girls. These girls were lucky to stay together, both because it was rare for a family to take two children, and because Georgia usually separated children from the same family. When such children asked about their siblings, she would insist that they were confused, that they were talking about their little friends in the orphanage. She milked her association with Hollywood for all it was worth, loving the attention and appearing in magazine articles alongside actors such as Dick Powell and June Allyson, who also adopted a child. She became so renowned that even Eleanor Roosevelt sought her advice on children's welfare and gave speeches lamenting the baby trade carried out by black market entrepreneurs. Georgia's fierce pride in being the daughter of a judge may have made her feel she was somehow above the law—or perhaps it had all become a game and she was able to blind herself to the deadly cost in human lives.

Breeders and Cows

Soon Georgia experienced a problem: demand was outstripping supply. The adoptive market was so large that to meet it she had to look for children beyond those in the orphanage. Rich pickings were to be found in hospital wards and the Family Court. Nurses were bribed to tell poor women and single mothers who'd given birth under anaesthetic that their babies had been stillborn. Georgia referred contemptuously to these women as 'breeders' and 'cows'. She paid several doctors in on the scam to tell other women that their babies were ill and needed special care. Once Georgia had the child, the doctor would tell the mother that the illness had been too severe and even the caring children's home had been unable to save it. In fact, many babies did die, through lack of proper care, abuse, and a cruel lack of accountability. In 1932 Memphis had the highest infant mortality rate of any city in the USA; many of those deaths were later to be attributed to Georgia Tann's system of 'care'.

Often children were given alcohol to subdue them; older children who had been surrendered into care were imprisoned in boarding houses and not allowed to attend school. Georgia carried on collecting money for the upkeep of many children even after they were sold—without their parents' knowledge. She would select the most beautiful babies, dress them up, put them in a basket, and try to sell them to people with soft hearts. To keep up the numbers, Georgia even kidnapped children from playgrounds and the front yards of their homes, assisted by a staff of six female 'spotters' as well as several social workers across the State, many of whom were deluded enough to believe they were doing the right thing. Georgia's activities were protected by her contacts in high places, people who were often reluctant to help but were open to blackmail, having themselves adopted one of Georgia's children. If she detected resistance she would drop into the conversation the fact that the birth mother had asked about the child only the other day. The horror these words aroused eliminated all opposition.

The Solitary Vulture

Georgia regularly attended the Shelby County Family Court of Judge Camille Kelley. Georgia was described by a court worker as 'sitting perched like a solitary vulture', waiting to swoop down on her prey. With her steel-rimmed eyeglasses and short-cropped grey hair she had the air of a stern schoolmistress. Unknown to court officials, Kelley herself was taking a cut and sending hundreds of children to the orphanage without reference to State laws. She frequently visited other County orphanages, seizing the most attractive children by court order and passing them on to Georgia. Her actions became so blatant that the nuns who ran many of the homes began to hide the prettiest infants immediately they saw Judge Kelley drawing near.

One of the most despicable aspects of Georgia's baby-trafficking scam was the way she managed to prey on everyone's vulnerability. The single mothers had no means of supporting their children, so it was pointless for them to protest; her rich customers were so delighted to have a child that they turned a blind eye to any apparent irregularities. Meanwhile, with no screening of the adoptive parents, other than how much money they had and their ability to pay, many children were adopted as 'workhorses' by unscrupulous couples or as 'toys' for paedophiles.

Georgia had also devised a system, which still exists in some States of the USA, whereby the adoption papers were shrouded in secrecy and not for public record. Consequently the adopted children stood little chance of knowing who their birth parents were, nor could the mothers who had been duped trace their children.

In the winter of 1945, an estimated forty to fifty children died in Georgia's care. At the same time the city of Memphis received a deluge of letters of complaint from wronged birth parents and adoptive parents who had by now realised what was happening and refused to keep silent. A Bill was introduced whereby adoptive parents would be screened, but Mayor Crump managed to step in at the last minute and put a stop to it; Georgia also blackmailed many of the policy-makers. But in 1948 the arrival of a new State Governor, Gordon Browning, saw the commissioning of a State of Tennessee investigation into the Children's Home Society. Georgia's power base began to crumble.

Judgment Day

Georgia's orphanage lost its funding from the Child Welfare League of America when Browning's investigation revealed that paperwork surrounding the adoptions was frequently destroyed. The findings were devastating but few paid the price for their crimes. Judge Kelley resigned from the bench and was never prosecuted, dying five years later. Mayor Crump was never brought to account for the profit he had made and the corrupt practices he had encouraged. As for Georgia, it was estimated that by 1950 she had made a million dollars and owned several properties, including a hotel. For almost thirty years she had been protected by influential people keen to keep the operation a secret. She died of cancer at the age of fifty-nine, three months after the investigation commenced and before its findings were announced. Even when her guilt was clear, people were reluctant to name her as a baby thief because too many of them had inadvertently become part of her illicit operation. It was a legal mess from which no one could see a way out. In the end, a law was passed making all five thousand adoptions legal. In effect, this meant that Georgia was exonerated and even those children who had recently been kidnapped remained in their new homes.

With cruel indifference, Georgia Tann changed the lives of thousands of people for ever. Despite the horror with which she is regarded, there is no avoiding the fact that she was responsible for inventing modern-day adoption. With that said, what she effectively did was to erase the birth histories of five thousand children, leaving a trail of adoptees forever questioning their ancestry and a generation of parents unable to offer any answers. Then there were the desperate families from whom children were snatched who were left in limbo, forever wondering what happened to their little ones, looking eagerly into the eyes of strangers and hoping for a flicker of recognition.

It took a long time for the Georgia Tann story to be told, and for many years no one was prepared to address the doubts and tormenting memories of her victims. Driven by her greed for power and position in society, she left a heartbreaking legacy and has become perhaps one of the most despised women in American history.

Madame Mao (Jiang Qing)
with husband Mao Zedong,
in their Communist
uniforms.

Madame Mao

The white-boned demon who almost ruled China

1914–1991

Few people suit her
taste. Only one—she
herself.

– Mao Zedong

Li Yunhe was studying the lines for her minor role in the next production at the drama academy. She knew she could captivate the audience if only she were given the chance. As usual, the male students were daring each other to sneak into one of the rooms of the temple and steal the headdress from the statue of Confucius. She listened to them, bored by this nightly ritual that never actually led to action. What good were mere words?

Rising abruptly, Li Yunhe stormed into the room and defiantly grabbed the headdress. The other students were astonished that a slip of a girl had been brave enough to commit an act that was tantamount to sacrilege. But while they could not help but be impressed by her courage, they were also wary. It was obvious to everyone that she delighted in being the centre of attention.

Later, having stood by her husband for forty years, the then Madame Mao firmly believed that on his death, the right to become the first Chairwoman of Communist China should automatically be hers. But China was never going to accept a woman as leader at that time. Thus it was that when Chairman Mao died, she not only failed to gain power but was also blamed for the entire Cultural Revolution. Madame Mao was ambitious, ruthless, and self-obsessed, but the Chinese ultimately viewed her as something far worse. Vilified as the 'White-boned Demon', she was held responsible for causing irreparable damage to Chinese history and tradition and being the cause of countless deaths. While her husband received a state funeral with the highest attendance figure in history, his wife was sentenced to death.

Crane in the Clouds

Jiang Qing, originally known as Li Yunhe ('Crane in the Clouds'), was born in Zhuzheng in eastern Shandong province in 1914, the daughter of hopelessly mismatched parents, a thirty-year age gap placing them in different generations. Her father was a violent drunk who, when Li Yunhe was six years old, abandoned his family, leaving his wife with little choice but to become a courtesan. Li Yunhe waited nervously at home as her mother returned night after night accompanied by yet another stranger. As the years passed, her mother transferred her attentions to men with fatter wallets, leaving her daughter in the care of her maternal grandparents in the city of Jinan.

Her childhood experiences gave Li Yunhe an early and ineradicable hatred of the traditional mores of Chinese society that gave men absolute power over a woman's fate. By the age of ten, she was already an independent and argumentative child, often singled out and subjected to bullying by other children. She longed to get away from Jinan and find a place where her opinions and forceful personality would receive the attention she felt they deserved. At the age of fourteen, when a travelling theatre troupe came to town, Li Yunhe decided that life in the spotlight as a famous actress could be the answer to all her dreams, and she ran away with the players.

An Actor's Life

Li Yunhe was soon to learn the harsh realities of life for an actress with aspirations to succeed in the theatre. Decisions as to who should get the starring roles were often made on the fabled 'director's casting couch'. Soon enough, as she blossomed into adolescence, she was asked to 'audition'. Remembering the horrors of the life her mother had been forced to lead, Li Yunhe was wary of what clearly smacked of prostitution, but she was nonetheless aware that success would depend on it. To a child who had been starved of affection, the rapturous applause of the audience was truly seductive, and Li Yunhe knew she would soon have to make a life-changing decision.

As luck would have it, her grandparents had so enjoyed the theatre troupe's previous performance that when they heard the troupe was returning to Jinan they hurried to buy tickets. The last person they expected to see stepping from the wings was their granddaughter; as the curtain fell, they made their way to the stage door to confront her and to take her home. Li Yunhe now gave one of the great performances of her life, wailing that her heart would break if she was torn away from her first love, the stage. Realising that they were unlikely to dissuade her, her grandparents struck a bargain—if she returned and lived safely with them, they would allow her to attend the Academy of Performing Arts in Jinan.

There Li Yunhe stood out from the other students in ways that made her feel inferior, although she reacted by assuming an air of bravado and superiority. Poorer than most, her clothes were visibly threadbare, while her feisty nature meant that she always chose to be contrary just to stir things up. People found her unpredictable, but still her talent shone through. In 1930, the Academy closed and Li Yunhe and several other students tried their luck in Beijing, where they found their Jinan accents worked against them. Li Yunhe was forced to return home, feeling that she had come full circle and failed to achieve her goal. At sixteen, probably encouraged by her grandparents, she took her first husband, but it was quickly apparent that she was not cut out to be a dutiful housewife. Her husband's parents claimed that she was lazy and were outraged by the fact she railed against her lowly position in the household. The marriage lasted only a few months, but it had served to demonstrate to Li Yunhe exactly what she did not want.

Li Yunhe divorced her husband, packed up her belongings, and set off to attend Qingdao University, an institution known for its vigorous support of theatre and the arts. Falling in love with a radical left-wing student, she began to dabble in Communist politics and felt that at last she had found a kindred spirit. She lived with him and underwent a modern marriage ceremony for which no certificate was needed. When her partner was thrown into prison for his political activism, Li Yunhe was distraught—but she was to feel even more devastated when on his release he chose to leave her and pursue his political agenda in Beijing. Lonely and rejected, Li Yunhe picked herself off the floor once more and set off for the bright lights of Shanghai.

Brave New World

In the 1930s China's largest city, Shanghai, the 'Paris of the East', was a melting pot of cultures and a place of decadence, tolerance and liberation, particularly for women. It also had a burgeoning movie industry, obviously the main attraction for an aspiring actress. Li Yunhe felt she had two choices: she could be a courtesan like her mother, dependent on men's favours, or a famous movie star like those she saw on the silver screen. Determined it would be the latter, she set about establishing herself in the underground theatre groups, performing in minor plays for little money. Like many young actors of the time, she dabbled in politics,

Former movie star Lan Ping (later Jiang Qing), right, pictured with her mother, left, c.1936.

distributing anti-government leaflets and appearing in anti-establishment plays, seeing herself perhaps as a romantic figure rebelling against oppression. But the dangers were real enough, for in 1934 Li Yunhe was imprisoned for subversive activities and spent three months behind bars. As the harsh regime sapped her health, she kept her spirits up by singing arias from the Chinese operas she had learned back in Jinan. On her release, in an attempt perhaps to find a new identity, she changed her name to Lan Ping, meaning 'Blue Apple', and decided to concentrate her efforts on becoming a movie star.

Against the odds, it turned out to be a good decision. In 1935, Lan Pin secured her greatest role in the theatre, one that would provide a springboard into the big time. She received rave reviews for her portrayal of Nora in Ibsen's *A Doll's House*, a role that revolved around a modern woman striving to break out from a soul-destroying marriage to an older man. Lan Pin was so outstanding that movie directors rushed to ask her to audition. But again the casting couch seemed an unavoidable clause in the contract. For many actresses sex and success went hand in hand, since they were often regarded as akin to prostitutes, but Lan Pin steadfastly refused to fall into the trap, taking strength from the new feminism that encouraged women to take control over their own bodies. To an extent this worked in her favour—her good looks and long flowing hair, together with her fierce streak of individualism, made her an engaging alternative to her more subservient contemporaries. She received many marriage proposals and started to achieve acclaim for her performances in various movies and stage plays. But she was never to act as well as when she played Nora, a performance that no doubt came from the heart.

For much of the four years she spent in Shanghai, Lan Pin was involved in a relationship with a well-known art critic, Tang Na, who regularly reviewed her films. They became inseparable and eventually married, but it was a tempestuous relationship, doomed to failure. Lan Pin always felt

Madame Mao meeting with artists and writers of the People's Liberation Army, 1970. After her own failed attempt as an actress, Jiang Qing always liked to involve herself in the world of theatre.

that she was meant for greater things, a belief fuelled by her political aspirations. She eventually left her husband, a separation that became public fodder as Tang Na's influential circle of journalist friends got their teeth into the matter. Lan Pin was portrayed as cold, heartless and driven by ambition; her name was blackened in the pages of their newspapers whenever the opportunity arose. Disillusioned by their vicious attitude, Lan Pin wrote an essay titled 'My Life', in which she condemned the movie industry for being unable to accept the individuality of actors and seeking to exploit them at every level. Lan Pin was finally finding a voice.

In 1937 the bustling city came to a complete standstill as the Japanese invaded Shanghai from all sides. Lan Pin recognised that this was the last act in her movie career and hurriedly packed her bags, heading for the town of Yan'an in Shaanxi province, the headquarters of the Chinese Communist Party. At twenty-four she was again setting off alone, with two failed marriages and a lost movie career behind her. But she knew now that it was politics, not movie stardom, that really attracted her, for in politics she saw the potential to change the world. And it was at this time that she was to meet the man who seemed to offer her the chance to realise her burning new ambitions.

A Vow of Silence

In Yan'an, however, Lan Pin at first found herself appearing in more plays. She began to fear that she would never escape what had begun to seem like a treadmill. But her performances, even if they were a shade lacklustre, soon won her a powerful new admirer. Mao Zedong was the leader of the Communist Party, a married man and father of eight children, but as soon as he saw Lan Pin he was smitten, driven to throw all caution to the winds. They became lovers, and their relationship immediately came under much critical scrutiny from the Party. Mao's wife, He Zizhen, commanded great respect, having just completed the Long March with her husband. Many of the cadres spoke out publicly against their alliance, spreading rumours that Mao was a sex maniac and Lan Pin merely a willing prostitute. However, Mao's enormous charisma meant that he was recognised as the only possible leader of the revolutionary movement. So when he stamped his feet at a meeting, insisting that he would be unable to carry on leading the revolution without Lan Pin by his side, the Party had no choice but to agree—but they insisted on several conditions. To Lan Pin one of these conditions was particularly monstrous: if she were to be with Mao, she was to stay out of politics for thirty years. It must have seemed a lifetime sentence at the age of twenty-four—but she agreed to it.

On Mao's advice Lan Pin changed her name, to symbolise a new beginning. She became Jiang Qing, meaning 'Green Waters', cut her hair to a close boyish crop, and took up the role of dutiful partner. But soon she began to feel like Ibsen's Nora, playing a subservient role, condemned never to voice her opinion in public or enjoy the independence she craved. Was she really to remain muzzled for thirty years? Her sense of self, always so strong, was being challenged. But when she gave birth to a daughter, Li Na, she began to rediscover her confidence, appreciating the importance of her position as wife of the Party Chairman. She became more extrovert and outspoken, and it became increasingly difficult for the Party to know what to do with her. Domesticity did not suit her, and her enforced abstinence from political activity led her to embrace numerous superficial projects. When a film director came up with the idea of doing a documentary on the couple, Jiang was delighted. She gave an accomplished performance, but Mao remained every bit the stiff politician—consequently the documentary ended up on the cutting-room floor. As the years passed, Jiang became more and more committed to Communist ideology but, forced to abide by the thirty-year ban, her frustration and resentment against those in power grew.

For two decades China had been embroiled in either international or civil wars. On 1 October 1949, the Communists claimed victory in the war against Chiang Kai-shek's Nationalists. The People's Republic of

China was established and Mao Zedong became Chairman Mao. But Mao was to make huge mistakes during his time as Party leader. A modernising campaign called the Great Leap Forward, which attempted to introduce industrialisation to rural areas at the cost of agriculture, resulted in up to thirty million deaths through starvation by the early 1960s. When the campaign was abandoned, other prominent members of the Party decided that Mao should become the symbolic head of state, and set themselves up as the leaders of the Party.

The Muzzle is Removed

Seeing her husband's power reduced, Jiang returned to his side after a period in Shanghai revisiting old haunts, establishing new networks, and spending time at the theatre and opera. Her relationship with Mao was now entirely platonic, for she had long accepted his voracious sexual appetite for young girls from the country. But she had not given up her ambitions to influence the way the country was run, and brought to Mao's attention a play which she suggested was undermining his authority. They discussed the power of the arts to influence politics, and concluded that anything intellectual or bourgeois, or that reflected traditional Confucian cultural values, flew in the face of Communism.

In 1966 they launched the Great Proletarian Cultural Revolution. It was not only a way by which Mao could maintain power, it was also the mouthpiece Jiang Qing so desperately desired. Her thirty years of silence were over and she had every intention of making up for every one of them. But in appointing his wife Deputy Director of the movement, Mao unwittingly released a monster. Among the other leaders of the Cultural Revolution were Zhang Chunqiao, Yao Wenyuan and Wang Hongwen, who with Jiang Qing were later known as the infamous Gang of Four. This extreme leftist group tried to influence

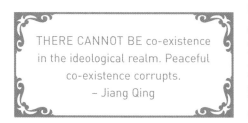

THERE CANNOT BE co-existence in the ideological realm. Peaceful co-existence corrupts.
– Jiang Qing

government policies in opposition to the conservative group led by Deng Xiaoping, their aim being to establish Jiang as Mao's successor.

In the name of the Cultural Revolution senior schools and colleges were closed down, and thousands of naïve young people who had never known anything but life under Communism were forced to enlist in the Red Guards. Numbering in the millions, this force became so large that for the next few years it was more powerful than the official military itself. The ideology of the Cultural Revolution turned against the old guard of the Communist Party, who were referred to as 'revisionists', and the Red Guards were ordered to destroy anything associated with privilege or with 'traditional' values. Teachers were killed or tortured, junior schools were closed, and people seen as members of the 'exploiting classes' were forced to shave half their heads and be doused in ink; unknown thousands of educated, 'wrong-thinking' people were sent to forced labour camps for 're-education', where an unimaginable total died. Cultural artefacts were destroyed wholesale. The Red Guards, fired by propaganda and indoctrination, turned indiscriminately on anything they considered to go against the grain of Communism. Whatever fine Communist ideals Jiang may have harboured at the outset vanished as she wielded unimaginable power, coldly indifferent to the fact that hundreds of thousands of her people were being persecuted and killed.

MADAME MAO WAS OFTEN filmed working side by side with the farmers. But it was said that she would always stop once the cameras were off, that this was merely part of her PR campaign. She traveled with a fur-trimmed toilet seat and as evening fell would demand that all the animals be locked up so that she could get a good night's sleep.

At the same time she was busily realising other ambitions, working to change the endings of contemporary plays and stories to reflect her ideology, and commissioning new works covering subjects that would reinforce the propaganda promoted by the Cultural Revolution, not just plays and books but musical works as well. She had glowing reviews of the new works published in the newspapers, and must have enjoyed avenging herself against those literary friends of her second husband who had given her such bad press all those years ago. She embarked on another personal vendetta, publicly humiliating any director, movie executive or politician who had let her down in the past.

When Jiang spoke 'to the masses' as she moved about the country, she did so with the experience and air of an accomplished politician, colouring her speeches with the light and shadow needed to entrance an audience. People said that it was as if Chairman Mao himself was speaking—or at least, those were the words they parroted, almost certainly too terrified to express their real feelings for fear of inspiring Madame Mao's wrath. In a triumphant realisation of ambition, as the sixties drew to a close, Jiang was appointed the first ever woman member of the Chinese parliament, the Politburo.

A Loose Cannon

As the seventies began, Jiang acted as if there was never enough time to get everything done. Undoubtedly her greatest fear was that Mao, twenty years older than she, would die and her power be taken from her. She seemed almost to be daring the Party to stop her. By 1974 she was quite openly taking lovers, and speaking up for women everywhere regarding their right to have as many partners as they wished. She became ever more unaccountable, and was viewed within the Party and by many in the wider population as a loose cannon. At one point she gave an interview to a foreign journalist, without Mao's permission, in which she marketed herself as a potential world leader. She said and did much else that displeased people, one of her worst sins being seen to sign photographs with red ink, traditionally a colour that only emperors could use. Possibly intended to demonstrate her continuing scorn for tradition, it may also have been an expression of the ambition that still burned within her.

Madame Mao at the trial of the 'Gang of Four' in Beijing, 1981, where she was sentenced to life imprisonment.

Eventually, unrest among the young conscripts of the Red Guards began to grow; in early 1976 this resulted in the imposition of martial law and the end to ten years of wanton destruction. As the hideous truth of what had been wrought in the name of the Cultural Revolution became apparent, Mao retreated into the shadows. Jiang could do no such thing and, since she had so grandly taken the applause, was forced to take the bad reviews.

When Mao Zedong died on 9 September 1976, he left no designated heir to rule China's eight hundred million citizens. The Gang of Four had planned to seize power through military coups in Shanghai and Beijing, but Deng Xiaoping moved first. On 6 October, guards broke into Jiang's room and arrested her, throwing her into Qincheng prison, where she was to remain for five years before being brought to trial. Still suffering from the effects of the Cultural Revolution, but feeling it was disrespectful to criticise Chairman Mao, the public chose to vilify his wife. Jiang Qing acquired her final title—the 'White-boned Demon'.

Throughout her trial Jiang maintained that she was no more than a mouthpiece for Mao: 'I was Chairman Mao's dog. Whomever he asked me to bite, I bit'. In 1981 she was sentenced to death, the sentence later commuted to life imprisonment. At the age of seventy-seven, she was diagnosed with throat cancer and admitted to hospital. Perhaps in a last attempt at control, on 14 May 1991 she hung herself from a rail in the hospital bathroom.

Whether Jiang Qing ever truly understood the enormity of the appalling crimes she had committed against her people in pursuit of a flawed ideology is uncertain. She also seems to have had a shaky grasp on the most basic principles of feminism and taken them to extremes, punishing those who had dared to suggest that she might have been better suited to a walk-on part in the drama of her own life. Mao once famously referred to her as a 'paper tiger'—'one blow and she's down'—but he entirely underestimated her burning need for public acclaim and, after the thirty years of enforced silence, her overwhelming hunger for power.

Imelda Marcos

The steel butterfly who plundered a nation's wealth

1929 –

Win or lose, we go shopping after the election.

– Imelda Marcos

Imelda Marcos pictured in 1988, two years after she fled the Philippines to the United States.

On 7 December 1972, a man smartly dressed in a dinner suit arrived at a glittering awards ceremony which was being broadcast live on television across the Philippines. Viewers watched in shock as the man produced a machete from his pocket. Guests were reluctant to intervene until he launched a savage attack upon the First Lady, Imelda Marcos, slashing at her viciously. By the time he was shot dead by guards, Imelda had received eleven wounds to her arms and hands which required seventy-five stitches. Later, horrified that the physical perfection she so prided herself on had been sullied, and alarmed that the scars were healing too slowly, Imelda contemplated plastic surgery. Her husband Ferdinand advised her to wear the scars as a 'badge of honour'—a notion which immediately appealed to this natural drama queen. Her obsession with beauty was such that she was later to wryly remark on the ugliness of the machete used in the attack: 'I thought, why such an ugly instrument to hurt me? Why couldn't he tie a little bow on it or something?'

Imelda Marcos, the Steel Butterfly, never formally convicted of crimes against her country, must share the blame with her husband Ferdinand Marcos for the economic and political disasters that plunged the Philippines into unprecedented poverty in the last decades of the twentieth century. While the majority of Filipinos were scraping a living below the poverty line, Imelda surrounded herself with riches and shamelessly chased the international jet set. Accused of plundering the national coffers, it has been estimated that the amount taken under her watch, and still unaccounted for, could have cleared the national debt. Yet somehow Imelda managed to keep out of prison—none of the charges of corruption laid against her were finally made to stick. Her buoyant personality, her overweening self-esteem, and her sense of having acted always for the common good, remain resolutely intact.

The Muse of Manila

Although born into one of Manila's leading families, Imelda Romuáldez grew up in the terrible poverty familiar to so many Filipino children, then and still. When her mother, Remedios Trinidad, met her father, lawyer Vincent Orestes Romuáldez, she took on five of his children from a previous marriage. As the family increased in size, Romuáldez's fortunes took a downward turn. He was made bankrupt and then was further devastated when his wife died after giving birth to their sixth child together. Living in a garage in the shadow of the Malacañang Palace in Manila, little Imelda now ran the streets barefoot and cared for her younger brothers and sisters.

When Imelda was ten, Romuáldez decided to escape the high cost of life in the city and moved his family to the province of Leyte. Imelda spent her adolescence in the town of Tacloban and studied hard, gaining a bachelor's degree in education. But it was her looks that were always her trump card. She began to enter beauty pageants and in 1953, aged twenty-four, she moved back to the capital, where she came second in a

The Marcoses with Emperor Hirohito and Empress Kojun, on a state visit to Japan, 1966.

beauty contest. She insisted, with characteristic insouciance, that despite her failure to win, she should still be given a title—the 'Muse of Manila' sounded perfect to her ears.

In 1954, Ferdinand Marcos, a dashing young congressman, met the stunning Imelda and, captivated by her beauty, style and charm, proposed marriage within thirty minutes. The impulsive couple married eleven days later. It seemed to them both that it was a match made in heaven, with Imelda the perfect muse to Ferdinand's political ambitions. Eleven years later, when he stood for presidential election, she campaigned tirelessly on his behalf, travelling the length and breadth of the country and successfully winning him one million votes. In 1965, Ferdinand became President of the Republic of the Philippines and Imelda, his First

Lady, revelled in the fact she was now queen of the palace she had regarded with such awe when she was a little girl. They seemed a fairytale couple then. Imelda proved herself an accomplished ambassador for her country, and was soon being hailed by the world press as the Jacqueline Kennedy of the Philippines.

A Conjugal Dictatorship

As Imelda grew in confidence and power in the years that followed, she began making up for those early years of poverty. Now she spent her time buying airlines, throwing lavish parties, bedecking herself in jewels and gorgeous clothes, and travelling the world in style.

When she discovered that her husband was having an affair, Imelda showed how well she had absorbed the lessons provided by international politicians manipulating situations to their own advantage. Ferdinand's affair had become public and the fallout was deeply embarrassing, with transcripts made from tapes of the lovers' conversations and Polaroid snapshots plastered over the front pages. Instead of adopting the role of downtrodden wife, Imelda began to promote herself as a possible replacement for her disgraced husband. With the country's long-standing social unrest increasing, she might well have managed to persuade a disenchanted electorate that she was a likely presidential candidate—had Ferdinand not taken the next drastic step.

In 1972, Ferdinand Marcos imposed martial law, claiming the risk of communist infiltration. In doing so he secured his position not only as President but also as Prime Minister. Ever the pragmatist, Imelda supported her husband, probably thinking she could play the guilt card over his affair whenever it suited her. Ferdinand might be in charge of the country, but Imelda was certainly pulling some of the strings. In one fell swoop, democracy was virtually abolished and an anti-subversion law was introduced that saw dissidents imprisoned, often for years at a time, just for questioning the motives of the government.

There were widespread rumours of torture and murder on political grounds, events for which the people blamed Imelda as much as her husband. Their leadership was now being referred to as a 'conjugal dictatorship', since the presidential couple appeared joined at the hip. Perhaps not coincidentally, the same year saw the assassination attempt on the First Lady at the awards ceremony. She was beginning to receive a lot more attention, and the initial adoration had soured.

During the first years of martial law, Imelda was an active member of the Cabinet, taking up government positions, such as Governor of Metro Manila, which held significant power. Her love of beauty meant that she embraced the arts, and she commissioned the building of a cultural centre in Manila which she claimed would revive Filipino art. Having experienced the delights of such famous establishments as the Lincoln Center in New York on her travels abroad, she wanted one the same for Manila. She became obsessed with creating 'beautiful' buildings, commissioning anything from theatres to luxury hotels, often siting them in the slums of Manila and claiming she was 'improving' the lives of the poor by giving them something nice to look at.

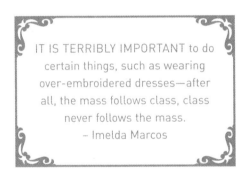

IT IS TERRIBLY IMPORTANT to do certain things, such as wearing over-embroidered dresses—after all, the mass follows class, class never follows the mass.
– Imelda Marcos

Imelda Marcos's lofty ambitions may have been applauded by the rich and influential, but she was deluded in her belief that the splendours she created would be seen by the poor as improving their lot. Her love of decadence was linked to the impoverished background she had escaped, and in her mind she 'edited out' the fact that ordinary people would never have access to these luxury hotels or be able to attend a night at the new Arts Centre. At one point she claimed, 'Here in the Philippines, we live in a paradise. There are no poor people as there are in other countries'. In fact, the majority of Filipinos were surviving on two dollars a day, living well below the poverty line. Imelda existed in a dangerous fantasy world, and her arrogance and egotism were to arouse fierce opposition and anger in the years to come. But meanwhile she was on a spending junket, the like of which had never been seen before.

All That Glitters

As Imelda travelled the major cities of the world, she became desperate to compete with the extravagance and sophistication she saw there. Greed now seemed the overwhelming motive for her actions and, with her husband a willing accomplice, she started to siphon off millions of government dollars to private Swiss bank accounts. The country's coffers were treated as a 'Marcos piggybank' and before long Ferdinand and Imelda were one of the richest couples in the world. She took shopping trips to New York, Rome and Copenhagen, and spent millions of dollars on her private art collection, adding works by such masters as Michelangelo and Botticelli—which she always insisted were meant for the museums of the Philippines. Imelda adored jewellery and by the late 1970s she had become the world's biggest private buyer of precious stones. But she always wanted at bargain—no matter what the item or the price, it was said that she always asked for a discount.

Perhaps in the circles of the world's wealthiest her excesses might have been acceptable, but in the slums of the third-world country from which she came, there was no appreciation of her extravagance. While Imelda and Ferdinand were bent on increasing their own wealth, and wining and dining the rich and famous, the political situation at home was rapidly deteriorating. People were sick of living in poverty while the First Lady showed off her wealth. Imelda seemed genuinely deluded in her approach to the image she felt she should portray. Explaining her ostentatious way of dressing

> THE BEST COMPLIMENT I ever got in my life came from Chairman Mao of China. When I went there, at a time when nobody wanted to touch China with a ten-foot pole, Mao told me that I'm beautiful because I'm a natural, and he said natural is perfection. So, no character assassination can diminish me and my perfection.
> – Imelda Marcos

Imelda Marcos adorned with rubies and diamonds, at her seventieth birthday party in Manila, 1999, to which more than a thousand guests were invited.

when visiting poverty-stricken communities in rural areas of the Philippines, she said, 'They need a star especially in the dark of night ... I had to be a star for the poor people, and at the same time, I had to be a slave. I had to enslave myself so that everybody became a star'.

For the most part the extravagant Imelda Marcos was admired by the rest of the world. Men in power enjoyed her company, and as Special Envoy she did a lot to promote her country. She was a lively personality who breathed fresh air into stuffy diplomatic circles, breaking through cultural barriers and often surprising world leaders by spontaneously breaking into song. She found an enthusiastic fan in Chairman Mao Zedong and succeeded in opening up relationships with China; she negotiated a cut-price oil deal with Saddam Hussein. Clearly those shopping skills where she demanded a discount were useful in the political arena too. She forged relationships with influential figures across the world, from Pope John Paul II to Henry Kissinger, and for years she was close friends with Ronald and Nancy Reagan, perhaps sharing with Ronald Reagan the sense of being an 'actor manqué'.

During the 1980s, the Marcos wealth became the stuff of legend. Setting off for New York on one particular shopping trip, Imelda had some big-ticket items on her list. Debating whether or not she should buy the Empire State Building, she decided it was too ostentatious, settling instead on the $51 million Crown Building and the $60 million Herald Center. She was officially named in the top ten richest women in the world list. It was claimed that between 1981 and 1983 a staggering $140 million was transferred by her from the Philippines into New York City real estate. Still obsessed with erasing all that reminded her of her early poverty, she knocked down the family home in Leyte and in its place built a palatial mansion with twenty bedrooms. She only spent one night there, but if people wanted to see where she had grown up, she had neatly repainted her history. Similarly, other scars left by those early years were covered up by a smooth publication relations team, bent on presenting her in an entirely new light and creating whatever fiction the First Lady dreamt up.

Power to the People

The corruption that had long plagued government in the Philippines escalated exponentially under the conjugal dictatorship and resulted in many political dissidents being forced to leave the country or face imprisonment. One of these was Benigno (Ninoy) Aquino, a popular left-wing senator and a fierce objector to the Marcos regime. Imprisoned for longer than any other political opponent, he was released after seven years to undergo heart bypass surgery in the United States, on the understanding he would not talk about conditions in the Philippines. During his time in prison, Aquino had become an international symbol of the wrongs of the Marcos dictatorship and the ongoing violation of human rights. (At the time 70 000 political detainees were hidden from the Filipino public.) Imelda and Ferdinand had control of the public television stations and the government-fed programs portrayed anything but the reality. 'Glamour and gloss' was the Marcos trademark; the true poverty and deterioration of the country was carefully airbrushed out.

The Philippines fell deeper into crisis when Ferdinand became seriously ill. Realizing that the self-serving Imelda was really ruling the country, Aquino believed that if he could talk to Marcos now, he might persuade him to lift martial law and give the country a chance to recover. On 21 August 1983, Aquino and a convoy of foreign journalists landed at Manila International Airport. Within minutes of landing he took a bullet to the head, a shocked world seeing the assassination live on television. In the knowledge that Ferdinand Marcos was out of action at the time, the mood of distrust was such that many suspected the First Lady had a hand in the murder, although the identity of killer remains a mystery to this day.

Culpable or not, Imelda might have believed that the problem posed by Aquino had been summarily dealt with, but it proved to be the beginning of the end. Aquino's wife Corazon (popularly known as Cory) took up her husband's cause, uniting anti-Marcos forces by using the moment to present herself as a presidential candidate. In December 1985, she won a snap election called by a recovering Marcos, whereupon, his hypocrisy knowing no bounds, Marcos denied her victory and accused her of fraud. These were by far the dirtiest, most fraudulent government-led elections that the country had ever seen, and Ferdinand's claim of victory was to cost him dearly. Ignoring his brazen announcement, Cory Aquino read the mood of the people correctly and herself held a victory rally at which she called for a 'national civil disobedience campaign'. This was to be the turning point in the Marcos regime.

The unthinkable now began to happen. Aware that the conjugal dictators had only 'triumphed' in the election through striking three million people off the electoral role and using intimidation tactics, a small group of rebel forces bunkered down in the Defence Ministry in Manila. Encouraged by Imelda, President Marcos impatiently ordered troops to march on them. As he did so, Radio Veritas, an independent radio station, called for the Filipino community to help the rebels and to gather on the EDSA highway, the main highway of Metro Manila. Things were suddenly slipping from Imelda's hands, and she could only watch helplessly from the palace windows.

Over the next four days people continued to congregate on the EDSA highway until finally there were tens of thousands present. Channel Four, a government-run television station, was taken off air midway through a Marcos speech and the whole country was made aware of what was happening as the opposition broadcast its own news reports. People parked buses across intersections and started to form a human barricade to halt the advancing troops. There was a festival atmosphere as families gathered, hawkers sold souvenirs, and demonstrators sang and danced. As the tanks rolled in, people stepped into their path and refused to move. Women hugged the advancing troops; young girls gave them flowers, cigarettes and candy. When the commander gave the order to move forward, priests and nuns knelt before the tanks, clutching their rosary beads. Not a shot was fired, and many of the troops began to weep, finally laying down their arms for the Peoples' Revolution.

Imelda and Ferdinand Marcos watched in a state of shock as their world crumbled around them. Their longtime ally, the United States, stepped in with some unwelcome and very pointed advice—relinquish power and leave the capital immediately. On 25 February 1986, after fourteen years in power, Imelda and Ferdinand reluctantly conceded defeat and, with their children, grabbed what valuables they could and fled the country under cover of night, airlifted out by a US military helicopter.

Diamonds and Diapers

With the presidential family leaving in disarray, the Malacañang Palace was opened to the public who gleefully fell upon everything they had left behind. There had been no time to pack, and Imelda's riches were on display for all to see. As the crowd reeled in shock at her extravagance, reports circulated the world of the three thousand pairs of shoes found in

A small selection from the now legendary shoe collection of Imelda Marcos, which numbered around three thousand pairs. After the Marcoses were overthrown in 1986, their palace, along with Imelda's closets and their decadent contents, was opened to the public.

her closet. Imelda later joked, 'When they went to my closet, they found shoes, not skeletons'. As well as shoes, there were bulletproof bras, gallons of perfume, 508 ball-gowns, over eight hundred handbags and hundreds of pairs of sunglasses. It was all the evidence of shameless excess that the people needed, and the country's woes were now laid firmly at the door of Ferdinand Marcos and his First Lady, a shopaholic clearly in a class of her own.

Forced to leave most of her possessions behind, it is said that Imelda arrived at US customs with nothing in her luggage but diamonds and diapers. The family was forced to live in Hawaii, where Ferdinand Marcos eventually died in exile, never really understanding why his great ally, the United States, had let him down. With Marcos dead it was left to Imelda to defend herself against accusations that the couple had defrauded the government of vast sums of money. At the end of their joint rule, the country was $27.5 billion in debt, and one in two Filipinos was out of work.

In 1990 Imelda faced trial in New York, accused of bringing $140 million of stolen money into the country for the purpose of buying real estate. But the unrepentant ex-First Lady still had a way with people and proceeded to charm the jury, who finally passed a 'not guilty' verdict. She celebrated her sixty-first birthday with the news that she had been found innocent on all counts and, by an extraordinary leap of the imagination, interpreted the result as a resounding victory for the underdog.

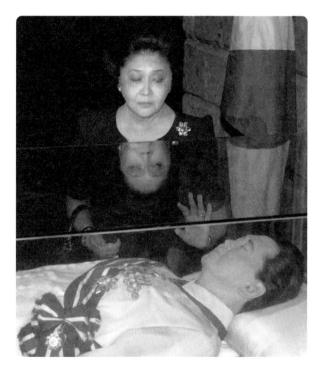

A mourning Imelda Marcos stands by the side of the remains of her husband, Ferdinand Marcos, on a visit to mark his eighty-eighth birthday anniversary. Marcos' body lies in a glass viewing case inside a refrigerated crypt, which is on constant view to the public in his home province of Luzon in the Philippines.

Most people in such circumstances would have chosen to remain in exile, or at least retire permanently from public life, but not Imelda. She fixed her gaze on the country she called home and decided to re-establish her power base. In 1992 she returned to Manila and stood as a candidate in the presidential elections. She was unsuccessful, but succeeded in gaining everyone's attention. The Philippine government and 10 000 civilians slapped her with lawsuits which, if they'd all been successful, would have seen her in prison for at least one hundred years. In 1993, Imelda was convicted of corruption and sentenced to more than eighteen years' imprisonment. Was the Steel Butterfly finally going to get her just deserts? It was not to be. First granted bail, in 1998 the guilty verdict was overturned after she convinced a jury that she was merely an innocent bystander with no knowledge of her husband's corrupt business and political affairs.

By the age of seventy-six, Imelda Marcos had been elected to Congress and had run two unsuccessful presidential campaigns. Of the 901 lawsuits filed against her, only three remained. She was surviving on a widow's pension of $90 a week in her high-rise Manila apartment, surrounded by bodyguards and limousines, and was once again the head of a political dynasty, since many of her family now held government positions. As time has passed, many have started to look back at the Marcos dictatorship with a perverse fondness, and the outrageous character that was the First Lady is celebrated, her shoe museum being a top tourist attraction in Manila.

Imelda Marcos remains the ultimate drama queen, a woman whose crocodile tears won the day on many occasions and whose rags-to-riches story can't help but strike a chord. Still stubbornly seeing herself as a mother to her country and a champion of the poor, she has asked that the words 'Here lies love' be engraved on her tombstone. Imelda seems to have achieved international celebrity status, and is perhaps forever destined to live in the shadow of the Malacañang Palace. And as to the estimated $684 million that went missing, one can only speculate where it went … that's an awful lot of shoes.

Leila Khaled

The pin-up terrorist
1944–

Leila Khaled passed through the final security gate at Rome airport, grenades in her pockets and the flight plan of the aeroplane tucked down her pants. Looking around at the passengers about to board Flight TWA 840 to Tel Aviv, she felt detached, as if all this was a dream. It was the moment she had been waiting for. She mustn't lose concentration now.

Almost as soon as the flight was airborne, Leila sprang into action. With her fellow-hijacker, Salim Essawi, she took control of the plane, forcing the American pilot to fly over her homeland of Palestine and to land the plane in Damascus. With a gun in one hand and a grenade in the other, she made jokes with the passengers, telling them the champagne was on her. By all accounts she seemed to enjoy putting on a performance, showing scant sympathy for the fearful hostages. As the plane flew over her home town of Haifa, she took over the radio and broadcast an anti-Israeli speech to the stunned control tower. For Leila that moment was sweet revenge for the hurried, shameful flight into exile that she and her family had endured so many years ago. How could she be labelled a terrorist? She was fighting for justice and to right a terrible wrong.

This famous photograph of Leila Khaled, taken in 1969, inspired an entire generation of activists and freedom fighters.

When the plane landed in Syria, all the passengers were allowed off except for six Israelis, in exchange for whom the Syrian government released thirteen political prisoners. Salim blew up the empty plane and in the confusion the two hijackers ended up on the same airport bus as the hijacked passengers. Elated that the mission had been a success and that no lives had been lost, Leila was in a mood for celebration but, conscious of the hostility not unnaturally emanating from the other bus passengers, she tried to placate them with cigarettes and candy. One woman plucked up the courage to speak. 'I don't understand', she said. 'Who are the Palestinians?' For Leila it was mission accomplished, for this was the very question the Popular Front for the Liberation of Palestine wanted the rest of the world to ask.

Leila Khaled carried out this successful hijacking as a freedom fighter for the Popular Front for the Liberation of Palestine on 29 August 1969. Almost immediately afterward, as one of the world's first female terrorists, she became a pin-up heroine for armed struggle. The passion she demonstrated for her cause, combined with her startling beauty, catapulted her onto the world stage and made her an icon for the previously ignored Palestinian movement.

There is that famous 1969 photo of Leila holding a gun in her delicate hands—the fringed keffiah over her head, on her finger a ring made out of a grenade pin and a bullet, and eyes seeming to focus with burning intensity on something just beyond the camera. In its time, it fired the imagination of an entire generation and saw Leila compete with her hero, Che Guevara, for space on the bedroom walls of activists around the world. That she moved from being a liberation fighter and hijacker to become a politician for the PFLP as a member of the Palestinian National Council, a woman whose autobiography has attracted worldwide interest and about whom an award-winning documentary was recently made, testifies to her charisma and her ability to walk through personal and political minefields with revolutionary principles intact.

Leila Khaled pictured with Yasser Arafat, Chairman of the PLO, at a Palestinian National Council meeting in 1987. After her career as a freedom fighter, Khaled went into politics and during the 1980s took up a new cause, the rights of Palestinian women and children.

Flight into Exile

In 1948, when the first Arab-Israeli conflict broke out, four-year-old Leila Khaled and her middle-class family, together with three-quarters of a million other Palestinians, were forced to leave their hometown of Haifa and flee into exile. Her father chose to stay behind and join the resistance movement, so Leila's mother fled with their children to a refugee camp at Tyre in Lebanon. It would be a temporary arrangement—or so they hoped. Leila missed her father desperately and even as a child appears to have been politicised, feeling herself an outcast in a place where nothing belonged to her. She vividly remembers her mother warning her she must not pick the oranges for 'we are in Lebanon now'.

Over a year later, Leila was excited to hear that her father was finally joining them, sure he was coming to take them home. But her excitement was dimmed by her first glimpse of the broken man who walked through the door. Her father seemed to have had all the fight drained out of him in the conflict that led to the state of Israel being created and thousands of Palestinians forever forced from their homeland.

As the years passed the growing Leila seethed with angry frustration, keenly feeling her people's defeat. She and her family were to remain in their cramped conditions, impoverished, struggling desperately to retain their self-respect, for the next sixteen years. Her family's disinheritance remained an open wound; as Leila grew up, tales of injustice, oppression and political division took the place of bedtime stories. They inspired her with a burning sense that her family and her people had been wronged and were now being 'edited out' of the collective memory. Always politically aware, she joined her older brothers and sisters in the Arab National Movement (ANM) when she was only fifteen. Her mother, a product of a deeply patriarchal society, was against her daughters taking part in political struggle, anxious to see them fulfil their roles as wives and mothers. But Leila's father was on her side. He might no longer have the strength to fight himself, but he understood the passion that drove her. Perhaps, too, he sensed that she was already moving beyond his control.

The Freedom Fighter

It was no great relief to Leila's mother when, in 1962, her spirited daughter won a scholarship to the American University in Beirut to study pharmacy, even though study would take her away from the ANM. But it seemed Leila had found a vocation, for she threw herself with her customary enthusiasm into university life. Before long, however, funds ran low and to her lasting regret she was never able to complete her degree, instead becoming an elementary teacher and taking up a position in Kuwait. But politics was in her blood and in

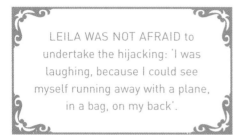

LEILA WAS NOT AFRAID to undertake the hijacking: 'I was laughing, because I could see myself running away with a plane, in a bag, on my back'.

1967 she joined the Popular Front for the Freedom of Palestine (PFLP), working hard to recruit members for the cause in Kuwait. Highly articulate and stunningly attractive, she was an instant success.

But Leila became increasingly interested in taking a more active part and becoming a freedom fighter. Why should the fact that she was a woman militate against that? In her autobiography, she describes how, 'In the beginning, all women had to prove that we could be equal to men in armed struggle so we wanted to be like men—even in our appearance'. Leila's skills as a communicator were particularly useful to the cause, and for two years she stayed in Kuwait, liaising between terrorist cells. Eventually her persistence paid off and she was accepted into a training camp to learn the skills she would need as a freedom fighter. Her new way of life was hard and she became used to a nomadic existence, always on the move to avoid being located and bombed by the Israeli militia. But the tough physicality, the sleep and food deprivation were all worthwhile. No sacrifice was too great if it meant that her beloved Palestine was finally to be liberated and families such as hers could go home. On one finger she now wore a ring made out of a bullet and the pin of the first grenade she had used in a training exercise, more a statement of intent than an article of adornment.

Leila's commitment to the Palestinian cause, and her courage under pressure, soon attracted the attention of those higher up, and she was chosen to carry out one of the PFLP's most dangerous missions, the hijacking of TWA Flight 840 from Los Angeles to Tel Aviv via Rome. The plan was to commandeer the plane after take-off from Rome, redirect the flight over Palestine, and land in Syria. No passengers were to be hurt. The overriding aim of the hijacking was to secure the freedom of a group of Palestinian prisoners and to draw the attention of the world to the Palestinian cause. But there was one hurdle still to be overcome.

The First Mission

Leila needed to know and understand everything about the plane she was to hijack so that if the worst happened she would be capable of piloting it herself. She leaped at the challenge, determined to master this new set of skills. In August 1969, after months of intensive training, she set off for Rome with her fellow hijacker, Salim Essawi. Arriving at the terminal, she felt strangely calm and detached. But as she waited to board and a few passengers chose to engage in idle conversation to fill the time, the only way to keep her nerve was to superimpose on their friendly faces the sorrowful faces of the thousands of Palestinian children incarcerated in refugee camps, their lives crippled by poverty and disease. The tactic worked. No one seeing the warm smile and captivating charm would have guessed the attractive young woman's deadly secret.

The mission was a resounding success. Leila and Salim, who was in charge of the explosives, forced the pilot to re-route the plane over Palestine and land in Damascus. From the window, Leila had looked down on her hometown of Haifa and felt a thrill of triumph. The fact that no passengers were injured in the course of their mission was a source of pride. She was able to discount the rather obvious dangers of holding a hand grenade and a gun to someone's head in mid-air and the fact that it could all have gone horribly wrong. To Leila, this was not terrorism but the struggle of the oppressed for a justice cruelly denied them.

Leila and Salim were detained for forty-five days by the Syrian government. This was a small price to pay. But after their release Leila became a number one target for Israel and the West—and an overnight celebrity. The PFLP milked her star status, exploiting the feverish attention given her by the foreign press and film crews to draw attention to the Palestinian cause. She travelled widely in the Middle East, attending conferences and giving speeches. The thrill she had experienced on board the plane, the belief that she had served the movement, and the accolades that followed provided an adrenaline rush. But Leila's notoriety and the fact that her photograph was plastered over the front pages of the world's newspapers and constantly appearing on television screens presented a challenge to her future.

Changing Face

The instant recognition factor made it impossible that Leila could ever again be active on the front line for the PFLP. One photo in particular had caught the public imagination, Leila standing with her face tilted away from the camera, shadows falling under her sharply defined cheekbones, one hand holding a gun and on her finger the ring made from the grenade pin and bullet. The Western world drew comparisons with the beautiful Audrey Hepburn, and the idea of a beautiful female freedom fighter resonated with the times, irrespective of political allegiance. But for Leila the photo was a disaster, and she decided that 'the face' must go. She underwent six plastic surgery procedures on her nose and chin that were to make her unrecognisable, an experience traumatic enough in itself, but she added another test of endurance. To remind herself of the pain suffered by her fellow Palestinians and affirm her commitment to the cause, she opted to have the operations done without anaesthetic.

Satisfied that her new look would fool press and customs officials alike, Leila began to prepare for her second mission. On 6 September 1970, three planes destined for New York were to be hijacked at the same time and flown to Dawson's Field in Jordan, which the terrorists referred to as 'Revolutionary Airport', an action aimed at freeing Palestinian prisoners from Swiss, German, and Israeli prisons. It was Leila's job to head up the hijacking of an El Al jet travelling from Amsterdam to New York. Things began to unravel from the start. Two of the four members of the team were prevented from boarding the plane (they bought tickets on a Pan Am flight instead and hijacked that). Posing as a married couple, Leila and the fourth hijacker, Nicaraguan Patrick Argüello, flashed Honduran passports under the noses of customs officials—and held their breath. Asked by a security guard if she had any dangerous weapons, Leila flirtatiously brushed the remark aside. 'Why would a girl like me have a dangerous weapon?' she teased. Heart hammering, she took her place next to her 'husband' in the first-class compartment.

Leila was elated that she had not been recognised and that while their bags had been thoroughly searched, customs officials had failed to check their pockets where the hand-grenades nestled. Nervousness seemed to make Patrick hungry—he kept complaining he wanted something to eat—but Leila insisted he should concentrate on the job in hand. She noticed two men glancing their way, which meant they had to act quickly. Signalling that it was time, Leila knocked on the cockpit door only a few steps away from her seat and, making as if to pull the pin from a grenade with her teeth, yelled at the pilot to open up.

But Captain Uri Bar Lev made a quick judgment call. He plunged the plane into a steep dive, so that everyone not in their seat was knocked off their feet. Patrick Argüello tumbled backward down the aisle, losing his grenade as he fell. Air marshals shot him four times in the back and someone crashed a bottle of whiskey down on his head. The passengers were screaming and shouting as the air marshals turned their attention on Leila. The last thing she remembered was being hit on the back of the head. Then blackness descended. When she surfaced, she was tied up and being kicked and pummelled and a woman was screaming, 'Stop the bloodshed!' Dazed, Leila muttered that the guns and grenades were there merely as a threat. But the PFLP had been involved in other armed actions which had led to civilian deaths, and the majority of the passengers didn't believe her; they became aggressive, and seemed willing to harm her.

With the hijackers restrained, the pilot made an emergency landing at Heathrow Airport in London. Fearing that the passengers were going to kill her, the air marshals literally threw Leila off the plane into the arms of the police waiting on the tarmac. Hustled into an ambulance with the motionless Patrick, she realised that he was fatally wounded; indeed, soon

Leila Khaled at a refugee camp in Beirut, 1975, still photographed with the customary gun. After having her face altered by plastic surgery in order to go unrecognised by the authorities, she later underwent further surgery to regain her original appearance.

afterward paramedics confirmed that he was dead. Leila was held at Ealing Police Station for three weeks. Even though she was devastated by the failure of her mission, she managed to make friends with the policewomen who guarded her. She was a natural communicator, chatting about life, death and the problems with men as if they were old school friends who had met up for a reunion. No one could quite believe this friendly, skinny, frail-looking girl could be the notorious Leila Khaled. But although her face no longer matched their files, there was no escaping the fact. Once the British press got wind of the identity of the prisoner in custody at Ealing, Leila was again accorded centrefold status. Marriage proposals flooded in.

On 9 September, three days after the failed hijacking, the PFLP had hijacked a fifth plane, BOAC Flight 775, en route from Bahrain to London via Beirut. Their main demand was the release of Leila Khaled. There were over three hundred passengers on board, sixty-five of them British. Britain suddenly found itself with an international crisis on its hands. A 72-hour ultimatum was issued to the British government—either Leila was released or the hostages died. And to prove they were serious, surrounded though they were by Jordanian tanks, the hijackers at Dawson's Field blew up the three previously hijacked jets on the tarmac. To America's disgust the British Prime Minister, Edward Heath, decided to negotiate, despite Britain having a no-tolerance policy towards hijackers. He was later to say that he could not afford to take the risk. On 30 September Leila was released and a potentially catastrophic situation was defused.

The Retired Terrorist

Months after the botched hijack, Leila made an attempt to settle down, marrying a PFLP comrade. But her turbulent, high-octane lifestyle made it hard for her to adjust, and two years later they divorced. She appears to have suffered some sort of an identity crisis, perhaps partly because looking in the mirror showed a stranger looking back. In any event, she decided she wanted her old face back and again underwent plastic surgery. Leila's days as a freedom fighter might have been over, but she would always remain a target, and her revolutionary past came at great personal cost. On Christmas Day 1976, her younger sister and her sister's fiancé were shot dead at Leila's home on the day of their wedding. It was thought it might have been a case of mistaken identity, and that the Israeli Secret Service had been targeting Leila. She had already found a bomb under her bed one night when she was looking for her slippers. In 1982 she married a second time and during the eighties embraced a new cause, championing the rights of Palestinian women and children.

In recent interviews she maintains she has no regrets, but always makes it clear that she does not condone violence.

THE CHARACTER OF the savage warrior Leela, from the British television cult classic *Doctor Who*, is named for Leila Khaled.

Leila Khaled justifies the hijacking missions she led as a necessary part of the heroic struggle for Palestinian liberation, a legitimate means of drawing attention to Palestinian anger at being driven out of their homeland. The fact that a single mistake could have resulted in the loss of hundreds of innocent lives should perhaps puncture some of the romantic rhetoric surrounding her exploits. Yet she remains an icon of liberation. The ring she fashioned out of a grenade pin and a bullet seems to symbolise her sense that she was married to her cause. She used her sexuality if necessary to get her through the security gates, sacrificed her beauty, and for all her claims that hostages were never intended to be harmed, appeared to embrace violence. She has never professed herself a feminist, claiming 'I am a Palestinian first, a woman second', but she effectively overcame the patriarchal restrictions of Arab society, proving at every turn that she was a freedom fighter more than equal to any man.

Phoolan Devi

Bandit queen, freedom fighter, politician

1963–2001

What others called a
crime, I call justice.
– Phoolan Devi

As the Bandit Queen walked out of the ravines of Chambal she took one last look at the place she had called home for so many years. It had been a perfect hideout for her dacoit gang, but now many had been killed and she herself was ill. Negotiating her surrender with the Indian authorities had seemed the only option. The local chief of police was waiting on the outskirts of the nearby town to take her into custody, which would be a real feather in his cap. As she approached the town, Phoolan heard a noise in the distance and paused for a second, unnerved. After years of living deep in wild jungle terrain, the sounds of the city were alien to her.

It was February 1983, and thousands of people had gathered to witness the surrender of the Bandit Queen. Stereos blared with celebratory music, local markets sold clay statues of their heroine, and women gossiped that she was an avatar of Durga, the active incarnation of the warrior goddess, Kali. At their first glimpse of Phoolan Devi the crowd went wild. Smaller than many had imagined, she was dressed in a new khaki uniform draped in a red shawl. She had a red bandanna, a symbol of vengeance, tied around her head, a bandolier slung across her chest, and an oversize rifle over her shoulder.

Phoolan Devi pictured in
1995, a year after she was
released from her eleven-
year jail term.

Phoolan Devi walked up the steps of the wooden platform especially built for the occasion, and stopped before the two pictures hanging there. Taking the garlands that had been provided, she placed one on the picture of Mahatma Gandhi and another on the picture of Durga, the giver of justice. Finally, she turned to the chief of police, draped a third garland around his neck and bowed at his feet. Turning to the crowd, she raised her gun in the air, held it for a moment and then placed it in front of the two portraits. Her reign as Bandit Queen was over.

When Phoolan Devi finally surrendered to the Indian police, she was wanted on fifty counts of murder. As leader of a band of dacoits, or bandits, she had stolen from the thakurs, the high-caste wealthy landowners, throughout the region and murdered anyone she deemed a sexual criminal. Embarking on a personal vendetta to avenge the murder of her lover by the vicious bandit leaders Shri Ram Singh and Lala Ram Singh, she was said to be responsible for the largest massacre by bandits in

By sixteen, Phoolan Devi had already escaped a violent husband and had served a short term in jail on a trumped-up robbery charge.

Indian history. But despite what seemed at the time to be an unquenchable thirst for blood, she came to be revered as their champion by women who had been oppressed, and elevated to the status of a goddess. She served eleven years in prison for her crimes. When she was released, she reinvented herself as a respected and highly effective politician, fighting for the rights of women and sending a stark message to their abusers. Her violent death in July 2001 in a high-security area near the Indian Parliament building sent shockwaves through the nation and touched a wider international world.

The Neem Tree

Born into the low caste of mullahs, a group who were considered untouchables, Phoolan Devi grew up in the small village of Ghura Ka Purwa in the northern Indian state of Bihar. From the moment she could walk, she knew she must do anything asked of her by the higher-caste thakurs and to gratefully accept every crumb of food they threw her way. Her mother brought her up to be proud and to stand up for what she believed in, but her father was more submissive, deeply pious, and desperate to avoid trouble. Each day the family worked in the fields belonging to Phoolan's uncle, who had callously cheated the family out of their inheritance and left them in the most abject poverty. The only item they owned of any value was a magnificent neem tree growing on their one acre of land. Phoolan's father often spoke of the money they would one day receive for its valuable timber, money which would pay for his daughters' dowries. Phoolan loved to rest beneath its shade, describing its trunk as being so large that she and her sister could barely encircle it with their arms outstretched. But these carefree childhood moments beneath the neem tree were to be brutally cut short.

While Phoolan's father was out in the fields one day, her uncle's son, Mayadin, arrived with some fellow villagers and chopped the tree down, carting it off for a quick sale. Then only nine or ten years old, Phoolan publicly accused her cousin of being a thief and attacked him, while her father, attracted by the commotion, stood by wringing his hands. Outraged at being challenged by this female firebrand, Mayadin retaliated by clouting her viciously with a brick, knocking her out cold. The loss of the precious neem tree and the antagonism resulting from Phoolan's attempt to stand up to her cousin made the family's situation ten times worse. But Phoolan was unrepentant—perhaps her mother had taught her rather too well to stand up for herself. Phoolan was fired up by a sense of the injustice at the hand she had been dealt.

Phoolan's childhood was soon at an end. When she was eleven, she was given in marriage to a man three times her age, from a distant village. Cast out from her home, traumatised, she was forced to submit to her new husband's voracious sexual demands despite being a child. As his abuse continued, an increasingly desperate Phoolan tried on several occasions to run away, but each time her husband tracked her down and subjected her to torture as punishment for her 'betrayal'. Eventually he abandoned her and she came back to her old village, hoping to find sanctuary. But her good looks and lithe figure, and the fact that she had been sexually used, attracted unwanted attention. She was constantly tormented by the son of the Sarpanch, the head of the village, finally being raped in front of her parents in their own house. Her mother, for all her advice about standing up for herself, now counselled Phoolan to keep her mouth shut, knowing that her daughter's status and that of the family would be further damaged if she spoke out.

But Phoolan believed passionately that she had been wronged. She reported the attack to the chief of a neighbouring village who had long been looking for an excuse to attack the Sarpanch of Ghura Ka Purwa. Phoolan might have won a measure of justice but, just as her mother had predicted, the family lost any status they might still have had in the eyes of their neighbours, being treated now as the lowest of the low. At a village meeting it was decided that, as punishment for her insolence, Phoolan should be forced to marry an old man who had had his eye on

Bandit Queen Phoolan Devi and her dacoit gang operated within an 20 000 square kilometre area of jungle.

her for a while. But one marriage had been more than enough for Phoolan. She fled the village where her life had become a torment and took refuge with her sister and brother-in-law, swearing that this time she would never return.

Mayadin and the son of the Sarpanch were furious that Phoolan had escaped, and began circulating rumours that she'd become a dacoit and stolen money from Mayadin's house. The police let it be known that her parents would suffer if she did not return to face her accusers. Left with no choice, Phoolan came back to her village, to be arrested and thrown into jail. The police repeatedly abused her until her sister finally arrived with evidence that Phoolan had been with her at the time of the alleged robbery. Worried that Phoolan might report them for false imprisonment, the police warned her to say nothing. But Mayadin decided her case should be tried in court, so she was once again dragged away from her family, and taken this time to the town of Orai. Phoolan was only sixteen, but the torment and abuse she had suffered must have seemed enough to fill a whole lifetime. Consumed by hatred for those who had hurt her, she had become a time-bomb primed to explode.

Breaking Point

When Phoolan was offered bail, her mother scraped together enough money to meet it and she was allowed to return to Ghura Ka Purwa. But the rumours that she was a bandit still held sway, and the villagers treated her with the contempt they might reserve for one of their pariah dogs. The Sarpanch ordered her parents to pay extra money if their daughter wished to use the same water as the other villagers, claiming they feared she would contaminate them. It became too much for Phoolan to endure. When a servant of the hated Mayadin told her that she and her father would not be paid for the day's work they'd just completed, she exploded in rage: 'You bastard dog, you're going to pay us … or I'll cut you to pieces!' To the startled onlookers Phoolan seemed a woman possessed.

The following day she confronted the Sarpanch and Mayadin, screaming that she was going to kill them. It was to be a turning point for her, a moment when she realised that, despite her diminutive stature, she could fight back and win. By now she had nothing more to lose. She was amazed by the effect of her fury on her bullying, brutal adversaries. 'From that moment on,' she said, 'I began to breathe again. I walked through the village without shame. I went to the river to bathe whenever I wanted. I had no more fear. I told my parents their daughter was dead.' It was a remarkable metamorphosis, marking the point where people began to believe that she had been touched by Durga, who brought justice to humankind by destroying evil. Phoolan enjoyed this sudden shift in their perception, feeling herself untouchable for a reason that had nothing to do with caste. Phoolan now did whatever she pleased within the village, enjoying the unaccustomed feeling of power, taunting Mayadin with what seemed like miraculous impunity. But the rumours which he had

After being kidnapped by the dacoit gang, Phoolan was subjected to abuse by the gang leader Baboo Gujar Singh. However, after his deputy, Vikram Mallah, shot him during an attempted rape, Phoolan was so touched that she began a relationship with Vikram that lasted until his untimely death.

viciously spread about her being a dacoit had reached the dacoits themselves, and they were intrigued to know what this new 'recruit' to their numbers was like. One night during the monsoon season, as torrential rain poured down, a gang of thirty turned up at her house and demanded to see her. At first, they couldn't believe their eyes. Here was a mere slip of a girl, nothing like the gun-wielding bandit they had imagined. What was her secret? Intrigued by the enigma, they snatched Phoolan and disappeared with her into the night.

Phoolan soon realised that the caste system operated even among the dacoits—the red-haired gang leader, the vicious Baboo Gujar Singh, was a thakur and his deputy, Vikram Mallah, a mallah like Phoolan. As the days passed, Baboo could not take his eyes off Phoolan and continually tried to abuse her. But Vikram would not join in and the tension between the two men began to build. Finally, when Baboo attempted to rape Phoolan one night, Vikram shot him and took over the leadership of the gang. In the following months, Vikram showed Phoolan a tenderness she had never known from a man, insisting that the gang treated her with respect and asking her if she liked him enough to marry him. Vikram had given Phoolan back her self-respect, her pride in herself as a woman, and her devotion to him was immediate and absolute.

So taken was Phoolan with Vikram that she embraced the dacoit lifestyle. For someone who had suffered so much at the hands of others, the idea of being a dacoit was empowering. Together they operated within a 20 000 square kilometre area of uncharted jungle terrain, spending their days negotiating the maze of ravines, swimming rivers, raiding villages and escaping the police. Vikram taught Phoolan to shoot a rifle, and initiated her into the strict code which the gang observed. Their purpose was to fight the caste war. When they entered a village, Vikram used a megaphone to warn the rich thakurs that they were a legitimate target and would have to pay. As well as training Phoolan, Vikram offered her a chance to wreak her revenge on those who had abused her. With the gang beside her, and dressed as they were in pseudo-police khaki uniform, Phoolan revisited all the men who had done her harm and made them pay for their crimes. Her first husband was beaten savagely, first by the gang and then by Phoolan, and a policeman who had taken part in a gang-rape was killed. She was like a wild thing, exhorting others to castrate her old tormentors so they could never perform such acts of abuse again.

The name of Phoolan Devi began to strike terror into the hearts of those who had degraded her in the past. Continuing her personal vendetta, she returned to her parents' village to search out the hated Mayadin. He had conveniently vanished, so she turned on the Sarpanch who had allowed his son to rape her. Not only had these men abused Phoolan, they were also a menace to the entire community, and the villagers were grateful that they'd been taught a lesson. No longer treating her as a pariah, they looked upon her now as a heroine and their champion. With a red shawl slung around her shoulders and her wide red bandanna, she seemed to them to resemble the goddess Durga even more, for Durga is depicted wearing red to show her active pursuit of justice.

Phoolan remarked wryly that the people were terrified of power and would worship anyone who possessed it.

But as their gang's notoriety increased, other gangs saw Phoolan and Vikram as a threat. In the dead of night, as Phoolan and Vikram slept side by side, a dacoit named Shri Ram Singh fired a volley of shots into their tent. Vikram died instantly. Waking in a confused state and feeling nauseous, Phoolan realised to her horror that she had been sedated with chloroform. It was the beginning of the worst nightmare of all. The only man she had ever loved lay dead, and she was too drugged to resist when Shri Ram Singh and his men carried her off to their boat and headed toward the nearby thakur settlement of Behmai. There, Shri Ram paraded her naked in front of the villagers, claiming that she was the one who had shot Vikram. First raping her himself, he announced that she was fair game for any man in the village who wanted her. Once again it seemed Phoolan had lost everything.

After three weeks of abuse and degradation, she managed to escape, swearing to avenge her husband's death. With many of her gang dead or on the run from the police, Phoolan set about reinventing herself. As she hid out in the Chambal ravines that she and Vikram had once leaped into hand in hand, she decided that from now on she would think and act as a man. She would call herself Phool, the male form of Phoolan, and reject every feminine feeling in herself that might make her weak.

Queen of Bandits

Deciding that she would answer to no one, Phoolan soon established her own gang. She had a stamp with the words 'Phoolan Devi Queen of Bandits', which she used to stamp on doors during a raid so that her victims would never forget her visit. Her extraordinary ability to give the authorities the slip meant that the reputation of the queen of the dacoits increased by the day. Phoolan and her men carried on their day-to-day business of robbery, but they also came to represent a type of rough social justice, fighting on the side of the oppressed. She set her sights on any men who were found to be abusing women. Women who were continually beaten, raped and treated as animals soon began to threaten their oppressors with Phoolan's name. If she found that a village was hiding a rapist, the villagers would all be punished; if she came across the rapist himself, she would torture him mercilessly.

Phoolan had a burning desire—that the people of Behmai who had abused her during those dreadful three weeks should pay the ultimate price. She was also determined to catch and kill Shri Ram Singh. When she heard that he was once again hiding out at Behmai she set about hunting him down. On 14 February 1981, seventeen months after her capture, Phoolan returned to Behmai with her new gang. With megaphone in one hand and gun in the other, she stormed through the streets, beating anyone who got in her way and demanding that her oppressors show themselves. When the men failed to appear and no one would admit to knowing the whereabouts of Shri Ram Singh, Phoolan flew into an uncontrollable rage, and ordered that twenty-two thakurs from the village be lined up and shot.

Phoolan always denied that she had anything to do with these killings, blaming other members of her gang for the outrage—but eyewitnesses say she was giving the orders. Perhaps at this moment she saw superimposed upon their terrified faces the gloating, jeering features of those who had raped her. Ultimately, it was enough that these men came from a higher caste and thought they could treat women like dogs. It was the largest massacre by bandits ever to have taken place in India and when news of it spread, Phoolan Devi became the country's number one criminal.

With a massive police manhunt underway and helicopters scouring the wild terrain, Phoolan hid out once again in the ravines of

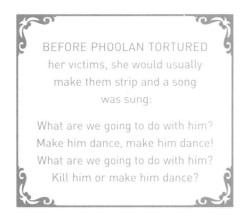

BEFORE PHOOLAN TORTURED her victims, she would usually make them strip and a song was sung:

What are we going to do with him?
Make him dance, make him dance!
What are we going to do with him?
Kill him or make him dance?

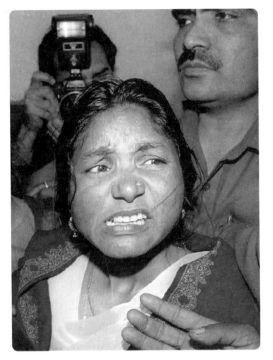

Phoolan Devi being escorted from jail, 1994. After serving eleven years of her sentence for the alleged massacre of twenty-two men, Phoolan was released early, due to the efforts of the lower caste chief minister of Uttar Pradesh.

Chambal. Two years later she still had not been found, and her elusiveness had become a serious embarrassment to the authorities. The government of Prime Minister Indira Gandhi decided they would have to negotiate her surrender. With many of her gang now dead, and in ill health herself, Phoolan realized that she had little choice but to give herself up, and drew up her list of conditions. She was not to be hanged, was to be tried for all her crimes at the same time, should receive no more than eight years and must be imprisoned with the members of her gang. These men and their families were to be given land and work on their release, and each provided with a gun permit for their own protection. Despite being illiterate, she seemed to possess the skills of a seasoned lawyer.

Months later the government accepted Phoolan's conditions and a date was set for her surrender. A frenzied media circus ensued. In February 1983, Phoolan Devi and the remaining members of her gang were met by an unarmed chief of police, who walked with them into the town of

Phoolan Devi, backed by her armed bodyguard and supporters, is pictured during a campaign stop in northern Uttar Pradesh, 1996. During this year Phoolan was elected to Parliament, her mission being women's rights and the plight of the lower castes.

Bhind. For someone accused of a massacre, the reception she received was extraordinary. Three hundred police, thousands of supporters, and countless representatives of foreign media all wanted to catch a glimpse of the legendary Bandit Queen. As the little procession approached the town, Phoolan felt certain she was going to be killed. Instead, a cheering crowd met her and her picture was flashed around the world in television news reports and on the front pages of countless newspapers.

In the end, the authorities ignored many of the conditions Phoolan had laid down for surrender. She faced thirty charges of dacoity but was never formally tried, and spent eleven years in prison, being freed in 1994. That year saw the release of the film *Bandit Queen*, in which she was immortalised on screen and her exploits and love affair with Vikram inevitably glamorised. Furious that her enemy Mayadin, the author of so many of her ills, was not portrayed in the film, and seeing it as a wildly inaccurate misrepresentation of her life, she successfully sued the producer. Phoolan was not about to allow the movie world the licence to reinvent her.

But now there was to be another metamorphosis. In 1996, after a vigorous election campaign, Phoolan became a member of the Lower House of Parliament, promising to stand up for women's rights and to fight for those from the lower castes. She was always worried that she would eventually be tried for her part in the Behmai massacre, but as a parliamentarian she had legal immunity and could not be sentenced. As it turned out, she would have been safer in prison. In July 2001, at the age of thirty-seven, having earned the respect of her political colleagues and of women who felt she had successfully drawn attention to their plight, she was gunned down by assassins outside her home in a high-security compound near the Indian Parliament.

Throughout her life, Phoolan Devi was driven by one powerful, all-consuming force; despite the appalling treatment she received through being born into one of the lowest castes, impoverished, robbed and degraded, she always refused to view herself as a victim. She fought back every inch of the way, wreaking vengeance on her abusers. At times her revenge was savage, and the massacre in Behmai could never be condoned. As a member of Parliament, and despite her lack of education, she made a spirited attempt to stamp out the exploitation of women and to fight caste oppression.

When members of the foreign press interviewed Phoolan, intent on creating a romantic heroine for the Western world, they quickly became disenchanted, claiming that she was discourteous and uncooperative. But Phoolan served no master, and the opinion of such people meant nothing to her. In her red bandanna and with her rifle on her shoulder, she remains an iconic figure in Indian history and an inspiration for those who are oppressed, demonstrating through her extraordinary courage that sometimes the spirit of one person can speak to multitudes.

Index

Acknowledgments

I would like to thank my editor and friend Ariana Klepac for coming up with such a captivating idea, and for her loyal support throughout the writing of this book. Thank you also to Carolyn Sally Jones, whose advice, guidance and comments were, as always, invaluable, and to Anne Savage for her careful copyediting. And finally I'd like to acknowledge all of the 'bad girls' that I have had the pleasure of knowing, who have always encouraged a healthy balance of work and play.

Picture credits

Corbis: p.11, p.13, p.25 & back cover, p.27, p.41, p.46, p.49, p.61, p.67, p.85, p.88, p.109, p.118, p.129, p.168, p.198, p.232, p.243, p.257, p. 267, p.268, p.271, p.273

Getty images: p. 2, p.7, pp.16–17, p.22, p.37, p.95, p.141, p.144, p.191, p.195, p.221, p.227, p.231, p.238, p.241, p.247, p.251, p.252, p.255, p.263, p.277, p.278

Image Works, The: p.97, p.106

National Library of New Zealand – Alexander Turnbull Library: p.157 [1/2-018586-F], p.159 [1/2-094204-F], p.163 [1/2-018527-F], p.164 [1/2-018527-F], p.166 [1/2-094176-F]

Photolibrary / Bridgeman Art Library: p.52, p.69, p.73, p.81, p.95, p.102, p.132, p.137, p.143, p.152, p.155

Press-Scimitar Photo/Mississippi Valley Collection/Special Collections/University of Memphis Libraries: p.215

Roger Vaughan picture library: cover image

State Records Authority of New South Wale, Department of Commerce: p.205 [3/6007] No.659

Photo research acknowledgments / special thanks to: Judith Bradbury and Amanda McKittrick

Further reading

Cleopatra

Blond, Anthony, *A Scandalous History of the Roman Emperors*, London: Constable & Robinson, 2000

Bradford, Enrnle, *Cleopatra*, London: Penguin, 2000

Burstein, Stanley M., *The Reign of Cleopatra*, Westport: Greenwood Press, 2004

Franzero, Carlo Maria, *The Life and Times of Cleopatra*, New York: Philosophical Library, 1957

Jones, Prudence J., *Cleopatra*, United Kingdom: Haus Publishing, 2006

Manley, Bill (ed.), *The Seventy Great Mysteries of Ancient Egypt*, New York: Thames and Hudson, 2003

Southern, Pat, *Cleopatra*, Stroud: Tempus Publishing, 2000

Messalina

Lewis, Naphtali and Reinhold, Meyer (eds), *Roman Civilization Volume II*, New York: Columbia University Press, 1990

McCabe, Joseph, *The Empresses of Rome*, New York: Henry Holt & Co., 1911

Scarre, Chris, *Chronicle of the Roman Emperors: The Reign-by-Reign Record of the Rulers of Imperial Rome*, New York: Thames & Hudson, 1995

Suetonius, *The Twelve Caesars*, translated by Robert Graves, London: Penguin, 2003

Wood, Susan E., *Imperial Women: A Study in Public Images 40 BC–AD 68*, Boston: Brill Academic Publishers, 2000

Boudica

Burke, Jason, 'Dig Uncovers Boadicca's Brutal Streak,' *Observer*, December 3, 2000

Cassius Dio

Fraser, Antonia, *Boadicea's Chariot: The Warrior Queens*, London: Weidenfeld and Nicolson, 1988

Lane, Richard J. and Wurts, Jay, *In Search of the Woman Warrior: Four Mythical Archetypes for Modern Women*, Boston: Element Books, 1998

Plutarch

Tacitus

Wood, Michael, *In Search of the Dark Ages*, London: BBC Books, 2005

Malinali

Dìaz del Castillo, Bernal, *The Conquest of New Spain*, translated by John M. Cohen, London: Penguin, 1963

Fehrenbach, T. R., *Fire and Blood: A History of Mexico*, New York: Da Capo Press, 1995

Foster, Lynn V., *A Brief History of Mexico*, New York: Facts on File Inc., 1997

Lanyon, Anna, *Malinche's Conquest*, St. Leonards: Allen & Unwin, 1999

Marks, Richard Lee, *Cortés: The Great Adventurer and the Fate of Aztec Mexico*, New York: Alfred A. Knopf, 1994

Taylor, John, 'Reinterpreting Malinche', http://userwww.sfsu.edu/~epf/2000/jt.html

Wood, Michael, *Conquistadors*, London: BBC Worldwide Ltd, 2000

Mary I

Loades, David, *The Chronicles of the Tudor Queens*, London: Sutton Publishing, 2002

Prescott, H. F. M., *Mary Tudor: The Spanish Tudor*, London: Phoenix Press, 2003

Weir, Alison, *Children of England*, London: Pimlico, 2005

Elizabeth Bathory

Thorne, Tony, *Countess Dracula: Life and Times of Elizabeth Bathory, the Blood Countess*, London: Bloomsbury, 1997

'Elizabeth Bathory the Blood Countess', http://www.bbc.co.uk/dna/h2g2/A593084

Catherine the Great

Alexander, John T., *Catherine the Great: Life and Legend*, New York: Oxford University Press, 1989

De Madariaga, Isabel, *Catherine the Great: A Short History*, New Haven: Yale University Press, 2002

Ranavalona

Bennett, Natalie, 'All the usual slanders are laid against a female queen', March 2006, http://philobiblon.co.uk/?p=1052

Laidler, Keith, *Female Caligula: Ranavalona, The Mad Queen of Madagascar*, Hoboken: John Wiley & Sons, 2005

Shi Xianggu

Cordingly, David (ed.), *Pirates: Terror on the High Seas from the Caribbean to the South China Sea*, Nashville: Turner Publishing Inc., 1996

Cordingly, David and Falconer, John, *Pirates: Fact and Fiction*, New York: Abbeville Press, 1992

Gosse, Phillip, *A History of Piracy*, New York: Tudor Publishing, 1946

Konstam, Angus, *The History of Pirates*, Guilford: The Lyons Press, 1999

Mary Ann Cotton

Appleton, Arthur, *Mary Ann Cotton: Her Story and Trial*, London: Michael Joseph, 1973

British History, BBC, http://www.bbc.co.uk/history/british/deary_gallery_05.shtml

Crime Library, http://www.crimelibrary.com/notorious_murders/women/cotton/1.html

Cixi

Haldane, Charlotte, *The Last Great Empress of China*, London: Constable, 1965

Laidler, Keith, *The Last Empress: The She-Dragon of China*, Hoboken: John Wiley & Sons, 2003

Paludan, Ann, *Chronicle of the Chinese Emperors: The Reign-by-Reign Record of the Rulers of Imperial China,* New York: Thames & Hudson, 1998

Seagrave, Sterling, *Dragon Lady: The Life and Legend of the Last Empress of China,* New York: Vintage, 1993

Warner, Marina, *The Dragon Empress: Life and Times of Tzu-Hsi 1835–1908,* London: Weidenfeld & Nicolson, 1976

Belle Starr

Armitage, Shelley, *Women's Work: Essays in Cultural Studies,* West Cornwall: Locust Hill Press, 1995

Rascoe, Burton, *Belle Starr 'The Bandit Queen,'* Lincoln: University of Nebraska Press, 2004

The HistoryNet, http://www.historynet.com/magazines/wild_west/3028036.html

Women in History, www.lkwdpl.org/wihohio/star-bel.htm

Amy Bock

Fiona Farrell, *Dictionary of New Zealand Biography,* http://www.dnzb.govt.nz/dnzb/default.asp?Find_Quick.asp?PersonEssay=2B30

McLintock, A. H., 'The Notorious Amy Bock, 1909', TRIALS, NOTABLE, *An Encyclopaedia of New Zealand,* 1966

Melville, Harvcourt, *A Parson in Prison,* Christchurch, Whitcombe and Tombs, 1942

Puke Ariki, Taranaki Stories, 'The Bridegroom Was a Woman', http://www.pukeariki.com/en/stories/lawandorder/amybock.asp

Robson, R. W., *The Adventures of Amy Bock: The Sensational Exploits of a Clever Adventuress, Who Recently Concluded a Career of over 20 Years of Crime by Masquerading as a Man, and Marrying a Port Molyneux Girl,* Dunedin: Daily Times Print, 1909

Mary Mallon

Bourdain, Anthony, *Typhoid Mary: An Urban Historical,* London: Bloomsbury Publishing, 2005

Leavitt, Judith Walzer, *Typhoid Mary: Captive to the Public's Health,* Boston: Beacon Press, 1996

Chicago May

Duignan, May, *Chicago May, Her Story: A Human Document by 'The Queen of Crooks',* 1928

O'Faolain, Nuala, *The Story of Chicago May,* London: Penguin, 2005

Mata Hari

Wheelwright, Julie, *The Fatal Lover: Mata Hari and the Myth of Women in Espionage,* London: Trafalgar Square, 1993

'The Execution of Mata Hari, 1917', EyeWitness to History, www.eyewitnesstohistory.com

Howe, Russell Warren, *Mata Hari: The True Story,* New York: Dodd Mead, 1986

Volkman, Ernest, *Spies: The Secret agents Who Changed the Course of History,* Hoboken: John Wiley & Sons, 1994

Keay, Julia, *The Spy Who Never Was: The Life and Loves of Mata Hari,* London: Michael Joseph, 1987

Tilly Devine

Blaikie, George, *Wild Women of Sydney,* Adelaide: Rigby, 1980

Writer, Larry, *Razor: A True Story of Slashers, Gangsters, Prostitutes and Sly Grog,* Sydney: Pan MacMillan, 2002

Georgia Tann

Raymond, Barbara Bisantz, *The Baby Thief: The Untold Story of Georgia Tann, the Baby Seller Who Corrupted Adoption,* North Sydney: Random House, 2007

The Diane Rehm Show, America University Radio, http://www.wamu.org/programs/dr/07/06/07.php#13215

Madame Mao

Clements, Jonathan, *Mao Zedong,* London: Haus Publishing, 2006

Lee, Lily Xiou Hong and Wiles, Sue, *Women of the Long March,* St. Leonards, Allen & Unwin, 1999

Terrill, Ross, *Madame Mao: The White-boned Demon,* Stanford: Stanford University Press, 1999

Imelda Marcos

Ellison, Katherine W., *Imelda, Steel Butterfly of the Philippines,* New York: McGraw-Hill, c.1988

McNeill, David, 'The Weird World of Imelda Marco', *Independent,* http://news.independent.co.uk/world/asia/article347541.ece

Pedrosa, Carmen Navarro, *Imelda Marcos,* London: Weidenfeld & Nicolson, 1987

Rempel, William C., *Delusions of a Dictator: The Mind of Marcos as Revealed in His Secret Diaries,* Boston: Little Brown, c.1993

Leila Khaled

Khaled, Leila and Hajjar, George (ed.), *My People Shall Live: the autobiography of a revolutionary,* London: Hodder and Stoughton, 1973

MacDonald, Eileen, *Shoot the Women First,* London: Fourth Estate, 1991

Morgan, Robin, *The Demon Lover: On the Sexuality of Terrorism,* New York: Norton, c.1989

Phoolan Devi

Devi, Phoolan with Cuny, Marie-Therese and Rambali, Paul, *I, Phoolan Devi: The Autobiography of India's Bandit Queen,* London: Little Brown, 1996

Sen, Mala, *India's Bandit Queen: The True Story of Phoolan Devi,* London: Pandora, 1993

First published in 2008 by Pier 9, an imprint of Murdoch Books Pty Limited

Murdoch Books Australia
Pier 8/9
23 Hickson Road
Millers Point NSW 2000
Phone: +61 (0) 2 8220 2000
Fax: +61 (0) 2 8220 2558
www.murdochbooks.com.au

Murdoch Books UK Limited
Erico House, 6th Floor
93–99 Upper Richmond Road
Putney, London SW15 2TG
Phone: +44 (0) 20 8785 5995
Fax: +44 (0) 20 8785 5985
www.murdochbooks.co.uk

Chief executive: Juliet Rogers
Publishing director: Kay Scarlett

Book concept: Ariana Klepac
Project managers: Ariana Klepac and Desney Shoemark
Editor: Anne Savage
Design: Annette Fitzgerald and Joanna Byrne
Production: Monique Layt

National Library of Australia Cataloguing-in-Publication Data

Stradling, Jan.
Bad girls & wicked women : the most powerful, shocking,
amazing, thrilling and dangerous women of all time /
author, Jan Stradling.
Sydney : Murdoch Books, 2008.
ISBN: 9781741960433 (pbk.)
Women--History.
Women--Biography.
Women.

305.40922

A catalogue record for this book is available from the British Library.

Printed by Midas Printing (Asia) Ltd in 2008. PRINTED IN CHINA.